Casebook of Arbitration Law

Also by John Parris

Law
THE LAW AND PRACTICE OF ARBITRATIONS
BUILDING LAW REPORTS (edited by John Parris)
COMMERCIAL LAW MADE SIMPLE

Autobiography
MOST OF MY MURDERS
UNDER MY WIG

History
THE LION OF CAPRERA
The biography of Guiseppe Garibaldi
PALERMO, 1860
*An edited translation of F. Brancaccio's
'Tre Mesi nella Vicaria di Palermo ne 1860'*

THE GRINGOES OF TEPEHUANES

CASEBOOK
OF
ARBITRATION
LAW

JOHN PARRIS
LLB(Hons), PhD

GEORGE GODWIN LIMITED
The book publishing subsidiary
of The Builder Group

First published in Great Britain by
George Godwin Limited, 1976

© Educational Copyrights Limited, 1976

ISBN 0 7114 3311 9

George Godwin Limited
The book publishing subsidiary
of The Builder Group
2-4 Catherine Street
London WC2

Typeset by
Inforum Limited of Portsmouth
Printed and bound in Great Britain
by Tonbridge Printers Limited
Peach Hall Works, Shipbourne Road
Tonbridge, Kent

Contents

Introduction

It would seem that my book *The Law and Practice of Arbitrations* met a real need, and I was fortunate to find reviewers universally kind to it. Indeed the only criticism was one made by a reviewer who complained that I had not mentioned that the Arbitration Act 1950 does not apply to Scotland or Northern Ireland. He apparently had not penetrated as far as page 2 of the text.

For the benefit of others similarly inclined, perhaps I should state in a prominent position that this book deals only with the law of England although, of course, the English law regarding arbitration has relevance in many jurisdictions.

Once again, this book is intended primarily for laymen rather than the lawyers. These have their own sources of information, confused and inadequate though they be.

For that reason, the cases reported here do not reflect the voluminous authorities on such strictly legal topics as when a step has been taken in an action or procedure after a case has been stated for the High Court. 'Other countries, the United States in particular, think very poorly of our system in arbitration of cases stated for the courts,' the Master of the Rolls, Lord Denning, has said. So do I. More space is therefore devoted to how to avoid a case stated than how to deal with one.

On the other hand, full treatment is afforded to what the courts have had to say about how an arbitrator should conduct himself and the arbitration, in the hope that this will prove a valuable reference book for an arbitrator to have at his elbow.

Since most of the words are not mine, I shall not be upset if the whole book is not read at a compulsive gallop. I have been at particular pains therefore to ensure that the index provides immediate and detailed references.

The learned editor of Hudson's *Building and Engineering Contracts*, Mr I.N. Duncan Wallace QC, has asked publicly why every opinion in the House of Lords now had to amount to a textbook in itself—'with the result that there are usually at least four conflicting textbooks in every case.' The appalling prolixity of modern judges is, indeed, a problem for the editor of a book such as this, both in the sheer volume he has to summarise and in the difficulty of discovering what is in fact the *ratio decidendi* of any particular case. Could not textbook writing be left to the textbook writers?

Perhaps it would help if present-day judges, like their predecessors up to 1825, were paid only by fees for the number of court cases of which they disposed: or if we invented a new system of remunerating them in inverse relation to the length of their judgments—so that any judge who merely said 'I agree' without feeling compelled to engaged in the work of supererogation by saying 'and have nothing to add' would take home the jackpot.

I would be less than gracious if I did not record my indebtedness to Mr Christopher Wright LLB, Barrister, who has helped in the task of checking proofs and who has prepared the tables of statutes and of cases; and to Mrs Maureen Webb, who has had to cope with my handwriting. If this book has any merit they are entitled to share of it; and where it has fault, it is mine alone.

JOHN PARRIS
Oxford

Note

This book is intended as a companion volume to *The Law and Practice of Arbitrations,* also by John Parris.

To help readers to follow up in greater detail the legal propositions given in this book, references have been included after the proposition to the relevant section in *The Law and Practice of Arbitrations* (1974 edition).

These references are shown in heavy type and have been abbreviated as *LPA.*

Case references: Cases are cited in the text by the date at which they were first reported. This may not necessarily be the same as the date judgment was given. Full report references to every case are given at the back of the book in the table of cases.

PART I

The nature of arbitration

'It is said to be called an Arbitrement either because the Judges elected thereon may determine the Controversie not according to the Law, but according to their Opinion and Judgment as honest men. Or else because the Parties to the Controversie have submitted themselves to the Judgment of the Arbitrators, not by Compulsion or Coertion of the Law but of their own accord. It is also called an Award, of the French word *Agarder*, which signifies to *decide* or *judge* and sometime in the Saxon or Old English, it was called a *Love-Day*, because of the Quiet and Tranquility that should follow the ending of the Controversie.'

Arbitrium Redivivam (1694)

Arbitration and valuation (see LPA 1.8)

Not every agreement to refer a matter to the decision of a third person is necessarily an arbitration.

At one time it was thought that a mere appraisal or valuation by a third party could never be an arbitration. The two cases that follow are included because they are commonly taken to support this view. It will be seen however that this is not so.

In the first case, Lord Esher is concerned solely with the point as to whether there was an arbitration agreement in writing or not; in the second, with the presumed intention of the parties. In the second case he concluded that there was no intention for arbitration because the parties did not intend a judicial hearing, but only that the third person should act on his own skill and judgment. This case however cannot be regarded as current law.

In re an Arbitration between Dawdy and Hartcup (Court of Appeal, 1885)

Dawdy was the tenant of Hartcup's farm who gave notice to quit. In accordance with the custom of the county of Suffolk, two valuers were appointed, one by the landlord and one by the tenant, for the purpose of ascertaining the sum the tenant was entitled to from the landlord on his outgoing. The valuers appointed an umpire and he held a hearing to receive evidence.

Application was made to enrol the award as a rule of court under the provision of section 17 of the Common Law Procedure Act 1854 (repealed) which were similar to those of section 26 of the Arbitration Act 1950.

Counsel for the appellant argued that the agreement provided that at the expiration of the tenancy the 'usual and customary valuation' should be made, and that this implied that the valuation was to be conducted according to the usual and customary rules, and by persons appointed in the usual and customary way. The usual and customary mode of making such a valuation was by appointing two valuers, who appointed an umpire if they could not agree. The subsequent words of the agreement contemplated the possibility of a dispute between the landlord and the tenant. There was a sufficient submission to arbitration. There was an agreement in writing, and, that being so, the court might look at the subsequent proceedings which are implied in the original agreement.

LORD ESHER MR: The only question which we have to decide is whether there is any submission in writing to arbitration which can be made a rule of court under the provisions of section 17 of the Common Law Procedure Act 1854.

That there was in this case in point of fact ultimately an arbitration between the parties I do not doubt; an umpire was appointed, and he had to arbitrate: the question is whether there ever was a written submission to arbitration. It has been admitted by [Counsel] in his very strenuous and able argument that, unless the agreement of 4 October 1882 contains a submission to arbitration, there has been no agreement in writing between the parties to submit the matters in dispute between them to arbitration. The only appointment of an umpire was a verbal one. The word 'arbitration' in section 17 of the Common Law Procedure Act has been construed as meaning an arbitration to be conducted according to judicial rules, where the person who is appointed arbitrator is bound to hear the parties, to hear evidence if they desire it, and to determine judicially between them. He must have a matter before him which he is to consider judicially.

As a consequence of this, it has been held that if a man is, on account of his skill in such matters, appointed to make a valuation in such a manner that in making it he may, in accordance with the appointment, decide solely by the use of his eyes, his knowledge, and his skill, he is not acting judicially; he is using the skill of a valuer, not of a judge. In the same way, if two persons are appointed for a similar purpose, they are not arbitrators, but only valuers. They have to determine the matter by using solely their own eyes, and knowledge, and skill.

We must, therefore, look at the agreement and see whether one or more persons are appointed to value, and in what way they are to act. The agreement says that there is to be the usual and customary valuation, but there is nothing to show the mode in which, or the persons by whom, the valuation is to be made. It means nothing more than that the usual and customary items are to be taken into account. Then it says that, when any valuation of the covenants shall be made between the tenant and the landlord, or his incoming tenant, the persons making the valuation shall take into consideration certain specified matters. I think the agreement contemplates the making of the valuation by the landlord and the tenant themselves; at any rate, the possibility of their making it. Obviously there are to be two persons, but I can see nothing in the first part of the clause other than this, that two persons are to be appointed as valuers, not arbitrators; that they are to be valuers in the ordinary sense of the word, ie, persons skilled in agriculture, who can determine the whole matter by the use of their own eyes, and knowledge, and skill. There is nothing to show that they are to hear the parties, and determine judicially between them. The case comes within the authority of *Collins v Collins* (1858) and *Bos v Helsham* (1866) which decide that persons so appointed are valuers, nor arbitrators. *In re Hopper* (1867) is not inconsistent; there the judges of the Court of Queen's Bench only said that, if those cases bore the construction which counsel had attempted to put on them, they could not agree with them; they did not say that they thought the cases had been wrongly decided. Blackburn J said:

'The cases of *Collins v Collins* and *Bos v Helsham* go to this extent, that, where compensation is to be settled by a particular person, that is not necessarily an award. In that I quite agree. An appraisement is not necessarily an award. If those cases are to be supposed to go as far as to decide that an agreement to assess compensation and ascertain value could not be a matter of arbitration, and there is to be no award, I should certainly pause before I concurred in them.'

In re Hopper, therefore, in no way takes away from the authority of *Collins v Collins* and *Bos v Helsham*. In the present case, I come to the conclusion, on the construction of the agreement, that the two persons who are indicated are to be mere valuers, not arbitrators.

A material provision contained in the agreement in *In re Hopper* is wanting in the present case; there was there a distinct provision in the agreement that, if the two valuers appointed by the landlord and tenant should disagree in their valuation, the amount of compensation to be paid to the tenant should be referred to the umpirage of such persons as the valuers should in writing appoint. The parties had agreed that, in case of difference, an umpire should be appointed to determine as arbitrator, and he was an arbitrator, if the valuers were not. We have no right to insert such a provision in the present agreement, unless it is a matter of necessary implication; it is not enough to say that there is a reasonable inference that the parties intended it. There is no such necessary implication, and therefore there is no agreement in writing to submit the matter in dispute between the parties to arbitration. The appointment of an umpire is not of itself a submission of arbitration; it is only a consequence of such a submission. The case does not come within section 17, and there is no power to make the agreement a rule of court. The decision of the Divisional Court was right.

In re Carus-Wilson and Greene (Court of Appeal, 1886)

Carus-Wilson sold land to Greene, the purchaser, to pay for standing timber at a price to be arrived at in the following manner:

'Each party shall appoint a valuer and give notice thereof by writing to the other party within fourteen days from the date of the sale. The valuers thus appointed shall, before they proceed to act, appoint by writing an umpire and the two valuers, or, if they disagree, their umpire shall make the valuation. Each party shall pay the charges of his own valuer, and one half the charges, if any, of the umpire. If either party shall neglect to appoint a valuer or to give notice to the other party within the time aforesaid, the valuer appointed by the other party shall make a valuation alone which shall be binding on vendor and purchaser.'

The valuers disagreed and the umpire thereupon determined the price. The vendor, being dissatisfied with the price, applied to the Divisional Court to set aside the award on various grounds. The Divisional Court held they had no power to do so since it was not an award but a valuation. The argument in the Court of Appeal on behalf of the vendor appellant is included, although unsuccessful, since the present author regards it as impeccable and it has been adopted in later cases as a correct statement of the law.

Counsel for the appellant argued: The umpire being appointed to settle a dispute which had arisen between the valuers of the respective parties is in the position of an arbitrator, not of a mere valuer. This case resembles that of *Turner v Goulden* (1873). It may be that the intention was not that he should hold a formal judicial inquiry and hear witnesses, but that he should decide upon inspection, relying on his own skill and knowledge; but it does not necessarily follow from this that he was not an arbitrator. No action would lie against him for negligence or want of skill in the performance of his functions: *Pappa v Rose* (1871) and *Tharsis Sulphur Company v Loftus* (1872). There is no contractual relation between the umpire and either of the parties, and therefore he could not be sued, whereas a mere valuer would be liable to an action for negligence or incompetence as for a breach of the contract to bring due skill and care to the performance of his functions. These considerations tend to show that the umpire was an arbitrator. Counsel also cited *In re Dawdy and Hartcup* (1885), *In re Hopper* (1867), *Bos v Helsham* (1866), *Collins v Collins* (1858) and *Stevenson v Watson* (1879).

LORD ESHER MR: The question here is whether the umpire was merely a valuer substituted for the valuers originally appointed by the parties in a certain event, or an arbitrator. If it appears, from the terms of the agreement by which a matter is submitted to a person's decision, that the intention of the parties was that he should hold an inquiry in the nature of a judicial inquiry, and hear the respective cases of the parties, and decide upon evidence laid before him, then the case is one of an arbitration. The intention in such cases is that there shall be a judicial inquiry worked out in a judicial manner. On the other hand, there are cases in which a person is appointed to ascertain some matter for the purpose of preventing differences from arising, not of settling them when they have arisen, and where the case is not one of arbitration but of a mere valuation. There may be cases of an intermediate kind, where, though a person is appointed to settle disputes that have arisen, still it is not intended that he shall be bound to hear evidence or arguments. In such cases it may be often difficult to say whether he is intended to be an arbitrator or to exercise some function other than that of an arbitrator. Such cases must be determined each according to its particular circumstances. I think that this case was clearly not one of arbitration, and that it falls within the class of cases where a person is appointed to determine a certain matter, such as the price of goods, not for the purpose of settling a dispute which has arisen, but of preventing any dispute. At the time when the umpire was appointed, it cannot be pretended that any dispute had arisen. The vendor and purchaser had respectively agreed to sell and to purchase the timber at a price to be fixed by valuation and, the price not yet being fixed, there was nothing in dispute between them. If the valuers could not agree as to the price an umpire was to be appointed, but nothing need be known to the vendor and purchaser about the matter; there cannot be said to be anything in dispute between them. It was said that there was no contractual relation between the umpire and the parties. I do not see that that is necessarily so. The parties may have delegated it to the valuers appointed by them respectively to employ the umpire for them and then there would be a contract. My reason for holding that the umpire here was not an arbitrator is that he was, in my opinion, merely substituted for the valuers to do what they could not do, viz, fix the price of the timber. He was not to settle a dispute which had arisen, but to ascertain a matter in order to prevent disputes arising. For these reasons, I think the decision of the court below was right.

LINDLEY LJ: I agree. This is an application to set aside what is called an award. But the question is whether this condition of sale provided for anything more than a mere valuation, which was to be made by two valuers, or, if they could not agree, by a third valuer to be appointed by them. A valuer may be, in one sense, called an arbitrator, but not in the proper legal sense of the term. In the ordinary cases of arbitration there is a dispute which is referred. The object of the valuation, on the other hand, is to avoid disputes. There is nothing in the nature of a dispute when the valuer is appointed. It is a term of the agreement for sale that the timber shall be valued and that the purchaser shall take it at the valuation. It is a mere matter of fixing the price, not of settling a dispute.

LOPES LJ: Whether an umpire is to be regarded as an arbitrator or a valuer must, in my opinion, depend on the circumstances and the documents in each case. Having regard to the circumstances and documents in the present case, I feel clear that the umpire was to be a mere valuer. I cannot see how he could be in any different position from that of the two valuers appointed by the parties respectively. He is merely substituted for them upon their being unable to fix the price. He is not called in to settle judicially any matter in controversy between the parties. No such controversy in fact existed. He is by the exercise of his knowledge and skill to make a valuation of the timber, the object being to prevent disputes from arising, not to settle them after they have arisen. For these reasons, I think the appeal must be dismissed.

Appeal dismissed

Quasi-arbitration (see LPA 1.9)

In the case that follows it was held that a person in the position of an arbitrator is not liable to either party for failing to use due skill in coming to an opinion about the quality of goods; but see now the views of Lord Salmon in *Sutcliffe v Thackrah* (post).

Pappa v Rose (Court of Exchequer Chamber, 1871)

> This was an appeal from the Court of Common Pleas. The defendant was a broker who was employed by the plaintiff to sell a quantity of Smyrna raisins for him. The contract note for the sale read: 'Sold by order and for the account of Mr D. Pappa to my principals, Messrs S. Hanson & Sons, to arrive, 500 tons black Smyrna raisins, 1869 growth, fair average quality in opinion of selling broker'. The buyers rejected the goods and the defendant inspected them and gave his opinion that they were not of fair average quality.
>
> The plaintiff, who was as a result obliged to sell the raisins at a lower price, brought an action for damages, alleging that the defendant had contracted to use 'due care, skill and diligence' in examining the goods. Bovill CJ held that the defendant was a quasi-arbitrator and was not therefore liable for want of skill in determining the quality. The Court of Common Pleas affirmed this decision. The plaintiff then appealed.

KELLY CB: If it were necessary for us to determine the question whether the contract in this case was for Smyrna raisins of the fair average quality of the growth of 1869, I should not hesitate to say that it was for raisins of the growth of 1869, and that they were to be fair average quality generally, and not of 1869, but that question does not arise here, but whether in undertaking to give his opinion as to the quality of the raisins the defendant, who was the selling broker, undertook not only to use due care, but also due skill in examining the raisins in order to form a correct opinion of their quality. Now I am clearly of opinion that there was no obligation on the defendant to exercise any degree of skill in the matter whatever. He had entered into a contract of an unusual character for a broker to make, and in order to carry out and give effect to such contract he must be considered impliedly to have undertaken to deliver an opinion as to the quality of the raisins sold, if called upon to do so. What more than this had he undertaken to do, unless perhaps it was to look at the raisins on which he had to give an opinion? I am of opinion that he was not bound to do more, and certainly not to bring any skill to the examination of the raisins for the purpose of forming his opinion on their quality. It was for the parties themselves to determine whether he was a person of competent skill to decide as to the quality of the raisins. The defendant has been treated as in the position of an arbitrator, but that has only been by way of illustration. If A and B agree to submit any question to the opinion of a third person that does not bind such third person to give any opinion at all, but if he contracts to give his opinion or award on the matter, he is as much bound to do so as A and B are bound to abide by it when it has been given. But though such arbitrator, when he has undertaken to give his award, is bound to give it, he is not bound to bring any skill in the matter, for that forms no part of his undertaking. There cannot be a better illustration of this than what often occurs in the case of an arbitration, where the parties have thought proper to refer the dispute, not to a lawyer, but to a surveyor or other lay person, and in the course of the enquiry before such arbitrator some important question of law has perhaps arisen. Has such arbitrator undertaken to possess any skill in the law in order to determine such question? Clearly not, and it is for the parties who submit the case to arbitration to take care that the person to whom they refer it is competent to deal with the matters which may come before him. The same principle applies here, and on the ground that there is no contract, express or implied, on the part of the defendant, to exercise any skill whatever in determining the quality of the raisins, I am of opinion that this action is not maintainable, and that therefore the nonsuit was right, and the judgment of the court below ought to be affirmed.

MARTIN B: I am of the same opinion. This is a case in which there was a contract for the sale of Smyrna raisins of the growth of 1869, and the contract contained these words — 'of fair average quality'. If those words stood alone, the question would have been whether the raisins delivered were of fair average quality, but the parties agreed that the selling broker should decide that matter. They were at liberty to do so if they chose, but there was no contract, express or implied, on the part of the selling broker to bring any skill in giving his decision. The parties were content to take him for better or worse, and he is not liable for a wrong decision if given without fraud.

BLACKBURN J: I also am of opinion that the judgment of the court below should be affirmed. I give no opinion on the first question, namely, as to whether the raisins were to be of the average quality as compared with those of other years generally, or as compared only with those of 1869, because the opinion I have arrived at on the second question renders it unnecessary to determine the first question. The second question is whether the defendant undertook to use any skill in forming his opinion as selling broker as to the quality of the raisins. In making the contract of sale, he made it part of the agreement that the raisins should be of fair average quality in the opinion of the selling broker, which must therefore be an undertaking that he was to give an opinion as to the quality of the raisins. I do not decide whether, under these circumstances, the defendant was an arbitrator or not, or what would be the liability he would incur if he were to misconduct himself, but I think he is not responsible for the opinion he gave, and it would be highly inconvenient if it were otherwise, and an action could lie against him by either of the parties to this contract. The case of *Jenkins v Betham* (1855) is very different, as there the defendant contracted to use proper skill as a valuer for the plaintiff. So here, if the cause of action had been shaped for not using proper skill as a broker, the defendant might have been liable for not possessing such skill.

MELLOR AND LUSH JJ. concurred.

Judgment affirmed

Note

In the case of *Jenkins v Betham* referred to, the defendants were held liable for negligence. They were employed exclusively by the plaintiff to value dilapidations or property belonging to the vicarage, as between the incoming and outgoing incumbents. Jervis CJ said:

> 'The cause of action is that the defendants by holding themselves out as valuers and surveyors of ecclesiastical property, represented themselves as understanding the subject, and qualified to act in the business in which they professed to act and this induced the plaintiff to retain and employ them.'

An architect's certificate (see LPA 1.10)

Nearly eighty years ago the Court of Appeal held that, when an architect gave his certificate under building contracts, he owed a duty both to the building owner and to the builder and he undertook to exercise judicial functions impartially between the parties in giving his certificates. Therefore he could not be sued for negligence by either party.

Mathew J in *Restell v Nye* (1901) held that an architect giving a certificate was in the position of an arbitrator and from this an appeal went to the Court of Appeal which was considered with the other appeal in:

Chambers v Goldthorpe & Restell and others v Nye (Court of Appeal, 1901)

The relevant clauses in the contracts under consideration were:-

'*Clause 20.* Where the value of the works executed, and not included in any former certificate, shall from time to time amount to the sum of £200, the contractors are to be entitled to receive payment at the rate of £75 per cent upon such value upon obtaining the architect's certificate, a further £15 per cent upon such value within one calendar month from the completion of the works, and of which completion the contractors shall then have obtained the certificate of the architect, and the remaining £10 per cent at the expiration of a further period of three calendar months from such last-mentioned certificate provided always that no final or other certificate is to cover or relieve the contractors from their liability under the provisions of clause 14 hereof, whether or not the same be notified by the architect at the time of or subsequently to granting any such certificate.

Clause 21. A certificate of the architect, or an award of the referee hereinafter referred to, as the case may be, showing the final balance due or payable to the contractors, is to be conclusive evidence of the works having been duly completed, and that the contractors are entitled to receive payment of the final balance . . . .

Clause 22. Provided always, that in case of any question, dispute, or difference arising between the employer, or the architect on his behalf, and the contractors attending the carrying out of the contract according to the true intent and meaning of the signed plans and specifications, or as to the works having been duly completed, or as to the construction of these presents, or the said specifications, or as to any other matter or thing arising under or out of this contract, or the execu-

tion of the works hereby contracted for (except as to matters hereinbe-
fore left during the progress of the works to the sole decision or
requisition of the architect), then such question, dispute, or difference
is to be from time to time referred to the arbitration and final decision
of ..... and the said referee's charges and costs of and incidental to
the reference shall be paid by such parties as the referee shall direct,
and the said reference shall be considered a reference to arbitration
within the meaning of the Arbitration Act 1889, or any statutory modification thereof, and no proceedings whatsoever shall be taken by the
contractors against the employer until the contractors shall have
obtained, and save upon, the award of the said referee, whose appointment shall be irrevocable.'

SMITH MR: These are two actions in each of which a question has been raised
as to the liability of an architect for negligence.

The first case is one in which an architect brought an action against the
building owner who had employed him, claiming fees for the work which he
had done, the fees being calculated at a percentage on the amount payable by
the owner to the builder who erected the houses. The owner counter-claimed
against the plaintiff, alleging that the plaintiff had been guilty of negligence in
certifying so large an amount as he did as being payable by the defendant to
the builder. The question thus raised is whether, in allowing and certifying the
amount payable by the defendant to the builder, the plaintiff was in the position of an arbitrator between the owner and the builder, or whether he was acting only as agent for the owner. If, in making out the certificate, the plaintiff
was acting merely as agent for the owner, he would be liable in case he should
have acted negligently. But if he were acting as an arbitrator between the two
parties, he would not be liable for negligence at the suit of the owner. There is
no suggestion in this case that the plaintiff acted fraudulently or in collusion
with the builder, so that the only question is as to his liability for acting negligently.

There can be no doubt that, in what the plaintiff did under several of the
clauses of the building contract, he was acting solely as agent for the owner.
He was employed by the owner to look after the builder, and to see that the
builder made use of proper materials. In those matters the plaintiff was acting
as agent for the owner — his position was adverse to the builder. In those
instances where his duty was simply to protect the interests of the owner he
was acting as agent for the owner, and would be liable to the owner if he acted
negligently. But the question in the present case has arisen out of what the
plaintiff did when acting under clause 20 of the building agreement. By that
clause the owner and the builder agreed to be bound by the final certificate to
be given by the plaintiff. Was the plaintiff, in giving that certificate, acting as
agent for the owner, or was it his duty to act impartially as an arbitrator
between the owner and the builder? I feel unable to hold that under clause 20
the sole duty of the plaintiff was to look after the interests of the owner as
against those of the builder. Under that clause he owed a duty to the builder
as well as to the owner. In agreeing to act under that clause, he undertook a
duty towards both of them which was to hold the scales fairly and to decide
impartially between them the amount which the builder was entitled to be
paid by the owner. Reference was made to the effect of clause 22 in the agree-

ment, and the judgment of Grove J in *Clemence v Clarke* (1879) was cited; but I do not see why, in case of a dispute arising under the contract, either party should not be entitled to go to arbitration under that clause. Under the contract in the second case now before the court, it seems clear that either party, in the case of a dispute, would be entitled to have it referred to arbitration. But the point does not seem to me material to the real question which we have now to decide. *Lloyd Bros v Milward* (1895), and *Clemence v Clarke (supra)*, seem to lead to the conclusion that, unless there is a dispute and a reference to arbitration under clause 22 before the architect has given his certificate, under clause 20 the certificate given by him is final between the owner and the builder.

What is the duty of the plaintiff in giving his certificate? The ascertainment of the amount to be paid by the owner to the builder is not a mere matter of arithmetic. The architect's duties are not merely ministerial or clerkly, to use the words of Lord Coleridge CJ in *Stevenson v Watson* (1879). The matter requires the use of professional knowledge, skill and judgment. In such circumstances *Stevenson v Watson* appears to show that the position of the architect is that of an administrator between the owner and the builder. It was argued that there could be no arbitration because no dispute had arisen between the owner and the builder. In my opinion, there can be an arbitration to settle matters although no dispute has actually arisen with regard to them if it is probable that a dispute will arise unless the arbitration takes place.

I will refer to *Tharsis Sulphur and Copper Co v Loftus* (1872) in which there was no more a dispute than there has been in the present case. There damage had occurred to a ship which required an average adjustment. There was no actual dispute as to the proportions in which the loss had to be borne by the various parties, but is was necessary that the question should be settled between them, and an average adjuster was asked to settle it. So in the present case when the builder had carried out his contract it became necessary that the question should be settled how much the owner ought to pay the builder. The claim in *Tharsis Sulphur and Copper Co v Loftus (supra)* was made against the average adjuster for negligence. It was held that he was not liable on the general principle that a person so employed is in the position of an arbitrator, and cannot be sued in respect of the manner in which he has exercised his functions, unless he be guilty of fraud or collusion. Bovill CJ. said:

'No authority has been cited to show that a person called upon to act as an arbitrator, or to settle disputes, or adjust accounts between parties, is liable to an action for negligence.'

Keating J said (ibid):

'Now, without deciding what is the proper definition of an arbitrator, it appears to me clear that the defendant is in the position of an arbitrator for the present purpose, inasmuch as he was a person by whose decision two parties having a grievance agreed to be bound. It appears to me that the safe rule, when parties agree to be bound by the decision of a third party on any matter, is that they take him in such a case for better or worse; and if he discharges his duty faithfully and honestly, they must be satisfied.'

Brett J. said (ibid):

> 'Then it is said that the defendant is liable because he was not an arbitrator, but only a person who had undertaken to adjust accounts between two parties. Now the case of *Pappa v Rose* (1871) decides that a person who undertakes to give a decision between two parties as to any matter, though he may not be an arbitrator in the strict sense of the word, as not being bound to exercise all the judicial functions for the purpose of deciding the matter in dispute that an arbitrator in the strict sense of the term would have to exercise, nevertheless is not liable to an action for want of skill. It appears to me that the reasoning employed in that case is equally applicable to an action for want of care, and that if an arbitrator in the strict sense of the word is not liable for want of care, it follows that a person who has undertaken to decide a dispute between two parties is also not liable.'

In my judgment, the present case is covered by those words. When acting under clause 20 of this building contract, the plaintiff was in the position of one who had undertaken to exercise judicial functions with regard to the questions that had arisen between the owner and the builder, and, therefore, he is not liable to an action for negligence in respect of the way in which he exercised those functions.

I will add a few words as to *Rogers v James* (1891) in which an architect was held liable in an action for negligence by his employer. That case is distinguishable from the one we have now to decide, though to some extent it supports the view I am now taking. The negligence there alleged was not properly supervising the work done under a building contract, which was the thing he was employed by the building owner to do. He was employed to do that supervision simply as agent for the owner, and his position was adverse to the builder. There was no arbitration in the matter at all. The case was simply one of a negligent breach of the duty owed by an agent to his principal. The question there decided has nothing to do with the present point.

For these reasons I think that the counterclaim raised by the defendant in the first of the two cases now under appeal is not maintainable, and that this appeal should be dismissed. The second case we have to decide is one in which a building owner has sued an architect for negligence of the same kind as that alleged in the first case. There may be some slight differences in the facts of the two cases, but they do not affect the principles to be applied in deciding them. The real point in issue in the two cases is the same, whether the architect in giving his final certificate of the amount due from the building owner to the builder was in the position of an arbitrator or of an agent to the building owner. For the reasons I have already stated I think that in the second case the action will not lie, and the appeal in this case must also be dismissed.

HENN COLLINS CJ: I am of the same opinion. The question in these two appeals is the same. The question is whether an architect who has undertaken the duties which were undertaken by the architects in the two cases now before us is in the position of what has been sometimes called a quasi-arbitrator. If he is, then it appears to me that upon the authorities no action is maintainable against him for negligence in the exercise of his functions. The question whether or not he is in that position depends upon whether, as was said by Channell J in the court below, he was placed in a position in which he was bound to exercise his judgment impartially as between the two parties to the building contract. It was argued that he was not in that position; that he was simply an agent of the building owner and, therefore, owed no duty whatever to the builder. The question is whether that view, or the view that he was bound to exercise his judgment impartially between the parties, is the correct one.

In my opinion, his position was that of a quasi-arbitrator. The construction of clause 22 of the contract has been the subject of a decision of this court in *Lloyd Bros v Milward (supra)* by which we are bound. It was there held that where a dispute had arisen—that is to say, where a dispute had actually been formulated between the parties—before the architect had given his certificate, the jurisdiction of the architect was ousted, and that of the arbitrator let in, but that, if no such formulated dispute had arisen before the architect had given his certificate, the jurisdiction of the referee was not let in, and the certificate of the architect was final and as binding as the award of a referee, as conclusive evidence that the works had been completed, and that the builder was entitled to the balance for which the certificate was given.

What is the position of an architect whose duty it is to give a certificate which is to be final and binding both on his employer and the other party to the building contract? Is he free from any obligation towards one of the parties, or is his position such that he is under the duty of exercising his judgment impartially between the two parties? It appears to me that he is in the last-mentioned position. The case seems to me to come exactly within the decision of *Stevenson v Watson*, which was decided in 1879. I have always looked on that case as the leading authority on the subject. It came after a series of cases in which the position of a lay person who has to decide a dispute between two parties had been discussed. Lord Coleridge CJ reviewed the preceding authorities, and laid down the law on a sound logical principle. He said that where a matter is left by two parties to the judgment of a third who is to determine their rights, and the task is not merely one of arithmetic, but involving technical skill and knowledge, that person is in the position of a quasi-arbitrator, and no action will lie against him for negligence in the performance of those duties.

In that case the question arose in demurrer, and the material clause of the contract, which was set out in the statement of claim, was as follows:

'The contractor and the directors will be bound to leave all questions or matters of dispute which may arise during the progress of the works or in the settlement of the account to the architect, whose decisions shall be final and binding upon all parties. The contractor will be paid on the certificate of the architect.'

That is substantially the same as what is contained in clause 20 in the contract in the present case. There was no formulated dispute in that case any more than there is here, but the certificate of the architect was to be final and binding. The builder sent in to the defendant accounts which showed a balance, after giving credit for certain sums, of £1,616 6s 7d, and it was alleged that the defendant, without calling on the plaintiff for any explanation, and without communicating to him on the subject, proceeded to ascertain what, in his judgment, was payable and gave a certificate to the effect that a balance of £251 14s 4d was due. There was, therefore, no formulated dispute any more than there is in the case now before us. Lord Coleridge, in delivering judgment, said he thought that, though no doubt the result was one of figures, yet, before it could be arrived at, there must be an exercise of professional knowledge, skill, and judgment. He then continued:

'Moreover, it seems to me that it is so provided for by the contract, and that the true view of the contract is that presented by [counsel], that before the plaintiff can recover sums of money from the building owner there must be the certificate of the architect to ascertain what sums are due from the building owner to the plaintiff. Now, if I have rightly described the position of the defendant with respect to the plaintiff, it follows from the decided cases that this action does not lie. Where, indeed, the building owner and the architect collude together, and in collusion the architect fraudulently abstains from doing his duty towards the builder, there is authority for saying that he can maintain an action against the building owner . . . . I think this case is within the authority of the cases cited which decide that where the exercise of judgment or opinion on the part of a third person is necessary between two persons, such as a buyer and seller, and, in the opinion of the seller, that judgment has been exercised wrongly, or improperly, or ignorantly, or negligently, an action will not lie against the person put in that position, when such judgment has been wrongly, or improperly, or ignorantly, or negligently exercised.'

It was contended that there can be no quasi-arbitration unless a dispute is in existence, but I think that there is a fallacy in that argument. There is a difference between a dispute formulated between the parties, so as to be within clause 22 of the contract as interpreted by the Court of Appeal in *Lloyd Bros v Milward (supra),* and that sort of possible difference which underlies an agreement between two parties, that what one is to pay and the other is to be paid in respect of a certain matter shall be ascertained by a third person. In such an agreement there is involved an underlying assertion of possible difference as to the rights to be so ascertained by the third person, and if he, having notice of the agreement, accepts the responsibility of deciding between the two parties he must, in my opinion, have duties towards both of them. It is not necessary that there should be a formulated dispute in order to put such a person in the position of a quasi-arbitrator.

Is, then, the architect in the two appeals now before us in that position? As the acts of the parties have not brought clause 22 into operation, it seems to me that the architect is in the position of a quasi-arbitrator—that is to say, his duty is to ascertain impartially the rights and liabilities between the building owner and the builder by the exercise of his skill and judgment. The matter seems to me to come well within the principles laid down in *Pappa v Rose, Tharsis Sulphur and Copper Co v Loftus,* and *Stevenson v Watson (supra).* Those cases seem to me not only to lay down the principle to be applied in the present matter, but to be clear authorities as to the terms of the contract now before us. As I have said, it was held in *Lloyd Bros v Milward (supra)* where there was a formulated dispute within clause 22, that the jurisdiction of the architect was ousted. And in *Clemence v Clarke (supra)*, where there was no such formulated dispute, it was held that the certificate of the architect was final, and it was spoken of by Grove J as an award. Taking those two cases together, it seems to me to be clearly established that, as the architect's functions were not ousted by anything done under clause 22, he was a person clothed with the duty of exercising his judgment impartially in deciding between two persons. I agree with the reasoning of my Lord and with that of Channell J in the court below.

As to *Wadsworth v Smith* (1871), the question there was whether a building contract, in which it was provided that the architect's certificate was to be final between the parties as to certain matters, was a submission to arbitration within the Common Law Procedure Act 1854, so as to admit of being made a rule of court, and it was to this point that the observations in the case were addressed. If such a contract were a submission, the architect would be, in the full sense of the term, an arbitrator. This is, presumably, the reason why in the subsequent cases the courts have been careful to refer to persons similarly situated as 'quasi-arbitrators'—that is, persons not acting under a formal submission, but, nevertheless, for certain purposes regarded as being in the same position as arbitrators. I see no material distinction between the facts in the two appeals now before us.

In the second case now before us it is to be observed that the judge was Mathew J who tried *Rogers v James* in 1891, where it was held that an action for negligence lay by the building owner against the architect. No one disputes that for many purposes the architect is the agent of the building owner, and so would be liable for negligence, but it is not inconsistent with his employment that he should for some purposes assume the role of quasi-arbitrator, and when acting in that position no action for negligence will lie against him. In *Rogers v James* the architect was not acting in the capacity of quasi-arbitrator, but as agent for his employer.

ROMER LJ dissented and sought to distinguish *Stevenson v Watson (supra)* because of what he termed 'the special nature of the clause in the contract: "The contractor and the directors will be bound to leave all questions or matters of dispute which may arise during the progress of the works or in the settlement of the account to the architect, whose decisions shall be final and binding upon all parties." '

Appeal dismissed

The House of Lords (Lords Reid, Morris, Hudson, Dilhorne and Salmon), however, overruled the previous case of *Chambers v Goldthorpe* (1901) in *Sutcliffe v Thrackrah and others* (1974).

Sutcliffe v Thackrah and others (House of Lords, 1974)

The facts are stated in the judgment of Lord Reid.

LORD REID: My Lords, the appellant in 1961 wished to have a high class dwelling house built on a site which he had acquired. He got in touch with the respondents who are a firm of architects. There were long and detailed discussions. Ultimately in 1963 the architects prepared the necessary documents for the invitation of tenders by contractors. The lowest tender, £22,368, was by a company David Walbank and it was accepted, the RIBA form of contract being used. There does not appear to have been any formal contract between the appellant and the architect but it is not disputed that they were aware that the RIBA form was to be used and that they undertook to carry out the duties of an architect under that form of contract.

The house ought to have been completed early in 1964 but progress was slow and the architect had occasion to make a number of complaints to the contractors. A number of interim certificates were issued to the contractors by the architects. The present case arises out of the issue of two certificates No 9 on 25 May 1964 for £2,620 and No 10 on 1 July 1964 for £1,837. These sums were duly paid by the appellant.

A short time thereafter it was decided to terminate Walbank's contract. It is not disputed that the appellant had adequate grounds for taking this step. Then Walbank became insolvent.

Later it was discovered that these interim certificates covered much defective work. The cost of remedying the defects could not be recovered from Walbank, so in 1968 the appellant sued the architects for the loss caused to him by negligence of the architects in issuing these certificates. After prolonged proceedings the official referee held in 1972 that the architects had been guilty of negligence and awarded damages to the appellant. What appears to have happened was that one of the architects was well aware of these defects before the certificates were made up but that he failed to pass this information to the quantity surveyor who assumed that all the work was satisfactory.

The case for the respondents (the architects) is that there is a rule of law which absolves architects from liability for negligence in issuing certificates. It is said that the architect's duty is only to act honestly, and it is not disputed that the respondents did act honestly. But it is said that in issuing certificates, an architect owes no duty to his client to exercise care or professional skill. There is authority for this rather startling proposition and the Court of Appeal with obvious reluctance felt bound to follow it. But your Lordships are free to reconsider the whole matter. If it is held that the architects did owe a duty to their client to exercise care and skill, then it is not now disputed that the respondents failed in that duty and it is agreed that damages should be assessed at £2,000.

The argument for the respondents starts from the undoubted rule, based on public policy, that a judge is not liable in damages for negligence in performing his judicial duties. The next step is that those employed to perform duties of a judicial character are not liable to their employers for negligence. This rule has been applied to arbitrators for a very long time. It is firmly established and could not now be questioned by your Lordships. It must be founded on public policy but I am not aware of any authoritative statement of the reason for it. I think it is right but it is hardly self-evident. There is a general rule that a person employed to perform duties of a professional character is liable in damages if he causes loss to his employer by failure to take due care or to exercise reasonable professional skill in carrying out his duties. So why should he not be liable if the duties which he is employed to perform are of a judicial character?

The reason must, I think, be derived at least in part from the peculiar nature of duties of a judicial character. In this country judicial duties do not involve investigation. They do not arise until there is a dispute. The parties to a dispute agree to submit the dispute for decision. Each party to it submits his evidence and contention in one form or another. It is then the function of the arbitrator to form a judgment and reach a decision.

In other forms of professional activity the professional man is generally left to make his own investigation. In the end he must make a decision but it is a different kind of decision. He is not determining a dispute: he is deciding what to do in all the circumstances. He may go wrong because he has at some stage failed to take due care and that may not be difficult to prove. But coming to a wrong but honest decision on material submitted for adjudication is rarely due to negligence or lack of care, and it is seldom due to such gross failure to exercise professional skill as would amount to negligence. It is in the vast majority of cases due to error of judgment and there is so much room for differences of opinion in reaching a decision of a judicial character than even the most skilled and experienced arbitrator or other person acting in a judicial capacity may not infrequently reach a decision which others think is plainly wrong.

But a party against whom a decision has been given that is generally thought to be wrong may often think that it has been given negligently, and I think that the immunity of arbitrators from liability for negligence must be based on the belief — probably well-founded — that without such immunity arbitrators would be harassed by actions which would have very little chance of success. And it may also have been thought that an arbitrator might be influenced by the thought that he was more likely to be sued if his decision went one way than if it went the other way, or that in some way the immunity put him in a more independent position to reach the decision which he thought right.

But whatever be the grounds of public policy which have given rise to this immunity of persons acting in a judicial capacity, I do not think that they have anything like the same force when applied to professional men when they are not fulfilling a judicial function.

The point can perhaps be most clearly illustrated by considering the case of a skilled man engaged to value some property or object. The circumstances may vary very much. The owner may wish to sell or insure the property and want to know its market value. No one doubts that in that case the valuer may be sued for negligence if his negligent valuation has caused loss to the owner. Or the owner may have reason to believe that a particular person A would buy the property from him and would accept a valuation by a skilled man. Or he may have agreed with A to sell at a price to be fixed by a skilled valuer, or by this particular valuer. And he may or may not have told the valuer about this when engaging him.

There is modern authority to the effect that if the valuer knows that his valuation will affect or bind another person besides his client, the owner, then he can claim an arbitrator's immunity. But why should that be? The valuer is in each case engaged by only one party and he has exactly the same task to perform in all these cases. He must, to the best of his ability, estimate the market price of the property. I do not believe that a professional man would approach his task in any different spirit or be influenced in any significant way because he knew that the interests of some other person besides his employer would be affected by the conclusion which he reached.

On the other hand, the valuer could be engaged by both parties as an arbitrator if there is a dispute about the value of certain property. The dispute would be submitted to him for decision and the parties would put their contentions before him. Then he would have to judge between them and have an arbitrator's immunity.

Now I can come to the position of an architect. He is employed by the building owner but has no contract with the contractor. We do not in this case have occasion to consider whether nevertheless he may have some duty to the contractor: I do not think that a consideration of that matter would help in the present case. The RIBA form of contract sets out the architect's functions in great detail. It has often been said, I think rightly, that the architect has two different types of function to perform. In many matters he is bound to act on his client's instructions, whether he agrees with them or not; but in many other matters requiring professional skill he must form and act on his own opinion.

Many matters may arise in the course of the execution of a building contract where a decision has to be made which will affect the amount of money which the contractor gets. Under the RIBA contract many such decisions have to be made by the architect and the parties agree to accept his decisions. For example, he decides whether the contractor should be reimbursed for loss under clause 11 (variation), clause 24 (disturbance) or clause 34 (antiquities); whether he should be allowed extra time (clause 23); or where work ought reasonably have been completed (clause 22). And, perhaps most important, he has to decide whether work is defective. These decisions will be reflected in the amounts contained in certificates issued by the architect.

The building owner and the contractor make their contract on the understanding that in all such matters the architect will act in a fair and unbiased manner and it must therefore be implicit in the owner's contract with the architect that he shall not only exercise due care and skill but also reach such decisions fairly, holding the balance between his client and the contractor.

For some reason not clear to me a theory has developed and is reflected in many decided cases to the effect that where the architect has agreed or is required to act fairly he becomes what has often been called a quasi-arbitrator. And then it is said that he is entitled to an arbitrator's immunity from actions for negligence. Others of your Lordships have dealt with the older authorities and I shall not say more about them than that they are difficult to reconcile and often unconvincing. They are not confined by any means to cases involving architects and one view of them has recently in *Arenson v Arenson* (1972) been succinctly expressed by Buckley LJ:

'In my judgment, these authorities establish in a manner binding upon us in this court that, where a third party undertakes the role of deciding as between two other parties a question, the determination of which requires the third party to hold the scales fairly between the opposing interests of the two parties, the third party is immune from an action for negligence in respect of anything done in that role.'

I can see no good grounds for this view. If there is any validity in my conjecture as to the reason of public policy giving rise to the immunity of arbitrators, those reasons do not apply to this situation. Persons who undertake to act fairly have often been called 'quasi-arbitrators.' One might almost suppose that to be based on the completely illogical argument—all persons carrying out judicial functions must act fairly, therefore all persons who must act fairly are carrying out judicial functions. There is nothing judicial about an architect's functions in determining whether certain work is defective. There is no dispute. He is not jointly engaged by the parties. They do not submit evidence as contentious to him. He makes his own investigations and comes to a decision. It would be taking a very low view to suppose that without his being put in a special position his employer would wish him to act unfairly or that a professional man would be willing to depart from the ordinary honourable standard of professional conduct.

The leading authority on which the respondents rely is *Chambers v Goldthorpe* (1901), where it was held by a majority of the Court of Appeal that an architect was not liable for negligence in ascertaining the amount due to the contractor under a building contract. A.L. Smith MR said that the question was whether the architect acted solely as the agent for the building owner to protect his interests as against the builder, or as an arbitrator between the building owner and the builder. Then he continued:

> 'I cannot think, as suggested by the defendant's counsel, that the plaintiff's duty was only to protect the interests of the building owner, in other words to cause the building owner to pay to the builder as little as possible for his work.'

If that was the argument for the owner I am not surprised that it failed. Then he dealt with some of the authorities but he never examined the difference of function between that of an arbitrator and that of an architect.

Collins LJ appears to have thought that the crucial question was:

> 'Can he address himself to his duty in the matter of giving that certificate free from any obligation towards that other party, or is he placed in a position in which it is his duty to exercise his judgment impartially as between the parties to the contract?'

This appears to mean that he had undertaken a duty to the contractor. But the architect had no contract with the contractor and in those days duty in this chapter of the law depended on contract.

I need not deal with the dissenting judgment of Romer LJ because I have already adopted a good deal of his reasoning.

There was nothing very new in the views of the majority. The importance of the *Chambers* case *(supra)* is that it is virtually indistinguishable on its facts from the present case. So if this appeal is allowed it must be overruled. I have the less hesitation in doing that because here and in other parts of the Commonwealth a number of judges have expressed doubts or disapproval of it.

With regard to the earlier cases I do not think that it is practicable to examine them and determine to what extent they are affected by the views of this House in this case. Many, probably most, of the decisions can be justified on their facts. And there are borderline cases where it is far from easy to determine whether there was a sufficient judicial element to require an arbitrator's immunity to attach. If that immunity is claimed, then it is for the person claiming it to show that the functions in the performance of which he was negligent were sufficiently judicial in character.

I would allow this appeal.

LORD MORRIS OF BORTH-Y-GEST From a consideration of conditions [30, 35] it would appear that in the case of a final certificate, unless either party requested arbitration before it was issued or unless the contractor requested arbitration within fourteen days after it was issued, the final certificate was 'conclusive evidence' that the works had been properly carried out and completed. In the case of interim certificates the contractor, subject to the arbitration provisions, would be entitled to be paid by the employer [the building owner] within fourteen days of presenting the certificate. The amount to be recorded in an interim certificate as being due was 'the total value of the work properly executed and of the materials and goods delivered.'

As in the contract there was an express provision for arbitration in the terms set out in condition 35(1) there would seem to be a strong indication that the named architect in the contract was not an arbitrator. But though there was provision in the contract for arbitration, does the fact that the architect had to issue interim certificates upon which the contractor would be entitled to receive and the employer be bound to pay and which would record the total value of the work 'properly executed' place him [the architect] in the position at least of being a 'quasi-arbitrator'?

The respondents were employed and paid by the appellant. The duties involved that the architect would act fairly: he was to act fairly in ensuring that the provisions of the building contract were faithfully carried out. He was to exercise his care and skill in so ensuring. But his function differed from that of one who had to decide disputes between a building owner and a contractor. When interim certificates were issued it was necessary to have regard to the contract terms and to exercise care and skill in certifying the value of work done. If the contractor thought that the sum certified was too little the contractor could call for arbitration. If the employer paid the amount certified and later found that there was over-certification as a result of the architect's negligence I can see no reason why, if loss resulted to him, he should not sue his architect.

As parties to a building contract or to a contract of sale are in general free to introduce whatever terms they wish into their contract, it follows that it is quite possible for them to arrange that someone, who at one stage is the agent of one party, may at another stage become an arbitrator as between the parties. But this must be a definite arrangement. The mere fact that an architect must act fairly as between a building owner and a contractor does not of itself involve that the architect is discharging arbitral functions . . . .

It is manifest that each case must depend upon its circumstances and upon the contents of the particular contract in the case. In *Tharsis Sulphur and Copper Co Ltd v Loftus* (1872) it was held that an average adjuster appointed by agreement between parties who were to accept his decision was in the position of an arbitrator and was not liable to be sued for want of care. It was pointed out in the judgments that *Pappa v Rose* (1871) had related to a claim for lack of skill against someone found to have been an arbitrator but it was held that there was equal immunity from a claim for lack of care; Bovill CJ said that there was no precedent to support a contention that a person called upon to act as an arbitrator to settle disputes or to adjust accounts between parties was liable to an action for negligence. If parties agree to be bound by the decision of a third party they take him, as Keating J put it, 'for better or worse' and 'if he discharges his duty faithfully and honestly they must be satisfied'. It was argued for the plaintiffs that in order that there may be a quasi-arbitrator it is necessary that disputes should have arisen between the parties and that it did not appear that any disputes had arisen. Bovill CJ interposed to say that the nature of the agreement set out assumed that the amount was in question between the parties. Keating J in his judgment said:

> 'Now, without deciding what is the proper definition of an arbitrator, it appears to me clear that the defendant is in the position of an arbitrator for the present purpose, inasmuch as he was a person by whose decision two parties having a difference agreed to be bound.'

I think, therefore, that the case can be regarded as one in which the appointment was by parties who had a difference or dispute. I express no opinion as to whether on the facts of that case the average adjuster ought or ought not to have been regarded as an arbitrator. The case merely shows that if it were assumed or if it was properly found that he was then he would be entitled to immunity.

In *Stevenson v Watson* (1879) the defendant was the architect of the building owner under a contract made between the owner and the plaintiff who was the contractor. The plaintiff and the defendant were therefore not in direct contractual relationship. Under the building contract the architect could order additions or deductions and the amount of such additions to or deductions from the contract were to be ascertained by the architect in the same manner as the quantities had been measured. A clause provided as follows:

> 'The contractor and the directors will be bound to leave all questions or matters of dispute which may arise during the progress of the works or in the settlement of the account to the architect, whose decisions shall be final and binding upon all parties.'

The contractor, who was to be paid on the certificate of the architect, complained of under-certification whereby he had suffered loss and in his action alleged that the defendant had not used due care and skill. The defendant demurred on the ground that the statement of claim showed him to have been an arbitrator and, there being no allegation of fraud or *mala fides,* that there was no cause of action. The demurrer was allowed. Lord Coleridge CJ drew a distinction between duties which he called 'merely ministerial and clerkly' and those which required the exercise of considerable skill and judgment. Lord

Coleridge CJ was prepared to say (this, be it noted, being in 1879) that though the defendant was no party to the building contract yet, having undertaken to perform certain work under it, he might have been liable to the plaintiff under some circumstances. He might have been liable if the true view of the case had been that the contract:

> 'imposed on him the duty of doing certain work requiring no judgment, no opinion, and requiring only the exercise of what I may call ordinary arithmetical powers, and the performance of his duty under that contract was necessary to the plaintiff's right to recover, yet the defendant had refused that duty.'

But as it was the defendant's duties were clearly not merely ministerial or clerkly. As Denman J said, they were very analogous to those of an arbitrator. Though there was no actual dispute between the building owner and the contractor the architect occupied the position of an arbitrator.

Though parties to a building contract may agree that as to some matters the architect of the building owner will be the person to whom disputes will be referred, and agree to accept his decision with the result that if and when he (the architect) is acting as arbitrator he will have the immunity which has been recognised by the courts, it does not follow that he will have any immunity if he is negligent while carrying out the duties for which he is employed by the building owner. In the present case the respondents were not, in my view, made arbitrators. If there was to be an aribtration, condition 35 prescribed who was to be arbitrator. When certifying, or when valuing, the respondents were, in my view, not exercising arbitral functions. But this view calls in question the decisions of the Court of Appeal in 1901 in *Chambers v Goldthorpe,* and in *Restell v Nye* (1901).

A situation where a building owner agrees with his contractor that he will pay on a certificate of his architect, which certificate he agrees is to be taken as certifying the total value of work done and as certifying that it has been properly done, is precisely the situation where, because he has so agreed, he may be involved in loss if his architect has negligently given the certificate. The fact that a building owner and contractor agree that they will treat the certificates of the owner's architect as conclusive evidence that work has been duly completed does not of itself establish that the architect was an arbitrator between them. Neither does the circumstance that by its very nature the architect's function involves that he will act impartially and fairly. He must certainly so act because, there being a contract for work to be done according to the terms of the contract, his function is to see that the contract is carried out. But that does not without more make him an arbitrator. His duty is to act fairly when exercising his professional skill in considering whether work done satisfied the contract requirements as to work to be done; if that circumstance constituted him an arbitrator then at almost every stage he would be an arbitrator. His duty to act fairly does not at all conflict with, but rather is a part of, his duty to safeguard and look after the interests of the building owner who has employed him . . . .

It is one part of the duty of an architect, to make an estimate of the value of work done. But to call him a valuer does not at all resolve the question whether he is or is not to be regarded as an arbitrator. In some circumstances a valuer may be an arbitrator just as in some circumstances an architect may be. It must depend upon the contract or arrangement which is made . . . .

In summarising my conclusions I must preface them by the observation that each case will depend upon its own facts and circumstances and upon the particular provisions of the relevant contract. But in general any architect or surveyor or valuer will be liable to the person who employs him if he causes loss by reason of his negligence. There will be an exception to this and judicial immunity will be accorded if the architect or surveyor or valuer has by agreement been appointed to act as an arbitrator. There may be circumstances in which what is in effect an arbitration is not one that is within the provisions of the Arbitration Act. The expression quasi-arbitrator should only be used in that connection. A person will only be an arbitrator or quasi-arbitrator if there is a submission to him either of a specific dispute or of present points of difference or of defined differences that may in the future arise and if there is agreement that his decision will be binding. The circumstances that an architect in valuing work must act fairly and impartially does not constitute him either an arbitrator or a quasi-arbitrator. The circumstance that a building owner and contractor agree between themselves that a certificate of an architect showing a balance due is to be conclusive evidence of the works having been duly completed and that the contractor is entitled to receive payment does not of itself involve that the architect is an arbitrator or quasi-arbitrator in giving his certificate. *Chambers v Goldthorpe* (1901) was wrongly decided.

LORD HODSON: My Lords, I am in full agreement with the opinion of my noble and learned friend, Lord Reid, that the appeal should be allowed.

VISCOUNT DILHORNE gave a lengthy opinion.

LORD SALMON: My Lords, I will not weary your Lordships by repeating the facts nor the relevant sections of the RIBA form of contract which had already been fully recited by my noble and learned friend, Lord Morris of Borth-y-Gest . . . .

It is well settled that judges, barristers, solicitors, jurors and witnesses enjoy an absolute immunity from any form of civil action being brought against them in respect of anything they say or do in court during the course of a trial. This is not because the law regards any of these with special tenderness but because the law recognises that, on balance of convenience, public policy demands that they shall all have such an immunity. It is of great public importance that they shall all perform their respective functions free from fear that disgruntled and possibly impecunious persons who have lost their cause or been convicted may subsequently harass them with litigation: *Rex v Skinner,* per Lord Mansfield CJ (1772); *Henderson v Broomhead* (1859); *Swinfen v Lord Chelmsford* (1860); *Marrinan v Vibart* (1962); and *Rondel v Worsley* (1967). This does not mean that the law fails to recognise the obligation of judges, barristers, solicitors, jurors and witnesses to exercise care. The law takes the risk of their being negligent and confers upon them the privilege from inquiry in an action as to whether or not they have been so. The immunity which they enjoy is vital to the efficient and speedy administration of justice.

Since arbitrators are in much the same position as judges, in that they carry out more or less the same functions, the law has for generations recognised that public policy requires that they too shall be accorded the immunity to which I have referred. The question is — does this immunity extend beyond arbitrators properly so called, and if so, what are its limits?

It is well established that, in general, persons such as doctors, accountants, barristers (acting in an advisory capacity), valuers and architects owe their clients a duty to exercise reasonable care and skill in rendering the services for which they are engaged. If they commit a breach of this duty which causes their client damage, then they are liable to compensate him for the loss which their negligence has caused him. This is obviously just. The heresy (as it seems to me) has, however, grown up that if a person engaged to act for a client ought to act fairly and impartially towards the person with whom his client is dealing, then he is immune from being sued by his client — however negligent he may have been. In short, liability to compensate your client for the damage you have caused him solely by your own negligence is excluded because of your obligations to act fairly and impartially towards someone else . . . .

Both in *Chambers v Goldthorpe (supra)* and *Finnegan v Allen (1943)* the Court of Appeal relied strongly upon a trilogy of cases which I do not find convincing and which indeed seem to conflict with other authorities to which I shall presently refer. The first of the trilogy was *Pappa v Rose (supra)*. The defendant signed a contract as selling broker in the following terms: 'Sold by order and for account of Mr D. Pappa, to my principals Messrs S. Hanson & Son, to arrive, 500 tons black Smyrna raisins — 1869 growth — fair average quality in opinion of selling broker . . . .'

As appears from the report:

> 'There was no evidence to show that there was any recognised standard by which to estimate the fair average quality of black Smyrna raisins generally, or the average of any given number of years — they being an article of very limited demand in the London market.'

Nor is there anything to suggest that the defendant received any fee beyond his ordinary broker's commission. The defendant refused to pass the first two consignments on the ground that they were not fair average quality of 1869 growth. At the trial before Bovill CJ there was conflicting evidence as to the quality of the raisins. The Chief Justice ruled that, on any view of the evidence or the contract, an action would not lie against the defendant because he had acted as judge or arbitrator in deciding the quality of the raisins. Accordingly he nonsuited the plaintiff.

The Court of Common Pleas upheld the nonsuit upon the grounds on which Bovill CJ relied. No authority was referred to in any of the judgments save *Jenkins v Betham* (1854) which the learned judges sought to distinguish.

The headnote in the report of the case [*Pappa v Rose, supra*] is misleading, for all the members of that court dismissed the appeal on the ground that the defendant had never held himself out as having any particular degree of skill in the valuation of black Smyrna raisins. Blackburn J said:

> 'I do not stop to inquire whether the defendant stood in the position of an arbitrator or not . . . The case of *Jenkins v Betham* does not affect this

question. There, the defendants declared themselves to be persons possessed of proper skill in valuations.'

In my view, this case, as it emerged from the Exchequer Chamber, in reality only decided, no doubt rightly, that a man who did not hold himself out as possessing any particular degree of skill in assessing the quality of certain goods, could not be taken to have warranted that he did possess such skill. Accordingly, if he was appointed to assess the quality of such goods (incidentally without a fee) and, owing to lack of skill, made an honest mistake in his assessment, no action would lie against him on that account.

The second case of the trilogy was *Tharsis Sulphur and Copper Co Ltd v Loftus (supra)*. This was decided by Denman J and the same three distinguished judges who had in the previous year decided *Pappa v Rose (supra)* in the Court of Common Pleas. The plaintiffs were the owners of a cargo being carried by sea. The ship and cargo were damaged in a storm and incurred certain general average and other losses. The defendant was an average adjuster. The plaintiffs and the shipowners jointly employed the defendant for reward:

'to investigate and examine the vouchers and accounts of the . . . losses . . . and to . . . prepare a statement showing the proportion of the . . . losses . . . to be contributed and borne by the . . . ship . . . and . . . cargo respectively, according to the usage and custom of Lloyd's . . . .'

The plaintiffs and the shipowners agree to abide by the defendant's apportionment. By their pleading the plaintiffs alleged that the defendant had acted with gross carelessness as a result of which they had paid the shipowners a sum far in excess of the amount due. They claimed this excess from the defendant as damages for negligence. The case came before the court upon demurrer and judgment was given for the defendant. The court, following its own decision in *Pappa v Rose (supra)*, held that the defendant was immune from action because he was acting as an arbitrator or quasi-arbitrator. It was said that the only distinction between the two cases was that the first concerned lack of skill, and the second, chiefly lack of care, and that this distinction was irrelevant—as no doubt it was. I find the decision in the *Tharsis Sulphur and Copper Co Ltd (supra)*, case difficult to accept. Contrary to what Bovill CJ suggested during argument, there does not seem to me to have been any dispute between the parties. They both knew that a loss had been suffered which had to be apportioned between them, but there is nothing to show that they had any idea, let alone conflicting ideas, of what the correct apportionment should be. Each of them might have engaged a separate average adjuster to advise him; had these not agreed, a dispute could have arisen between the parties which they might have submitted to arbitration—a somewhat unusual course in business of this kind. Instead, they sensibly decided to avoid disputes and differences by jointly employing one average adjuster to advise them upon how the loss should be apportioned and agreed to accept and act upon his advice. I do not agree that he was employed solely to give his honest opinion. It was undoubtedly, in my view, an implied term of his contract that he would use the care and skill to be expected of a reasonably experienced and competent average adjuster: see *In re Hopper* (1867). He may well have done so — but that is beside the point. He was engaged upon the ordinary business of an average adjuster in making his appraisal. I do not understand how public policy could in these circumstances possibly demand that he should be invested with an immunity against a claim for damages for a breach of the implied term in his contract. Moreover, the doctrine laid down by the Court of Common Pleas in *Pappa v Rose* and the *Tharsis Sulphur and Copper Co Ltd's* case *(supra)* is very difficult to reconcile with *Jenkins v Betham (supra)* and *Turner v Goulden* (1873). In each of those cases there was a sum admittedly due from A to B. The only question was as to the amount of that sum. A and B each appointed a valuer on the basis that if the valuers agreed a sum, then that was the sum which should be paid but that, if the valuers failed to agree, an umpire should be appointed. Both valuers knew that, if they agreed a value, then their valuation would be final and conclusive as between A and B. In each case the valuers did agree and the sum agreed was paid. Then one of the parties sued the valuer he had employed for negligently agreeing that sum and thereby causing him to suffer a loss. In both cases it was decided that the action would lie. In *Turner v Goulden (supra)*, Lord Coleridge CJ cited with approval what Cockburn CJ had said in *In re Hopper (supra)*:

> 'The authorities . . . no doubt established the proposition that, where the matter to be determined by the referee is merely one of value, that is not, strictly speaking, an arbitration. I am not at all disposed to quarrel with the cases . . . but I think they must not be taken to comprehend every case of compensation or value: as where, in ascertaining the value of the property or amount of compensation to be paid, the matter assumes the character of a judicial inquiry, to be conducted upon the ordinary principles upon which judicial inquiries are conducted, by hearing the parties and the evidence of their witnesses. If it be the intention of the parties that their respective cases shall be heard, and a decision arrived at upon the evidence which they have adduced before the arbitrator, it would be taking too narrow a view of the subject to say that, because the object to be arrived at was the ascertaining of the value of property or the amount of compensation to be paid, the matter was not properly to be considered as one of arbitration.'

Lord Coleridge CJ then said, and I would echo his words in the present case: 'There is nothing of that sort here.' Nor was there in *Pappa v Rose,* nor in the *Tharsis Sulphur and Copper Co Ltd's* case *(supra)*.

In *In re Hopper (supra)* Cockburn CJ, with whom Blackburn and Lush JJ agreed, was in effect saying that the question as to whether anyone was to be treated as an arbitrator depended upon whether the role which he performed was invested with the characteristic attributes of the judicial role. If an expert were employed to certify, make a valuation or appraisal or settle compensation as between opposing interests, this did not, of itself, put him in the position of an arbitrator. He might, for example, do no more than examine goods or work or accounts and make a decision accordingly. On the other hand, he might as in *In re Hopper (supra)*, hear the evidence and submissions of the parties, in which case he would clearly be regarded as an arbitrator. Everything would depend upon the facts of the particular case. I entirely agree with this view of the law.

The third case of the trilogy was *Stevenson v Watson (supra),* in which the plaintiff, a builder, sued the architect appointed under a building contract for negligently failing to certify sums alleged to be due to the builder by the building owners. The court in allowing a demurrer and giving judgment for the defendant relied upon what had been said by the Court of Common Pleas in the first and second case of the trilogy. I think that the decision in the third case was probably right, but not because of anything said in the first two cases. Under the very special terms of the contract in *Stevenson v Watson* 'all questions or matters in dispute which (might) arise during the progress of the work or in settlement of the account' had to be left to the architect 'whose decision (was to be) final and binding upon all parties'. It seems to me that this architect may well have been put in the position of an arbitrator under the exceptional terms of the contract. Moreover, since there was no contractual relationship between the architect and the builder, it is difficult to see how any action based on a duty of care could be got up on its feet against him; in those days the law of negligence was in a very early stage of its development.

In *Stevenson v Watson* Lord Coleridge CJ drew a distinction between a professional duty and a clerkly duty. He concluded that the liability of a professional man to be sued for negligently giving a certificate or making a valuation or appraisal which he knew would be binding as between two others depended upon whether he was called on to use skill and judgment or only to exercise an administrative or clerkly function. In the first case he could not be sued; in the second he could. Lord Denning MR made short work of that proposition in his dissenting judgment in *Arenson v Arenson* (1973). I respectfully agree with and adopt every word he said on that topic.

For the reasons I have indicated I have come to the conclusion that the trilogy of cases which were so strongly relied upon in *Chambers v Goldthorpe* (1901) and *Finnegan v Allen* (1943) afford only a tenuous, if indeed any, support for the decision reached in those two cases.

I recognise that for many years the doctrine which those cases enunciated has been generally accepted. As my noble and learned friend, Lord Reid, has said, it is succinctly expressed by Buckley LJ in *Arenson v Arenson* (1973):

> 'where a third party undertakes the role of deciding as between two other parties a question, the determination of which requires the third party to hold the scales fairly between the opposing interests of the two parties, the third party is immune from an action for negligence in respect of anything done in that role'.

My noble and learned friend, Lord Morris of Borth-y-Gest, has cited passages from speeches in your Lordships' House from which it seems that the doctrine, being then unchallenged, was perhaps acceptable even here. This appeal is, however, the first occasion upon which your Lordships' House has had an opportunity of deciding whether or not the doctrine is good law. Clearly it is not a doctrine to be lightly overthrown, however fragile its foundations. Nevertheless I am convinced that, for the reasons I have given, it is contrary alike to principle, sound authority, reason and justice and that therefore we are obliged to overthrow it.

My Lords, I would accordingly overrule *Chambers v Goldthorpe* and allow the appeal.

Appeal allowed

An auditor who is appointed to value shares fairly as between two parties is not protected from an action for negligence by either party. A majority of the House of Lords held that before a valuer could be so protected, there had to be a formulated dispute between the two parties referred for a judicial decision, but Lord Kilbrandon saw no reason why any arbitrator chosen for his skill and judgment should be protected from an action for negligence.

Arenson v Casson Beckman Rutley & Co (House of Lords, 1975)

LORD SIMON OF GLAISDALE. My Lords, the question in this appeal is whether an accountant/auditor of a private company who on request values shares in the company in the knowledge that his valuation is to determine the price to be paid for the shares under a contract for their sale is liable to be sued if he makes his valuation negligently.

The first defendant, Archy Arenson (who has taken no part in the proceedings which have led to the instant appeal), was the controlling shareholder and chairman of a private company, A. Arenson Ltd. He took his nephew, Ivor Arenson, the plaintiff in this action and the appellant before your Lordships, into the business; and Archy Arenson and his wife gave the appellant a parcel of shares in the company. By two documents ('the contract letters') dated 18 March 1964 and 1 October 1968 the appellant agreed with the first defendant, *inter alia*, as follows, the terms being common to both letters:

'5. In the event of my employment with the Company terminating for whatsoever reason, I will offer to sell my Shares to [the first defendant] and it is agreed that he will purchase them from me at the Fair Value ...
6. "Fair Value" shall mean in relation to the Shares in A. Arenson Limited, the value thereof as determined by the auditors for the time being of the Company whose valuation acting as experts and not as arbitrators shall be final and binding on all parties.'

The respondents to this appeal, a firm of chartered accountants, were at all material times the auditors of the company. They are the second defendants in the action.

On 4 April 1970 the appellant's employment by the company ceased. It appears that the secretary of the company thereupon orally requested the respondents to value the appellant's shares (though the detailed terms of this communication are not before your Lordships). The respondents replied to the company secretary by letter dated 13 May 1970, referring to the contract letters, and giving the 'fair value' of the shares as £4,916 13s 4d. On 11 June 1970, in reliance on that valuation, the appellant transferred his shares to the first defendant and received payment of £4,916 13s 4d.

A few months later the company 'went public', the transaction involving a report by the respondents. The appellant alleges that the transaction showed that the shares which he had sold were worth six times their value as assessed by the respondents. In consequence on 19 August 1971 the appellant brought the action from which this appeal arises. Alleging that the said 'valuation was misconceived and erroneous in one or more fundamental respects and was made on a wrong basis or wrong bases', he in effect claimed from the first defendant the difference between what he had been paid for the shares and the sixfold sum which he asserts was their true value. Further or in the alternative, the appellant claimed damages from the respondents, alleging that they 'were negligent in making the said valuation'.

By summons dated 21 October 1971 the respondents applied for an order, under Rules of the Supreme Court, Order 18, rule 19, and the inherent jurisdiction of the court, that the statement of claim should be struck out and the action dismissed as against themselves (the respondents), on the ground that the statement of claim disclosed no reasonable cause of action against them. The matter was adjourned to Brightman J who delivered a reserved judgment. He held that a clear line of authority — *Pappa v Rose* (1871); *Tharis Sulphur and Copper Co Ltd v Loftus* (1872); *Stevenson v Watson* (1879); *Chambers v Goldthorpe* (1901); *Boynton v Richardson* (1924); *Finnegan v Allen* (1943)—established a principle whereby the appellant's claim against the respondents was misconceived and bound to fail. Brightman J stated the principle as follows:

> '. . . where a person (although not an arbitrator) is in the position of an arbitrator, with a duty to hold the scales evenly of his own judgment a matter that is not agreed between them, it is not expedient that the law should entertain an action against the opinion-giver alleging an error, whether negligent or not.'

I shall presume to call this 'Brightman J's formulation'. Although he did not use the term expressly, it is apparent that the learned judge considered the rule to be one of public policy.

The appellant appealed to the Court of Appeal. By reserved judgments delivered on 22 February 1972 they dismissed the appeal, Lord Denning MR dissenting. The majority (Buckley LJ and Sir Seymour Karminski) relied on the same authorities as Brightman J, Buckley LJ summarised their effect in a passage which I presume to call 'Buckley LJ's formulation':

> '. . . these authorities establish in a manner binding on us in this court that, where a third party undertakes the role of deciding as between two other parties a question, the determination of which requires the third party to hold the scales fairly between the opposing interests of the two parties, the third part is immune from an action for negligence in respect of anything done in that role.'

Later in his judgment Buckley LJ reformulated the principle in such a way as to elucidate that by 'question' he meant 'matter in dispute or on which other parties have opposed interests'. A clear distinction, in his opinion, was to be drawn between the position of a third party who is required to adjudicate in such a way and one to whom the parties delegate the function of ascertaining some matter of fact. Buckley LJ held the rule to be based on public policy, which, though not precluding a duty from arising gives immunity from the consequences of its breach. Sir Seymour Karminski delivered a short concurring judgment.

It will be noted that there is some difference between Brightman J's and Buckley LJ's formulations. Buckley LJ's as elucidated involves either 'a dispute' or 'opposed interests'; while Brightman J's goes no further than 'a matter which is not agreed between them'. Buckley LJ's formulation was approved by my noble and learned friend, Lord Salmon, in *Sutcliffe v Thackrah (1974)* as an accurate distillation of the authorities relied on; though he disapproved of the reasoning of these authorities and of Buckley LJ's resultant formulation of principle.

Apparently it had been suggested to the Court of Appeal (though not to Brightman J) that the statement of claim might be so amended as to preclude the drastic expedient of striking out. The Court of Appeal was willing to consider such an application on production of a draft of the proposed amendment. This was produced on 9 July 1973, when the Court of Appeal gave leave to amend. The Court of Appeal's order of that date in effect:(1) declared that the (unamended) statement of claim disclosed no reasonable cause of action against the respondents; (2) ordered that the appellant should be at liberty to amend the statement of claim in accordance with the draft produced; (3) ordered that, on the footing of such amendment, Brightman J's striking out order should be discharged; (4) gave the appellant liberty to apply for leave to appeal to your Lordships' House. The costs of the application to Brightman J and to the Court of Appeal were to be the appellant's in any event. The allegation of and claim in negligence against the respondents therefore remained on the record, though with a declaration that it thereby disclosed no cause of action. I apprehend that the Court of Appeal took this course because they considered that the issue might ultimately be appealed to your Lordships; and that, against such an event, it would be desirable for the trial judge *de bene esse* to make findings of fact in relation to the allegation of negligence against the respondents. But the procedure involves the trial judge hearing and ruling on evidence which a Court of Appeal judgment in the very case held to be irrelevant. The allegations contained in the amendment to the statement of claim do not affect the issue before your Lordships, and I desire to say nothing about them.

On 12 February 1974 your Lordships' House gave judgment in *Sutcliffe v Thackrah.* The plaintiff there had employed builders, who subsequently went into liquidation, to build a house for him, the contract being in the standard RIBA form. The defendants were appointed architects and quantity surveyors under the contract. The plaintiff brought an action in negligence against the defendants for, inter alia, over-certifying interim sums due from the plaintiff to the builders. The Official Referee found for the plaintiff and awarded him damages against the defendants. The Court of Appeal reversed the decision on the ground that the defendants were acting in an arbitral capacity and were accordingly absolved from liability for negligence. Your Lordships'

House restored the judgment of the Official Referee. It will be necessary to refer to the opinions in greater detail later. At this stage it is sufficient to state: (i) the Court of Appeal in *Sutcliffe v Thackrah* relied on the line of authority which the majority of the Court of Appeal followed in the instant case; (2) your Lordships' House expressly overruled *Chambers v Goldthorpe,* which was directly in point, in that line of authorities; (3) the majority of the appellate committee expressly disapproved of Buckley LJ's formulation in the instant case (see Lord Reid; Lord Hodson, concurring; Lord Salmon).

In consequence of the decision in *Sutcliffe v Thackrah,* the instant appellant applied to the Court of Appeal for leave to appeal immediately to your Lordships' House against their order of 9 July 1973 ; and, despite the respondents' opposition, the Court of Appeal, on 22 July 1974, acceded to that application—obviously considering that the legal issue raised by the striking-out application could now most conveniently be decided at an interlocutory stage.

Formally, the appeal to your Lordships is only against the costs order made by the Court of Appeal. But it has been rightly treated as raising the point of law which I posed at the outset of this speech—the legal issue falling to be decided on the basis that the facts set out in the statement of claim are correct. Although it would be deplorable were there to be a further appeal in point of law between the appellant and the respondents, the procedure by which the matter has come before your Lordships is an unusual, and in many ways an inconvenient, one for disposing of all the legal issues which may arise between the appellant and the respondents.

Counsel for the respondents, with the ratio decidendi of the majority of the Court of Appeal in the instant case no longer tenable, had perforce to support by a new formulation the actual decision that no action against the respondents lay in negligence. This he did with force and ingenuity—all the more exacting in view of decisions that a 'mere valuer' is not immune from suit in negligence by the person who employs him in the valuation; *Jenkins v Betham (1855); Turner v Goulden (1873); Re Carus-Wilson and Greene (1886); Re Hammond & Waterton (1890).* Counsel founded his argument on four propositions:(1) judges and arbitrators enjoy immunity from suit in negligence in respect of their decisions; (2) such immunity is conferred by law on grounds of public policy, namely the desirability of speedy and final settlement of disputes; (3) Lord Reid in *Sutcliffe v Thackrah* (Lord Hodson concurring) considered that 'many, probably most' of the decisions on which the Court of Appeal relied in that case, as in the instant one, could be justified on their facts, and only Lord Salmon specifically disapproved of any other than *Chambers v Goldthorpe (supra);* (4) the generic nature of the immunity recognised in those cases not specifically disapproved was marked by the longstanding and reiterated use of the phrase 'quasi-arbitrator' (which Lord Morris of Borth-y-Gest and Viscount Dilhorne cited in *Sutcliffe v Thackrah* without apparent disapproval)—thereby according recognition that the role of the person concerned has some essential characteristic akin to that of an arbitrator. Counsel then went on to ask what this essential characteristic could be. Why should judges and arbitrators enjoy immunity from suit in negligence? Because, said counsel, they are in a particularly vulnerable situation; in the nature of things their decisions are liable to be displeasing to at least one of the parties affected thereby; as counsel put it, 'they are liable to be shot at by both sides'. This, then, is the first essential characteristic which is shared by arbitrator and 'quasi-arbitrator', and the first prerequisite to constitute a person who is not an arbitrator under the Arbitration Act 1950 a 'quasi-arbitrator' so as to enjoy immunity from suit. The second such characteristic of an arbitrator, and prerequisite for immunity from suit, is that two or more parties have agreed to be bound by his decision on the question between them. The respondents satisfied both prerequisites; accordingly, they are 'quasi-arbitrators' and immune from suit in negligence in respect of their decision. So far as public policy is concerned, no logical distinction can be drawn between the speedy and final settlement of disputes by an arbitrator and the obviation of disputes by a valuer in the position of the respondents: if public policy requires immunity in the one case, so it must also in the other.

Skillfully though this argument was deployed, I find it less than compelling. My main objections are that the journey starts at the wrong place and arrives at a wrong place. It starts with the immunity conferred on the arbitrator for reasons of public policy. But in my judgment this is a secondary and subordinate consideration of public policy. There is a primary and anterior consideration of public policy, which should be the starting-point. This is that, where there is a duty to act with care with regard to another person, public policy in general demands that such damage should be made good to the party to whom the duty is owed by the person owing the duty. There may be a supervening and secondary public policy which demands, nevertheless, immunity from suit in the particular circumstances (see Lord Morris of Borth-y-Gest in *Sutcliffe v Thackrah*). But that the former public policy is primary can be seen from the jealousy with which the law allows any derogation from it. Thus a barrister enjoys immunity, but only in respect of his forensic conduct (since his duty to the court may conflict with and transcend his duty to his client): *Rondel v Worsley (1967).* And a diplomatic envoy enjoys immunity, but only so long as he is in his post (plus a reasonable time thereafter for him to wind up his official affairs): *Musurus Bey v Gadban (1894).*

It is, in my view, wrong in principle to freewheel by analogy from the arbitrator's immunity, as if it were not exceptional, and as if the primary rule were not one of responsibility.

Not only does the argument start from the wrong place, it arrives at an impossible place. The respondents' contention would leave the instant case in absurd discrepancy with *Sutcliffe v Thackrah* and throw the law into hopeless confusion. The only ways that *Sutcliffe v Thackrah* can be distinguished are, first, that the architect there was for many purposes the building-owner's agent whereas the instant respondents were agents of neither the appellant nor the first defendant, and, secondly, that the RIBA contract contained an arbitration clause. As for the former consideration, it is true that Lord Morris of Borth-y-Gest and Viscount Dilhorne mentioned that relationship of agency, but they did not do so as the start or any intermediate part of their process of reasoning, but rather as its conclusion: since the architects were not made arbitrators they remained throughout agents of the building-owner, and as such liable to him on the general principle of responsibility for negligence.

As for the arbitration clause, both Lord Morris of Borth-y-Gest and Viscount Dilhorne attached importance to it as showing that the architect was not an arbitrator but remained the agent of the building-owner. Lord Salmon also mentioned the point; but I do not think that it formed part of his *ratio decidendi* which was to answer the comprehensive question:

> '. . . namely, the limits of the immunity which the law affords against claims in respect of negligence in general. . . . The question is—does this immunity extend beyond arbitrators properly so called, and if so, what are its limits?'

Lord Reid did not even mention the arbitration clause.

Moreover, all the members of the appellate committee which decided *Sutcliffe v Thackrah* invoked the analogy of a valuer. Lord Reid (Lord Hodson concurring) said:

> 'But whatever be the grounds of public policy which have given rise to this immunity of persons acting in a judicial capacity, I do not think that they have anything like the same force when applied to professional men when they are not fulfilling a judicial function. The point can perhaps be most clearly illustrated by considering the case of a skilled man engaged to value some property or object. The circumstances may vary very much. The owner may wish to sell or insure the property and want to know its market value. No one doubts that in that case the valuer may be sued for negligence if his negligent valuation has caused loss to the owner. Or the owner may have reason to believe that a particular person A would buy the property from him and would accept a valuation by a skilled man. Or he may have agreed with A to sell at a price to be fixed by a skilled valuer or by this particular valuer. And he may or may not have told the valuer about this when engaging him. There is modern authority to the effect that if the valuer knows that his valuation will affect or bind another person besides his client, the owner, then he can claim an arbitrator's immunity. But why should that be?'

Lord Morris of Borth-y-Gest quoted with approval from the dissenting judgment of Romer LJ in *Chambers v Goldthorpe (supra):*

> 'Suppose a person undertakes for reward to value or estimate for another work about to be done for his principal by a third person; in my opinion, he does not, so far as his principal is concerned, become in the position of an arbitrator in regard to his valuation or estimate, merely because he knows that his principal and the third person have no contract between them agreed that, in default of dispute previously arising with regard to the matter, his valuation or estimate is to be taken as conclusive, and as determining the price to be paid by his principal for the work to be done by the third person.'

Since *Hedley Byrne & Co Ltd v Heller and Partners Ltd (1963)* it cannot be a pre-condition for liability that the valuer has undertaken the valuation 'for reward'. Viscount Dilhorne cited with approval the same passage from Romer LJ's judgment. Lord Reid (Lord Hodson concurring) stated that he had adopted a good deal of Romer LJ's reasoning. Lord Salmon actually founded his argument on the example of a valuer:

'A well-known dealer in eighteenth century English paintings is brought an eighteenth century English painting to value for a handsome fee. He is not told why his client requires the valuation. It may be because he intends to sell it or insure it, or perhaps just out of curiosity. The dealer values the picture (entirely honestly but wrongly) at £500. Relying on this valuation, the client asks £500 for the picture, and sells it for that sum. It is subsequently established that the picture was worth £50,000 and that this should have been obvious to anyone in the dealer's position who had exercised reasonable care and the skill which he professed. In such circumstances, the client would have an unanswerable claim against the dealer in negligence. Now suppose exactly the same facts, save that when the client brought the picture to the dealer he told him that the valuation was wanted because he was going to sell the picture to a friend, and the friend had agreed to buy the picture for the value which the dealer put on it, providing he could afford to do so. It would appear on the authority of certain cases to which I will refer later, that the dealer would then be immune from being sued by his client because of his additional duty to act impartially and fairly towards his client's friend. It is said that this factor, of itself, puts the dealer in the same position as if he were performing the functions of a judge or arbitrator; and accordingly, so the argument runs, public policy requires that he should have complete immunity in respect of his undoubted negligence, which had admittedly caused his client a loss. I am afraid that I can find no sensible basis for such an astonishing proposition.'

Lord Salmon tested the position of the architect in *Sutcliffe v Thackrah* by reference to that of the valuer:

'I confess that I can see no more reason for regarding the architect as being in the same position as a judge or arbitrator than there is for so regarding the valuer.'

These passages emphasise the final reason why, as it seems to me, the argument for the respondents not only starts from the wrong place but also ends up in a wrong place—namely, that it is liable to cause injustice without in any way advancing justice. A person adversely affected by a negligent valuation (possible for rich reward) is left without a remedy. He is, in fact, in a worse position than under a formal arbitration, where he has the right to demand a case to be stated for the opinion of the court.

Furthermore, several of the intermediate steps by which the respondents' argument proceeds seems to me to be on shaky ground. Lord Reid did indeed say that 'Many, probably most, of the decisions can be justified on their facts'. But he went on to make it apparent that those were cases in which 'there was a sufficient judicial element to require an arbitrator's immunity. (I shall have to return later to the concept of 'sufficient judicial element'.) Similar were the explanations of *Pappa v Rose* and *Tharsis Sulphur & Copper Co v Loftus (supra)* by Lord Morris of Borth-y-Gest and Viscount Dilhorne. Lord Salmon regarded *Pappa v Rose* as correctly decided on a ground irrelevant to the issue before your Lordships and *Tharsis Sulphur & Copper Co v Loftus* as wrongly decided. With regard to *Stevenson v Watson (supra),* Lord Morris of Borth-y-Gest, Viscount Dilhorne and Lord Salmon all regarded the architect there as having been appointed by 'the special terms' of a building contract to occupy the position of arbitrator. So much for the cases relied on as yielding a principle favour of the respondents.

Then there is the alleged criterion of liability to be 'shot at by both sides'. This could, however, arise in the case of a 'mere' valuer—ie, one admittedly not a 'quasi-arbitrator'. Thus, it has never been doubted that *Jenkins v Betham* (1855) was correctly decided. An incoming rector was entitled to payment for dilapidations from his predecessor. Each appointed a valuer with a view to agreeing the figure. They did agree, but on a common incorrect basis, so that the figure was much too low. The incoming rector was held to be entitled to damages from his own valuer. But, since *Hedley Byrne v Heller (supra),* the outgoing rector's valuer also might well have been held to be jointly liable to the incoming rector.

Finally, there is the alleged criterion of immunity that the valuation etc should be final and conclusive between the parties, such being, it was argued, a characteristic of arbitration. But that is not necessarily so. An arbitrator's award may be subject to review, if he has been appropriately requested to state a case; and there are some other controls over arbitrators by the courts. Finality and conclusiveness do not seem to me be so characteristic of arbitration as to suggest that anyone not an arbitrator whose decision is final and binding is a 'quasi-arbitrator' enjoying immunity from suit in negligence . Even strictly judicial decisions are generally subject to review by way of appeal or rehearing.

I think that a good part of the difficulty which has arisen in this branch of the law has come from the use of the word 'quasi-arbitrator'. 'Quasi' is all too apt to confuse and to mask valid juridical distinctions. 'Quasi-arbitrator' could mean any of the following: (1) such person as is described in Buckley LJ's formulation; (2) such person as is described in Brightman J's formulation; (3) such person as satisfies the two criteria put forward by counsel for the respondents; (4) an arbitrator at common law in contradistinction from one under the Arbitration Act 1950; (5) a person who is not an arbitrator under the Arbitration Act 1950 but nevertheless 'acts in a judicial capacity' or 'character', or 'fulfils a judicial function'.

Meaning (1) is excluded by *Sutcliffe v Thackrah. A fortiori* meaning (2), since it does not necessitate the 'quasi-arbitrator' acting in any way judicially apart from acting fairly—a criterion shown by *Sutcliffe v Thackrah* to be insufficient. I have already given my reasons why I have not been able to accept meaning (3). I am inclined to think that meanings (4) and (5) are merely different ways of putting the same essential concept. But (5) was the way it was considered in *Sutcliffe v Thackrah,* and it was the 'judicial function' which was discussed in argument before your Lordships.

The main issue in this part of the case was whether it was of the essence of a judicial decision that it answers a question (the respondents' contention) or decides a dispute (the appellant's contention). The latter seems to me to be the right view both in principle and on authority. It is true that judges sometimes answer questions. Examples are references by the Home Secretary to the Court of Appeal, Criminal Division, certain references to the Judicial Committee of the Privy Council, and summonses by executors or trustees for the construction of a will or settlement. But these are exceptional, and not the characteristic, activities of judges. The general judicial role in society is to resolve disputes which the parties themselves cannot resolve by conciliation, compromise or surrender.

That is, indeed, the theme that runs throughout the speeches in *Sutcliffe v Thackrah*. It is only necessary to cite a few passages. Lord Reid said:

> 'There is a general rule that a person employed to perform duties of a professional character is liable in damages if he causes loss to his employer by failure to take due care or to exercise reasonable professional skill in carrying out his duties. So why should he not be liable if the duties which he is employed to perform are of a judicial character? The reason must, I think, be derived at least in part from the peculiar nature of duties of a judicial character. In this country judicial duties do not involve investigation. They do not arise until there is a dispute. The parties to a dispute agree to submit the dispute for decision . . . On the other hand, the valuer could be engaged by both parties as an arbitrator if there is a dispute about the value of certain property. The dispute would be submitted to him for decision and the parties would put their contentions before him. Then he would have to judge between them and have an arbitrator's immunity.'

Lord Morris of Borth-y-Gest said:

> 'If there is no arbitration to which the provisions of the Arbitration Act 1950 apply but if two or more people informally agree to refer a disputed matter to the decision of some person of their own selection they may place him in the position of quasi-arbitrator and the common understanding of them all may be that the chosen person in accepting the charge does not expressly or implicitly undertake to do more than to give his honest opinion . . . One of the features of an arbitration is that there is a dispute between two or more persons who agree that they will refer their dispute to the adjudication of some selected person whose decision on the matter they agree to accept . . . A valuer may not be exercising any judicial function. There may be a situation in which two people wish to know the value of some property with a view possibly to their making some contract in regard to it. They may have no dispute because neither has any precise idea as to the value.'

Lord Morris expressly dissented from the view of Collins LJ in *Chambers v Goldthorpe (supra)* that 'no formulated dispute is necessary before such "third person" has both the duties and also the immunities of a quasi-arbitrator'.

Viscount Dilhorne said:

> 'That persons who are appointed as arbitrators, or as it has been called quasi-arbitrators, to resolve a dispute which has arisen or which may arise cannot be sued for negligence in respect of their decisions is, I think, clear law.'

Viscount Dilhorne expressed the view that *Pappa v Rose* and the *Tharsis* case *(supra)* were only correctly decided if on the true view of the contracts in those cases the broker and the average adjuster respectively 'were appointed . . . to resolve disputes . . . which might arise or had arisen'.

Lord Salmon said:

'. . . there are the most striking differences between the roles of the valuer and architect in the circumstances to which I have referred and the role of a judge or arbitrator. Judges and arbitrators have disputes submitted to them for decision.'

The reason why Lord Salmon thought that the *Tharis* case was wrongly decided was that there did not seem to him to be any dispute between the parties.

There may well be other indicia that a valuer is acting in a judicial role, such as the reception of rival contentions or of evidence, or the giving of a reasoned judgment. But in my view the essential prerequisite for him to claim immunity as an arbitrator is that, by the time the matter is submitted for him for decision, there should be a formulated dispute between at least two parties which his decision is required to resolve. It is not enough that parties who may be affected by the decision have opposed interests—still less that the decision is on a matter which is not agreed between them.

Counsel for the respondents relied strongly on *Finnegan v Allen*. It may be that there was a dispute between the parties there. Lord Morris of Borth-y-Gest in *Sutcliffe v Thackrah* seems to have thought that *Finnegan v Allen* was rightly decided, on the basis that on the 'somewhat special' facts the valuer was 'fully in the position of an arbitrator', having had 'a formulated point of difference' referred to him. Lord Salmon seems to have doubted *Finnegan v Allen*. None of the other learned Lords mentioned it; although Lord Reid must have disapproved it along with Buckley LJ's formulation in the instant case unless he thought that it could be supported on the lines of Lord Morris of Borth-y-Gest's explanation. Certainly much of the language of the judgment in *Finnegan v Allen* (which Buckley LJ's formulation followed closely) cannot stand with the speeches in *Sutcliffe v Thackrah*; and I think the decision can only be supported as viewed by Lord Morris of Borth-y-Gest—that there was a formulated point of difference (ie, a dispute) which was referred to a person who was constituted an arbitrator by the terms of the contract.

My Lords, in this speech I have done no more than attempt to answer the question which I posed at its outset, and to declare that in my opinion the statement of claim is not misconceived and bound to fail as against the respondents. But the facts as they are judicially determined may differ from those alleged in the statement of claim. It will then still be open to the respondents to show that their role was a judicial one (as I have tried to explain it), so that they were appointed arbitrators—though in the nature of things they will have to overcome the obstacle that the contract letters declared that their valuation was to be made 'acting as experts and not as arbitrators'. If the respondents succeed in this, they can claim immunity. Even if they fail, it does not follow that they are liable in damages. It will be for the learned trial judge to determine the nature of the duty of care owed by the respondents and whether they were in breach of it. As Lord Salmon said in *Sutcliffe v Thackrah*: '. . . there is no topic about which greater differences of informed opinion may exist than the value of shares in a private company . . .' But, in the meantime, the question before your Lordships is whether the statement of claim discloses a cause of action against the respondents. In my opinion it does, and I would therefore allow the appeal.

LORD WHEATLEY. My Lords, the full narration by my noble and learned friends, Lord Simon of Glaisdale and Lord Salmon, of the essential facts and of the somewhat strange history of this case resulting in its arrival in your Lordships' House renders it unnecessary for me to set them out again.

Whatever other considerations underlie it, the simple issue in this case is whether the order of the Court of Appeal dated 22 February 1973 which declared that the original, ie, the unamended, statement of claim disclosed no reasonable cause of action against the respondents was well founded. If it was not, or even if it was premature, and in the result the case has to be sent to trial on the basis that the case on the unamended statement is still a live issue, then the anomalies in relation to the admission or rejection of evidence which might have arisen under that order of 22 February 1973 would disappear.

Your Lordships were presented with an anthology of cases which concluded with *Sutcliffe v Thackrah.* I do not propose to examine the earlier cases in detail. They have now to be looked at in the light of the decision and of the speeches in your Lordships' House in the case of *Sutcliffe v Thackrah.* But of that more anon. In my opinion the proper and simple approach to the issue is to consider what the respondents, the auditors of the company, were called on to do, what were their legal obligations in that regard, and whether, in the event of their failure to carry out these obligations with consequential loss to the appellant, the latter is precluded from the legal remedy of damages which he seeks by reason of an immunity which the law has conferred on persons in the position of the respondents. At this stage the pleadings of the appellant have to be accepted *pro veritate.* In the event which occurred the appellant and Archy Arenson had agreed by the letters of 18 March 1964 and 1 October 1968 that the fair value of the shares to be transferred from the appellant to Archy Arenson would be determined by the auditors of the company acting as experts and not as arbitrators, and that this valuation would be final and binding on both parties. A verbal request was made by the secretary of the company to the respondents asking them to place a value on the shares in accordance with the letters of 18 March 1964 and 1 October 1968. The respondents undertook the request and in due course provided a non-speaking valuation. In that situation certain duties of care in relation to the valuation were incumbent on the respondents. That is not in dispute. Since *Hedley Bryne & Co. Ltd v Heller and Partners Ltd (supra)* it is clear, if it ever was in doubt, that all persons who express an opinion which is negligent are liable for that negligence to persons who are within a relationship which is recognised by the law and who have suffered damages as a result thereof. Again it is not disputed that the appellant's pleadings bring this case within that category. The respondents, however, successfully argued in the courts below that, be that as it may, they were free from any legal liability through the operation of what is known as the immunity doctrine. This is a doctrine which provides immunity to persons for the consequences of negligence in the exercise of their legal duties by reason of the position which they occupy. This immunity has been given to judges and extended to arbitrators and semble to quasi-arbitrators. Since it is a defence to what otherwise would be a good claim for damages on the ground of negligence, the onus is on the party claiming the immunity to establish it: cf Lord Reid in *Sutcliffe v Thackrah*. Their Lordships in that case recognised that the existence or non-existence of the immunity will depend on the circumstances of the particular case. Accordingly, in the present case the respondents can only succeed at this stage if *ex facie* of the appellant's pleadings they can establish a case for their immunity. Looking to the terms of the letters which constituted their appointment, and particularly to the specific provision that they were to act as experts in the valuation and not as arbitrators, and to what they were being called on to do, it seems to me that the respondents could not extract from these documents or from the appellant's pleadings as a whole the foundation of a case of immunity, unless they could satisfy your Lordships that in all cases a valuer acting as an expert is entitled to the immunity irrespective of the terms conditions and purposes of his appointment. This extreme proposition was not advanced by the respondents' counsel, although they stoutly maintained that the circumstances in the present case provided that immunity. With this latter point I disagree. I am accordingly of the opinion that the appellant's case of negligence on his unamended claim should be allowed to go to trial. Even if the appellant's pleadings and associated documents do not disclose *ex facie* a case of immunity for the respondents, facts may emerge at the trial which cast a different light on the situation. I accordingly consider that the appropriate course is to allow the facts to be elicited and then to consider and apply the law. On that narrow ground alone I would allow the appeal.

However, since it is reasonable to infer that the Court of Appeal granted leave to appeal to your Lordships' House on 22 July 1974 in order that the majority decision of 22 February 1973 could be reconsidered in the light of the decision and speeches in *Sutcliffe v Thackrah* which had subsequently been delivered, and since this involves a general review of the law in this field, it is manifestly desirable that such a course should be followed. In that exercise I feel that I can avoid a good deal of unnecessary repetition, as, having had the benefit of seeing in draft the speech of my noble and learned friend, Lord Simon of Glaisdale, I find it unnecessary to deal with the law in detail, being in agreement with what he has said and concurring with it. I therefore content myself with a number of observations.

(1) It is clear from the speeches of Lord Reid, Lord Morris of Borth-y-Gest and my noble and learned friend, Lord Salmon, in *Sutcliffe v Thackrah* that while a valuer may by the terms of his appointment be constituted an arbitrator (or quasi-arbitrator) and be clothed with the immunity, a valuer simply as such does not enjoy that benefit.

(2) It accordingly follows that when a valuer is claiming that immunity he must be able to establish from the circumstances and purpose of his appointment that he has been vested with the clothing which gives him that immunity.

(3) In view of the different circumstances which can surround individual cases, and since each case has to be decided on its own facts, it is not possible to enunciate an all-embracing formula which is habile to decide every case. What can be done is to set out certain indicia which can serve as guidelines in deciding whether a person is so clothed. The indicia which follow are in my view the most important, though not necessarily exhaustive. They are culled

from the speeches in *Sutcliffe v Thackrah* cited by my noble and learned friend, Lord Simon of Glaisdale, and from several other passages therein. In particular I would refer to the following passages.

Lord Morris of Borth-y-Gest said, after pointing out that the circumstances of his appointment (including the determination of a dispute) might place a person in the position both of a valuer and arbitrator:

'But it by no means follows that everyone who has a duty of valuing, a duty which obviously must be fairly and honestly discharged, is an arbitrator. A valuer may not be exercising any judicial function.'

Then my noble and learned friend, Lord Salmon, said:

'As in the case of the valuer, it is said that the architect is performing much the same functions and must, therefore, be regarded as being in the same position as a judge or arbitrator and must accordingly be accorded the same immunity. I confess that I can see no more reason for regarding the architect as being in the same position as a judge or arbitrator than there is for so regarding the valuer. No reason has ever been suggested. I suspect that this is because none exists. The descriptions "quasi-arbitrator" and "quasi-judicial functions" have been invoked but never defined. They cannot mean more than in much the same position as an arbitrator or judge. In reality, however, there are the most striking differences between the roles of the valuer and architect in the circumstances to which I have referred and the role of a judge or arbitrator. Judges and arbitrators have disputes submitted to them for decision. The evidence and contentions of the parties are put before them for their examination and consideration. They then give their decisions. None of this is true about the valuer or the architect who were merely carrying out their ordinary business activities.'

Then later, Lord Salmon, after quoting a passage from Cockburn CJ in *Re Hopper (1867)* said:

'In *Re Hopper* Cockburn CJ, with whom Blackburn and Lush JJ agreed, was in effect saying that the question whether anyone was to be treated as an arbitrator depended on whether the role which he performed was vested with the characteristic attributes of the judicial role. If an expert was employed to certify, make a valuation or appraisal or settle compensation as between opposing interests, this did not, of itself, put him in the position of an arbitrator. He might, eg, do no more than examine goods or work or accounts and make a decision accordingly. On the other hand, he might, as in *Re Hopper,* hear the evidence and submissions of the parties, in which case he would clearly be regarded as an arbitrator. Everything would depend on the facts of the particular case. I entirely agree with this view of the law.'

I likewise agree with my noble and learned friend's summation of the law.

The indicia are as follows: (a) there is a dispute or a difference between the parties which has been formulated in some way or another; (b) the dispute or difference has been remitted by the parties to the person to resolve in such a manner that he is called on to exercise a judicial function; (c) where appropriate, the parties must have been provided with an opportunity to present evidence and/or submissions in support of their respective claims in the dispute; and (d) the parties have agreed to accept his decision.

(4) Applying the foregoing tests to the present case, it is clear to me that the respondents here cannot pray in aid the appellant's pleadings to satisfy the requirement of immunity. On the contrary, they appear to negative the claim. In this regard I agree with and adopt the analysis and rejection by my noble and learned friend, Lord Simon of Glaisdale, of the submission of counsel for the respondents in support of his contention that the requirements for immunity have been satisfied in the present case. I agree with counsel for the appellant's submission that the valuation here was not to decide a dispute or difference but to avoid a dispute or difference. There is nothing in the appellant's pleadings and relevant documents to suggest that a dispute or difference between the parties existed and was being remitted to the respondents for a judicial (or quasi-judicial) determination, and nothing to suggest that the remit was so treated.

(5) The validity of the decisions from *Pappa v Rose* onwards on which the respondents' counsel relied has to be considered and tested against (a) what was said in *Sutcliffe v Thackrah*, particularly in the rejection of *Chambers v Goldthorpe*, and (b) the indicia to which I have referred. So viewed, I find them difficult to justify. I will only deal with *Finnegan v Allen*, because it is said that for over 30 years it has been the guiding basis on which valuations such as the present one have proceeded, and to overturn it could lead to unfortunate and possibly serious repercussions in relation to past transactions where an action based on negligence may still be open. I recognise that this would be unfortunate and that your Lordships' House would be slow to interfere with an understanding of the law which has regulated such transactions over a long number of years, but if the law has to be restated in a manner which seems to run contrary to that decision, then your Lordships' House will not be deterred from restating it because of the consequences. In my opinion the law requires to be restated, and the consequences may not be so grievous as they might appear to be at first blush, since negligence of a certain nature has to be established before a claim for damages can succeed in circumstances where immunity cannot be established. In my opinion *Finnegan v Allen* cannot pass the test unless, as envisaged by Lord Morris of Borth-y-Gest in *Sutcliffe v Thackrah* there were present there special facts which placed the valuer in the position of an arbitrator. It would appear from what was said by Lord Greene MR in *Finnegan v Allen* that there was a dispute between the parties, and as each case has to be decided on its own facts that factor may have justified the decision although I personally have doubts about that.

However, *Sutcliffe v Thackrah* and the present case should provide the authoritative guides for the future and I am prepared to leave it at that. I would accordingly allow the appeal.

LORD KILBRANDON. My Lords, I agree that the respondents are not immune from suit at the instance of the appellant on the ground of negligence, that the question whether they were guilty of negligence must, along with the allegations of fraud which have been made by amendment, be sent to trial, and that as a consequence of these decisions the appeal must be allowed. It is more in the matter of the implications of these decisions, and in the nature of their philosophical foundations, that I have experienced doubt and difficulty. Since these disabilities do not affect the result at which I arrive, I will try to state them shortly.

I will begin with the position of the valuer, observing parenthetically that I am as mistrustful of the phrase 'mere valuer' as I know some of your Lordships are of the office of 'quasi-arbitrator'. Not infrequently the duties undertaken by an arbitrator or even by a judge are found on inspection to involve nothing more than the making of a valuation. As to the liability of a valuer in negligence I need not requote the old authorities, but will confine myself to the compelling passage in the speech of my noble and learned friend, Lord Salmon, in *Sutcliffe v Thackrah* in which his Lordship instances the giving of a valuation by an expert on pictures. My Lords, I entirely agree that it would be absurd if the situation were that, when an expert is asked by one customer to value a picture, he is liable in damages if he is shown to have done so negligently, but that if two customers had jointly asked him to value the same picture he would have been immune from suit. The latter is precisely the situation displayed here, leaving out, what I think is not relevant at this stage, that the formal request was made by a third party (the company) on behalf of the customers. Two people wanted to know, for reasons which are immaterial, the value of a parcel of shares. They had contracted with one another that in such a situation a particular expert should be asked to give his opinion, which opinion they were bound to accept as final in accordance with their contract. This is just the same as two customers employing a valuer. It does not matter whether there has arisen between the customers and the valuer, a relation of 'neighbourhood' which fixes on the latter an obligation to act with reasonable care, or whether—and more rationally as I would have thought—one holds that the contract between them and the valuer includes an implied term that he will exercise proper skill and care. The formality that the secretary of the company made the contract on behalf of the 'customers' (shareholders) is of no significance. He made it for the shareholders, not for the company. It is not a case of looking for a cause of action in the shareholders on a contract between the valuer and a third party. The result, whether in tort or contract, is the same—a liability in damages arising out of negligence—and conceptual subtleties, however edifying, are not helpful.

I do not think there can be much doubt as to the nature of the relationship from which such liability, at least in a case like the present, must be held to arise. It is seen in a wide range of activities, and can by no means be confined today to the relation between a professional man and his client. If I engage a man to exercise his expertise on my behalf, and it matters not whether he is to prepare a conveyance of land or to drive a straight furrow across it, then *spondet peritiam artis, et imperitia culpae adnumeratur.* That there have been recognised some exceptions to this rule the authorities testify, as do they to the gradual narrowing of such pleadable immunities. What the limits of these immunities are, granted that they do not cover the situation of the respondents, must, I think, be considered before a decision can be reached today, since it is in my view necessary to find some satisfactory statement of principle which will explain and justify the boundary lines which have now to be drawn.

The question which puzzled me as the argument developed was: what was the essential difference between the typical valuer, the auditor in the present case, and an arbitrator at common law or under the Arbitration Acts? It was conceded that an arbitrator is immune from suit, aside from fraud, but why? I find it impossible to put weight on such considerations as that in the case of an arbitrator (a) there is a dispute between parties; (b) he hears evidence; (c) he hears submissions from the parties, and that therefore he, unlike the valuer, is acting in a juridical capacity. As regards (a), I cannot see any juridical distinction between a dispute which has actually arisen and a situation where persons have opposed interests, if in either case an impartial person has had to be called in to make a decision which the interested parties will accept. As regards (b) and (c), these are certainly not necessary activities of an arbiter. Once the nature and limits of the submission to him have been defined, it could well be that he would go down at his own convenience to a warehouse, inspect a sample of merchandise displayed to him by the foreman, and return his opinion on its quality or value. I have come to be of opinion that it is a necessary conclusion to be drawn from *Sutcliffe v Thackrah* and from the instant decision that an arbitrator at common law or under the acts is indeed a person selected by the parties for his expertise, whether technical or intellectual, that he pledges skill in the exercise thereof, and that if he is negligent in that exercise he will be liable in damages.

If this conclusion were to be established by law, I do not think the consequences would be dramatic or even noticeable. It would become a generally accepted term of a reference to arbitration—because the referee would insist on it—that he be given by the parties immunity from suit for negligence at the instance of either of them. I am afraid I cannot go along with my noble and learned friend, Lord Salmon, when he suggests that such insistence would be damaging to a man's professional reputation. I think he would be saying something like this: 'I will accept your reference. I shall take every care and give you the whole benefit of my skills. But probably one of you will be dissatisfied with my award. I decline absolutely to accept the risk of having to defend a negligence suit, even though I be confident that I have not been negligent. I have no ambition, nor can I afford, to be a successful defendant, even in a leading case.' So commercial life would go on very much as before.

If, then, arbitrators are not immune from suit, what about the judges? Here I believe one is in a different region to which different principles apply. I do not rely on considerations of public policy, although no doubt it is the general acceptance of the principles which has caused a public policy to be adopted. The whole subject has recently been reviewed in *Sirros v Moore* (1974). I am aware that in trying to formulate a principle I am straying more towards contract than towards tort, but as I explained earlier I am not distressed by that. The state—I use the word for convenience—sets up a judicial system, which includes not only the courts of justice but also the numerous tribunals, statutory arbitrators, commissioners and so on, who give decisions, whether final or not, on matters in which the state has given them a competence. To these tribunals the citizen is bound to go if he wants to maintain particular rights or to obtain an opinion carrying authority ultimately enforceable by the public agencies; like as before them the citizen must appear to answer claims or complaints made against him. (This is subject to the rights citizens may have to make agreements one with another to submit their civil differences elsewhere.) The citizen does not select the judges in this system, nor does he remunerate them otherwise than as a contributor to the cost of government. The judge has no bargain with the parties before him. He pledges them no skill. His duties are to the state: it is to the state that the superior judge at least promises that he will do justice between all parties, and behave towards them as a judge should. I do not suppose that there is any English lawyer, and he would be a bold Scottish lawyer, who would say that here there is a contract between the state and the judge with a *jus quaesitum tertio* in the litigant. It is for the state to make such arrangements as may be necessary for the correction of careless or erroneous judicial decisions; if those arrangements are deemed to be inadequate, it is for Parliament to put the matter right. And if it be necessary to state the matter in terms of the law of tort, litigants are not persons to whom judges owe a legal duty of care—a duty which does not exist in the abstract, but only towards persons in particular relationships. The fact that he is under a moral duty is *nihil ad rem*. Judges in this context include, of course, persons forming tribunals and other bodies such as I referred to above. You do not test a claim to immunity by asking whether the claimant is bound to act judicially; such a question, as Lord Reid pointed out in *Sutcliffe v Thackrah*, leads to arguing in a circle. Immunity is judged by the origin and character of the appointment, not by the duties which the appointee has to perform, or his methods of performing them. I say nothing here about the immunity of counsel and witnesses, which again raises quite different and, to this appeal, irrelevant considerations.

I have, I fear, been led rather far from the actual substance of this appeal, but my reason is this. Since I can find no satisfactory distinction between the liability for negligence of persons in the position of the respondents and that of arbitrators, had I not been of opinion that arbitrators at common law or under the acts have no immunity, I would have been unable to agree that the appeal should be allowed.

LORD SALMON. My Lords, Mr Archy Arenson was the chairman, managing Director and controlling shareholder of a private company called A. Arenson Ltd. In 1964 he took his nephew, the appellant, into his company's employment. He also made a gift to his nephew of a small parcel of shares in the company on the terms of a letter dated 18 March 1964 which read as follows:

'18th March 1964

Dear Mr. and Mrs. Arenson,
A. Arenson Limited
In consideration of your procuring the Company to continue to employ me, I hereby agree the following arrangements concerning the Shares of which you have made me a gift:—

1. I will not sell the Shares other than to Mr. Arenson or to Mrs. Arenson should he predecease her.

2. Should I wish to dispose of my Shares, Mr. Arenson will purchase them from me at the Fair Value, but I shall not require him to purchase from me for five years from the date hereof.

3. Should I wish to sell the Shares after the death of Mr. Arenson I will

first offer them for sale to Mrs. Arenson, who shall have the right to purchase them at the Fair Value but she shall not be under an obligation so to do.

4. Should Mr. Arenson decide to dispose of his Shares in the Company, then I hereby agree to sell my Shares in the Company to Mr. Arenson at the same price per share as Mr. Arenson will be receiving in respect of his Shares.

5. In the event of my employment with the Company terminating for whatsoever reason, I will offer to sell my Shares to Mr. Arenson and it is agreed that he will purchase them from me at the Fair Value. Should Mr. Arenson be dead then Mrs. Arenson shall have the option to purchase the Shares from me at the Fair Value.

6. "Fair Value" shall mean in relation to the Shares in A. Arenson Limited, the value thereof as determined by the auditors for the time being of the Company whose valuation acting as experts and not as arbitrators shall be final and binding on all parties.

Please indicate your acceptance of the above conditions by signing the carbon copy sent herewith, and returning it to me.

Yours sincerely,
I. ARENSON.

Enc. We agree to the above terms and conditions.

(signed over 6d. stamp)'

Another letter in precisely the same terms, dated 1 October 1968, later passed between the appellant and his uncle. The appellant's employment with Arenson Ltd was terminated on 4 April 1970. Some time prior to 13 May 1970 the company's secretary verbally asked the company's auditors, Casson, Beckman, Rutley & Co, the respondents, to place a value on the shares held by the appellant. From the respondents' letter of 13 May 1970 it appears that they had been put in possession of copies of the letters of 18 March 1964 and 1 October 1968 to which I have referred. The respondents wrote to the company's secretary on 13 May 1970 as follows:

'Casson Beckman Rutley & Co.
27 Queen Anne Street,
London, W1M 0DA.
13th May 1970.

AB/PDB
The Secretary
A. Arenson Ltd.,
Lincoln House,
Colney Street,
St. Albans, Herts.
  Dear Sir,

Valuation of Shares—I. Arenson

1. We refer to your verbal request to place a value on the shares held by Mr. I. Arenson in your company in accordance with the letters of the 18th March 1964 and the 1st October 1968.

2. The shares held by Mr. I. Arenson in the company are as follows:—1,750 Ordinary Shares of £1 each fully paid 500 6% Non-Cumulative Preference Shares of £1 each fully paid.

3. In our view the fair value of these shares on the 4th day of April 1970 was as follows:—

(a) The 500 6% Non-Cumulative Preference Shares of £1 each fully paid at a valuation of £166.13.4.

(b) The 1,750 Ordinary Shares of £1 each fully paid at a valuation of £4,750.

Yours faithfully,'
[signed]

We do not know whether the respondents were asked to make the valuation on behalf of the company (which presumably was interested in the value of its own shares) or on behalf of Mr Archy Arenson and the appellant; nor do we know whether the respondents charged any fee for this valuation and if so, to whom, or whether they made their valuation as part of their ordinary duties as the company's auditors. Nor do I think that this matters because, since the decision of this House in *Hedley Byrne & Co Ltd v Heller & Partners Ltd* (*supra*), it is clear that quite apart from any contractual obligation, the respondents must have owed a duty both to Mr Archy Arenson and to the appellant to use reasonable care and skill in making their valuation. On 11 June 1970 the appellant, in reliance on the respondents' valuation, transferred his shares to his uncle for £4,916 13s 4d. About three months later, on 10 September 1970, a holding company was incorporated to acquire all the issued share capital of A. Arenson Ltd. After about a further four months the shares in the holding company were offered for sale to the public by a prospectus dated 14 January 1971. The prospectus included an accountant's joint report prepared and signed by the respondents and another firm of accountants which placed a value on the company's share capital of £1,699,983. This value, if applied pro rata to the shares formerly owned by the appellant would have made them worth not less than £29,500, that is to say six times more than the value put on them by the respondents only seven months previously. There is an apparently striking disparity between the value placed on the shares by the respondents' valuation of 13 May 1970 and the valuation placed on them by the prospectus of 14 January 1971. This disparity might be attributed to the fact that there is normally a substantial difference between the value per share of a small minority holding and the value per share of the entire holding in a private company; whether this factor could account for a difference of 600 per cent is a question which will have to be decided at the trial. There may also have been a remarkable improvement in the company's fortunes between 13 May 1970 and 14 January 1971, entirely unforeseen on the earlier date, which may help to explain the disparity between the two valuations. However this may be, shortly after the publication of the prospectus, the appellant issued a writ against his uncle and the respondents. The only part of the appellant's claim which is relevant to this appeal is that part which claims damages for negligence against the respondents in relation to their valuation of 13 May 1970. For the purposes of this appeal it must be assumed that the allegations of fact in the statement of claim are correct: that the respondents were negligent in preparing their valuation of 13 May 1970 which as a result was a gross undervaluation causing the appellant substantial damage. On this hypothesis, the important question for your Lordships to decide is whether, in the circumstances, the law confers an immunity on the respond-ents against being sued for the damage which they caused the appellant by their negligence.

The respondents, relying on their alleged immunity from suit, applied for the statement of claim to be struck out as disclosing no cause of action against them and for the action to be dismissed as against them. Brightman J con-cluded that, by authority binding on him, the respondents were immune from suit and he accordingly granted their application. The appellant then appealed to the Court of Appeal which, on 22 February 1973, by a majority (Lord Denning MR dissenting) upheld Brightman J's decision that the respondents were immune against any claim based on negligence and that accordingly the statement of claim, as it then stood, disclosed no cause of action against them. The Court of Appeal, however, held over the further hearing of the appeal so as to give the appellant an opportunity of applying for leave to amend his statement of claim by pleading a reasonable cause of action against the respondents on some ground other than negligence.

On 9 July 1973 the Court of Appeal: (1) gave leave to the appellant to re-serve an amended statement of claim which added, amongst other things, a claim alleging fraud against the respondents and collusion between them and Mr Archy Arenson; (2) discharged the order of Brightman J on the footing that the statement of claim should be so amended and re-served; and (3) ordered that all the costs hitherto incurred should be borne by the appellant in any event. The amended statement of claim was re-served on 11 July 1973.

On 12 February 1974 the appeal to your Lordships' House in *Sutcliffe v Thackrah* was allowed. In that case, the majority of your Lordships carefully considered and strongly criticised that part of the decision of the Court of Appeal in the present case which held on 22 February 1973 that the respond-ents were immune against the claim in negligence. On 22 July 1974 the Court of Appeal gave leave to the appellant to appeal from its order of 9 July 1973. Thereupon the appellant presented a petition to your Lordships' House pray-ing for a declaration that the unamended statement of claim did disclose a rea-sonable cause of action against the respondents and for an order reversing the order of the Court of Appeal relating to costs.

This appeal now comes before your Lordships in somewhat peculiar cir-cumstances. The only order made by the Court of Appeal on 9 July 1973 was in respect of costs. But that order was clearly based on the majority decision of the Court of Appeal delivered on 22 February 1973, holding that the unamended statement of claim disclosed no cause of action against the respondents because, in the circumstances of the case, the respondents were immune against any claim based on their alleged negligence. When the Court of Appeal granted leave on 22 July 1974 for an appeal to your Lordships' House, they clearly did so because of your Lordships' decision in *Sutcliffe v Thackrah* and in order to enable your Lordships to consider and rule on their decision of 22 February 1973. In my view, it is clearly desirable both in the interest of the parties (as counsel have agreed) and in the public interest that your Lordships should now clarify the law by ruling whether or not the Court of Appeal's majority decision of the 22 February 1973 was correct.

In *Sutcliffe v Thackrah* the immediate question which arose for decision was whether an architect who had been engaged by a building owner under the RIBA form of contract and had caused his client damage by negligently issuing an interim certificate for substantially more than the amount due, enjoyed the same immunity from suit as a judge or arbitrator. The Court of Appeal rightly considered that it was bound by its own majority decision in *Chambers v Goldthorpe* to uphold the architect's alleged immunity and with marked reluctance did so.

Your Lordship's House then unanimously reversed the decision of the Court of Appeal and overruled *Chambers v Goldthorpe*. My noble and learned friends, Lord Morris of Borth-y-Gest and Viscount Dilhorne, confined their opinions strictly to the question whether the law afforded immunity to an architect on the facts of that particular case Lord Morris of Borth-y-Gest expressly stated that he found it unnecessary to consider whether the Court of Appeal's decision in the present case was correct. Viscount Dilhorne did not refer to it. The majority of your Lordships however thought that the question relating to an architect's immunity should not be considered in isolation and could best be solved in the context of the wider issue, namely; what are the limits of the immunity which the law affords against actions for negligence in general? Such immunity can only exist when there are strong grounds for holding that public policy demands it. This rarely occurs because the law recognises that there is normally an overriding requirement of public policy that those who cause damage by a breach of their legal obligations to take reasonable care should be answerable in the courts to compensate those to whom they have caused damage by their negligence. Sovereign states, monarchs and their accredited representatives enjoy immunity from suit on grounds of a public policy founded on international comity. Judges, barristers, solicitors, jurors and witnesses also enjoy immunity in respect of anything they say or do in court during the course of a trial. The law recognises that such an immunity is vital to the efficient and speedy administration of justice and therefore necessary on grounds of public policy. The law also accords the same immunity to arbitrators when they are carrying out much the same functions as judges.

The question which arose in *Sutcliffe v Thackrah* and arises on the present appeal is: does this immunity extend beyond such arbitrators and if so, what are its limits? I think that your Lordships' House decided that this immunity is not afforded to any so-called arbitrator or quasi-arbitrator who claims it unless he can show that the functions in the performance of which he was negligent were, in reality, judicial in character. Clearly all your Lordships were confident that the functions of the architect employed under the RIBA form of contract were not judicial in character, nor, according to the majority of your Lordships, were the functions of valuers such as those performed by the respondents in the present case. In none of the authorities forming the basis of the Court of Appeal's decision was any cogent reason given for extending immunity from suit beyond the limits which I have enunciated and which had been clearly laid down in *Re Hopper (supra)*. Buckley LJ was accordingly constrained to attempt to distil a principle from those authorities which might justify the decisions at which they arrived and by which the Court of Appeal was bound. He said:

'In my judgment, these authorities establish in a manner binding on us in this court that, where a third party undertakes the role of deciding as between two other parties a question, the determination of which requires the third party to hold the scales fairly between the opposing interests of the two parties, the third party is immune from an action for negligence in respect of anything done in that role.'

I respectfully agree with Lord Reid's criticism of that passage when he said:

'I can see no grounds for this view. If there is any validity in my conjecture as to the reason of public policy giving rise to the immunity of arbitrators, those reasons do not apply to this situation. Persons who undertake to act fairly have often been called "quasi-arbitrators". One might almost suppose that to be based on the completely illogical argument—all persons carrying out judicial functions must act fairly, therefore all persons who must act fairly are carrying out judicial functions.'

Lord Hodson entirely agreed with Lord Reid's speech. It has been ingeniously argued on behalf of the respondents that when Lord Reid expressly disagreed with the passage in Buckley LJ's judgment stating the ground on which the majority of the Court of Appeal decided to uphold the immunity claimed by the respondents, Lord Reid was merely disagreeing with the grounds of the decision but not with the decision itself. I entirely reject that argument; it seems to me untenable, especially having regard to what Lord Reid had previously said.

I hope that in my speech in *Sutcliffe v Thackrah* I also made it plain that, in my opinion, for the reasons fully set out (which I need not repeat), the functions of the architect in that case, just like the functions of the respondents in the present case, were entirely different from the functions performed by a judge and that there were therefore no grounds of public policy which could possibly justify the immunity claimed being accorded to the architect in the one case or to the valuers in the other.

It is plain that the letters of 18 March 1964 and 1 October 1968, which apparently were shown to the respondents before they made their valuation, stated that in making the valuation they would be 'acting as experts and not as arbitrators'. It seems to me that these words were only stating the obvious; and I do not wish to place too much emphasis on them, particularly as to do so might encourage attempts to distinguish the present case from future cases in which these words are omitted but in which it is nevertheless equally obvious that the valuers were discharging no function even remotely resembling a judicial function.

Since the principle promulgated by Buckley LJ on which he attempted to justify the old decisions had been completely rejected by your Lordships' House in *Sutcliffe v Thackrah*, it was of necessity abandoned on the hearing of this appeal and a new ground had to be improvised for supporting the Court of Appeal's decision that public policy demanded that so-called quasi-arbitrators in the position of the respondents should enjoy immunity against being sued for damages caused by their own negligence. It was accordingly argued that without such immunity it would be very difficult, if not impossible, to persuade accountants to make valuations in circumstances such as the present; and thus contrary to the public interest the commercial community would be deprived of a very valuable service. The suggested reason for this supposed reluctance to make such valuations was that accountants would not accept the risk, as counsel put it, of being 'shot at from both sides'. It was one thing for an expert to express his opinion on value in circumstances such as the present. In one case, he was risking being sued for negligence only by his client; in the other, either the buyer or the seller might be dissatisfied with the valuation, and the expert would therefore be exposing himself to the wholly unacceptable dual risk of being sued by both. In spite of the remarkable skill with which this argument was developed I cannot accept it. Were it sound, it would be just as relevant in *Sutcliffe v Thackrah* as in the present case. The architect owed a duty to his client, the building owner, arising out of the contract between them to use reasonable care in issuing his certificates. He also, however owed a similar duty of care to the contractor arising out of their proximity: see the *Hedley Byrne* case *(supra)*. In *Sutcliffe v Thackrah* the architect negligently certified that more money was due than was in fact due; and he was successfully sued for the damage which this had caused his client. He might, however, have negligently certified less money was payable than was in fact due and thereby starved the contractor of money. In a trade in which cash flow is especially important, this might have caused the contractor serious damage for which the architect could have been successfully sued. He was thus exposed to the dual risk of being sued in negligence but this House unanimously held that he enjoyed no immunity from suit. The fallacy of the argument based on dual risk is, however, best exposed by the facts of the present case in which the respondents, apparently without any marked reluctance, took on not only a dual but a multiple risk of being sued in negligence when they signed the report in the prospectus issued to the public on 14 January 1974. If they had negligently over-valued the shares, they could have been sued by all those members of the public who had bought shares on the faith of the negligent over-valuation. If they had negligently under-valued the shares they could have been sued by their clients. This is the kind of risk which has been accepted by innumerable firms of accountants ever since the decision of this House in the *Hedley Byrne* case, apparently without any injury to themselves or to the public interest.

I attempted an exhaustive analysis of almost all the relevant authorities on this branch of the law in my speech in *Sutcliffe v Thackrah* which I now adopt without repeating it. I would sum it up by stating that it was long ago rightly decided in *Re Hopper (supra)* that a valuer enjoys the immunity of a judge or arbitrator only if what he does assumes the character of a judicial enquiry, eg by the parties submitting their dispute to the valuer for adjudication and the valuer listening to or reading the contentions made by or on behalf of the parties and to any evidence which they may put before him and then publishing a decision which is final and binding save for any appeal which the law allows: see also *Re Carus-Wilson and Greene (supra)*.

The immunity relates not only to claims for damages for negligence. It relates to all kinds of civil claims including, eg, claims for damages for defamation. It exists not for the protection of judges and arbitrators but for the protection of the public in cases in which truly judicial functions are being discharged.

The heresy adopted by the majority of the Court of Appeal derives from the trilogy of cases consisting of *Pappa v Rose, Tharsis Sulphur and Copper Co Ltd v Loftus and Stevenson v Watson (supra)*. For the reasons I explained in *Sutcliffe v Thackrah*, the first has been misunderstood, possibly as a result of the inaccuracy of the headnote in the report of the appeal. As it emerged from the Exchequer Chamber, no question of immunity arose in that case; the second case was wrongly decided, and the third case was probably rightly decided because of the exceptional terms of the contract which may well have put the architect in the position of an arbitrator appointed to discharge a truly judicial function. These three cases formed the basis of the decision in *Chambers v Goldthorpe (supra)* which your Lordships' House has recently overruled and together with *Chambers v Goldthorpe* formed the basis of the decision of the Court of Appeal in *Finnegan v Allen (supra)* which for the reasons which I gave in *Sutcliffe v Thackrah* was, in my view, wrongly decided. *Finnegan v Allen* is indistinguishable from the present case save that counsel for the appellant in that case seems to have admitted in argument that no action would lie for want of care or skill in making the valuation. In my opinion, that case should be overruled. In that case Goddard LJ, for whose views I have always had the greatest respect, stated that if a dispute arose between a buyer and a seller, eg as to whether goods sold and delivered corresponded with the sample or were of merchantable quality, an expert appointed as an arbitrator to inspect the goods and decide the question in dispute was automatically immune, in any circumstances, from being sued in negligence by either party. This may be so, but I prefer to offer no concluded opinion on this question. Undoubtedly such an expert may be formally appointed as an arbitrator under the Arbitration Acts, notwithstanding that he is required neither to hear nor read any submission by the parties or any evidence and in fact, has to rely on nothing but his examination of the goods and his own expertise. He, like the valuer in the present case, has a purely investigatory role; he is performing no function even remotely resembling the judicial function save that he finally decides a dispute or difference which has arisen between the parties. If such a valuer who is appointed as arbitrator makes a decision without troubling to examine the goods, surely he is in breach of his duty to exercise reasonable care, so would he be if he made only a perfunctory and wholly careless examination.

I find it difficult to discern any sensible reason, on grounds of public policy or otherwise, why such an arbitrator with such a limited role, although formally appointed, should enjoy a judicial immunity which so called 'quasi-arbitrators' in the position of the respondents certainly do not. Such an arbitrator, like any accountant who signs a report in a prospectus, could always protect himself against action for negligence, if he wished to do so, by stipulating that he is willing to act only on condition that he should be under no obligation (which the law would otherwise impose) to use reasonable care. I do not suppose, however, that insistence on such a condition would be likely to improve his chances of obtaining business; and that no doubt is why such a condition is so rarely imposed.

The question whether there may be circumstances in which a person, even if he is formally appointed as an arbitrator, may not be accorded immunity does not, however, arise for decision in the present case; but it may have to be examined in the future. Whatever the true answer to that question may be, I am convinced for the reasons I have indicated that the respondents, who were certainly not formally appointed arbitrators, do not in law enjoy the immunity which they claim and that accordingly the majority decision in the Court of Appeal cannot be upheld.

My Lords, I would accordingly allow the appeal.

LORD FRASER OF TULLEYBELTON: My Lords, I agree that this appeal should be allowed. It has long been established in both England and Scotland that judges are immune from actions for negligence in the performance of their duty. The reason no doubt is that public policy requires that they should not be liable to harassment for actions by disappointed litigants; 'otherwise no man but a beggar, or a fool, would be a judge [Stair, *Institutions*, BK 4, tit 1, s5]. Immunity against actions for negligence is enjoyed by arbitrators for much the same reason; in *Lingood v Croucher* (1742) Lord Hardwicke LC quoted a dictum by Lord King LC that if arbitrators were liable to be sued that 'would effectively discourage persons of worth from accepting of being arbitrators'. But the immunity of judges and arbitrators forms an exception to the general rule that a person who professes special skill or knowledge is liable for negligence if he fails to show such knowledge and skill and to take such care and precautions as are reasonably expected of a normally skilled and competent member of the profession or trade in question. The question in this case is whether that immunity extends beyond arbitrators and includes persons in the position of the respondents, who, when they made their valuation of the appellant's shares, undoubtedly had a duty to act fairly and impartially between the appellant, as vendor, and the purchaser of the shares. Persons in such a position are sometimes called (ungrammatically but conveniently) 'mutual' valuers and I shall so refer to them. There may, of course, be cases where, either by statute, or by contract, the liability of a mutual valuer for negligence is expressly excluded, but we are here concerned with the principle which applies in the absence of such express exclusion.

The respondents rely on a line of cases starting with *Pappa v Rose (supra)*. The effect of these cases was summarised by Buckley LJ in his opinion in the present case in the Court of Appeal, thus:

> 'In my judgment, these authorities establish in a manner binding on us in this court that, where a third party undertakes the role of deciding as between two other parties a question, the determination of which requires the third party to hold the scales fairly between the opposing interests of the two parties, the third party is immune from an action for negligence in respect of anything done in that role. He may be liable for fraud or collusion with one of the opposed parties, but if he acts honestly he is immune'.

Buckley LJ's judgment was delivered on 22 February 1973 and at that date the statment that I have quoted was, in my opinion, well founded. But on 12 February 1974 in *Sutcliffe v Thackrah (supra)* this House held that an architect who certified the amount payable by the owner of a building to the builder was not entitled to the same immunity as an arbitrator and Lord Reid, with whose speech Lord Hodson agreed, expressed disapproval of the statement which I have quoted from the judgment of Buckley LJ. So did Lord Salmon. As a result of the decision of this House in *Sutcliffe v Thackrah* the statement of claim in the present case was amended and the plaintiff with leave of the Court of Appeal has appealed to your Lordships' House.

It is unnecessary for me to refer particularly to *Pappa v Rose* and the cases that followed it. My noble and learned friend, Lord Salmon, examined these cases in his speech in *Sutcliffe v Thackrah* and I agree with him that the decision of the Exchequer Chamber in *Pappa v Rose* has been misunderstood. One of the cases which followed it, *Finnegan v Allen (supra)*, was a claim against auditors who were alleged to have made a negligent valuation of shares, and it is, in my opinion, indistinguishable from the present case. Insofar as it was decided by applying the doctrine of *Pappa v Rose* it cannot help the present respondents, and the position of the mutual valuer must now be considered afresh.

The force of the argument for the respondents seems to lie in the difficulty of stating a logical reason for denying to a mutual valuer, who is instructed to assess the value of property, knowing that the vendor and purchaser have agreed in advance to be bound by his valuation, the same immunity as is given to an arbitrator. It seems to me, with all respect to my noble and learned friend, Lord Salmon, that their functions are in many ways similar. Both are giving decisions which will bind parties with conflicting interests. Both have a duty to act impartially between the parties. Both can reach their decision by using their own skill and judgment without hearing evidence, and, unless they have immunity, both are liable to be shot at from opposite sides. The main difference between them is that the arbitrator, like the judge, has to decide a dispute that has already arisen, and he usually has rival contentions before him, while the mutual valuer is called in before a dispute has arisen, in order to avoid it. He may be employed by parties who have little or no idea of the value of the property to be valued and who rely entirely on his skill and judgment as an expert. In that respect he differs from some arbitrators. But many arbitrators are chosen for their expert knowledge of the subject of the arbitration, and many others are chosen from the legal profession for their expert knowledge of the law or perhaps because they are credited with an expertise in holding the balance fairly between parties. It does not seem possible, therefore, to distinguish between mutual valuers and arbitrators on the ground that the former are experts and the latter are not. I share the difficulty of my noble and learned friend, Lord Kilbrandon, in seeing why arbitrators as a class should have immunity from suit if mutual valuers do not. It may be, as my noble and learned friend, Lord Salmon, has suggested, that a person, even if he is formally appointed as an arbitrator, ought not in all cases to be accorded immunity. But, as both parties accepted the immunity of arbitrators, we heard no argument on that matter and I express no opinion on it.

There is even greater difficulty in distinguishing, so far as immunity is concerned, between the mutual valuer and a valuer who is instructed by a single client. The latter is undoubtedly liable for negligence in accordance with the general rule. Why should the former be immune? It cannot be because a valuer who is instructed by a single client is only liable for negligence to his own client because, as *Hedley Byrne (supra)* showed, he may be liable also to other people if he knew or ought to have known that they would rely on his skill and judgment. So the mutual valuer is by no means unique in being open to attack from several quarters. In my opinion no sufficient reason has been shown for treating him as an exception to the general rule of liability for negligence. I would allow the appeal.

Appeal allowed.

PART II

Agreements for arbitration

'There are five things incident to every Award or Arbitrement:
1.   Matter of Controversie.
2.   Submission to Arbitrator.
3.   The Parties to the Submission.
4.   The Arbitrator or Umpire.
5.   The manner of the Award or Yielding up of their Judgment.'

Arbitrium Redivivam (1694)

Is a signature necessary? (see LPA 1.2b)

Signatures to an arbitration agreement are not necessary where the parties have adopted the agreement.

Hickman v Kent or Romney Marsh Sheep-Breeders' Association (King's Bench Division, 1915)

> The articles of a limited liability company, an association not for profit, provided for the reference of disputes to arbitration. It was claimed that since the parties had not signed the articles there was no sufficient submission to arbitration within the meaning of section 4 of the Arbitration Act 1889, which as will be seen from the judgment below, was in all respects similar to section 4 of the Arbitration Act 1950 except that, instead of the words 'an arbitration agreement', the words 'a submission' were used.

ASTBURY J: Section 4 of the Arbitration Act 1889 says:

> 'If any party to a submission, or any person claiming through or under him, commences any legal proceedings in any Court against any other party to the submission, or any person claiming through or under him, in respect of any matter agreed to be referred, any party to such legal proceedings may at any time after appearance, and before delivering any pleadings or taking any other steps in the proceedings, apply to that Court to stay the proceedings, and that Court or a judge thereof if satisfied that there is no sufficient reason why the matter should not be referred in accordance with the submission, and that the applicant was, at the time when the proceedings were commenced, and still remains, ready and willing to do all things necessary to the proper conduct of the arbitration, may make an order staying the proceedings.'

Then section 27 says:

> ' "Submission" means a written agreement to submit present or future differences to arbitration, whether an arbitrator is named therein or not.'

The defendants' first contention is that article 49 is, on the authorities, a written agreement within the meaning of this Act.

In re Lewis (1876) it was held that a document containing the terms of an agreement as to the amount of costs payable by a client to his solicitor, assented to by the client but signed by the solicitor only, is not an 'agreement in writing' within the Attorneys and Solicitors Act 1870, section 4. Lord Coleridge CJ said:

> 'It is quite clear that there was no agreement in writing within section 4 of the Act'; and, later on, he says: 'An "agreement in writing" within section 4 must be an agreement by both parties, and both parties must sign their names upon the agreement.'

In *Caerleon Tinplate Co v Hughes* (1891) an action for the price of goods sold, the bought note signed by the defendants contained a provision for arbitration in case of dispute, whilst the sold note signed by the plaintiff contained no such provision. It was held that there was no submission within the meaning of the Act, for an agreement to submit to arbitration must be in writing and signed by both parties. *In re Lewis (supra)* was referred to, and Denman J, referring to section 27 of the Arbitration Act, said:

> 'In my judgment there can be no written agreement unless in writing signed by the parties as their agreement, and that "written agreement" means one in which the terms on both sides are reduced into writing. It is useless to discuss the documents here, for the bought and sold notes differ in the essential particular that the former contains a provision which is wholly absent in the latter.'

Then Wills J said:

> 'Supposing there were a contract and the parties were *ad idem*' — which in fact they were not in this case — 'yet there was no submission under the Act unless there were an agreement in writing by both parties. *In re Lewis (supra)* is conclusive on this point. In the present case the agreement is to be in writing under section 27 and we must hold that both parties must sign their names to it; otherwise there might be a conflict of evidence, and a discussion as to what was understood by either party.'

In *Baker v Yorkshire Fire and Life Assurance Co* (1892) an action was brought on a fire policy which was executed in the usual way by the company but not by the assured, and it was held that the policy, though not signed by the plaintiff, amounted to a submission to arbitration within the meaning of the Act.

Lord Coleridge CJ, who had been a party to the case of *In re Lewis (supra)* said:

> 'The plaintiff sues on the policy, and by so suing affirms it to be his contract; he cannot disaffirm a part of the very contract on which he is suing. He contends that, in order to bring into operation the arbitration clause contained in the policy, the policy must be signed by both parties; but the Act of Parliament says nothing of the kind, and the only apparent justification for the contention is to be found in *Caerleon Tinplate Co v Hughes (supra)*. That decision must be interpreted, however, with regard to the particular facts of that case. There was there no complete contract;

the two documents constituting the contract differed materially in their terms, and the court said it was plain that the parties never were *ad idem*.'

Then A.L. Smith J said:

'It is said, however, that by the interpretation clause a submission must be a written agreement to refer disputes to arbitration. This, however, is not a higher interpretation than was necessarily put on the language of the old Act, under which it was the universal practice to refer these cases, and does not mean that in all cases the written agreement to refer must be signed by both parties. It is quite unnecessary to say more as to the decision in *Caerleon Tinplate Co v Hughes (supra)* than that it turned entirely upon the peculiar facts of the case.'

The result of these decisions is, I think, that if the submission is in writing and is binding on both parties as their agreement or as the equivalent in law to an agreement between them the statute is satisfied.

Agreements for 'suitable arbitration' (see LPA 2.1)

An agreement to submit to 'suitable arbitration' is one that the courts will enforce.

Hobbs Padgett & Co (Reinsurance) Ltd v J.C. Kirkland and Kirkland (Court of Appeal, 1969)

> A contract between insurance brokers contained the words 'Clause 16: Suitable arbitration clause'. On an action to reverse an order by a Queen's Bench Master that an action arising out of the contract should be stayed, it was argued that (a) the clause was so vague that there was no contract, and (b) alternatively, that it was meaningless, as were the words in *Nicolene Ltd v Simmonds* (1953), and could therefore be ignored.

SALMON LJ: We are concerned with clause 16 of that agreement, which is commendably short, and reads: 'Suitable arbitration clause'. We are concerned with it because, when the plaintiff company sued J.C. Kirkland Ltd and Mr Kirkland personally for £2,500 (being one of the instalments due by the defendant company under the contract and guaranteed by Mr Kirkland), the defendant company and Mr Kirkland applied to stay the action on the basis that there had been a valid submission to arbitration contained in clause 16 of the contract.

The case for J.C. Kirkland Ltd and Mr Kirkland was that they had deposited the £2,500, but were not satisfied that they were then obliged to pay because the plaintiffs had not carried out their part under the agreement. Master Diamond stayed the action, but on 5 June 1969 Mr Justice Mackenna reversed the Master's order and removed the stay. The defendants now appeal to this court against that order of the learned Judge.

I understand that there are two points taken on behalf of the plaintiffs in relation to clause 16. First, it was suggested that the parties had never agreed as to what was a suitable arbitration clause and, therefore, clause 16 was merely an agreement to agree and it would follow that the document which they signed, namely, the so-called contract, since it contained a term which had not been agreed, was itself no contract.

That contention seems to me to be quite impossible as far as these plaintiffs are concerned. The plaintiffs are suing upon the contract in the action and they are, therefore, affirming it to be a contract. When it is pointed out by the defendants that the contract contains what they contend is manifestly an arbitration clause, the plaintiffs say that it never was a contract because the document contains a term about which they were never *ad idem*. It is impossible to blow hot and cold to that extent. Therefore, the first point, in my opinion, is quite clearly hopeless.

The second point raised is more interesting, but, despite the very attractive arguments addressed to us by Mr Myers and by Mr Bathurst,[counsel for the plaintiffs], I think that it has almost as little substance in it as the first point. The argument is that clause 16 is meaningless and can be ignored. I understand that some reliance is placed on the case of *Nicolene Ltd v Simmonds* (1953). That was a case in which a contract for the sale of a quantity of reinforcing steel bars was expressed to be subject to the 'usual conditions of acceptance'. After the sellers repudiated the contract, the buyers brought an action claiming damages for wrongful repudiation, and they won. On appeal, the sellers contended that the trial judge was wrong because the 'usual conditions of acceptance' had never been agreed as between them and the buyers and, therefore, there was no contract. It was conceded that there were no 'usual conditions of acceptance' in the trade carried on by the buyers and the sellers. This court decided that there was a contract but that, since there were no 'usual conditions of acceptance', the words were meaningless and could be ignored.

Lord Justice Denning (as he then was) pointed out that the clause was so vague and uncertain as to be incapable of any precise meaning. He said that it could be 'rejected without impairing the sense or reasonableness of the contract as a whole, and it should be so rejected'.

It seems to me quite impossible to say that there can be no suitable arbitration clause. It may be that in the trade concerned with the sale and purchase of reinforcing steel bars there are no 'usual conditions of acceptance', but it certainly cannot be suggested, in a contract such as this, that there can be no suitable arbitration clause; nor, in my view, that it would make any business sense of the contract to strike out that clause. If ever there was a type of contract in which businessmen would want to include an arbitration clause, this must be a prototype of such a contract. Here is a dispute between what are, in effect, partners in a reinsurance broker's business who decided to split and go their divers ways. Should there by any dispute in future concerning the meaning of the contract which effected this divorce, I should have thought it very unlikely that ordinary businessmen would want that ventilated in public and their business affairs perhaps exposed to the eyes of their competitors.

The fact that the clause is very short does not seem to me to make it any less meaningful. In the case of *Tritonia Shipping Inc v South Nelson Forest Products Corporation* (1966), this court had occasion to consider a contract where the arbitration clause was almost as short. It merely read: 'Arbitration to be settled in London'. This court held that that was an enforceable arbitration clause, and that it meant: 'Any dispute under this charter-party to be settled by arbitration in London'. I cannot think that if the clause in that contract had merely stated 'arbitration', without the words 'to be settled in London', it would have made the slightest difference. The Arbitration Act 1950 provides under sections 6, 10 and 32, to which I need not refer in detail, for what is to occur when there is an arbitration clause which does not specify any method of selecting an arbitrator; it gives the court power to appoint an arbitrator.

It seems to me that 'suitable arbitration clause' means that these parties have agreed that, if any dispute arises between them under the contract, including any dispute as to the meaning of the contract, that dispute should be referred to arbitration rather than to the courts. If the parties cannot agree upon an arbitrator, then they can invoke the terms of the Arbitration Act 1950, and an arbitrator will be appointed by the court.

In this case it is said that the addition of the word 'suitable' makes the clause entirely meaningless. I fail entirely to understand, when considering whether clause 16 can be given any meaning, how the fact that the word 'suitable' is added to it makes its meaning uncertain. If, for example, one side wanted an arbitrator appointed by the Chairman of Lloyd's, no one, I suppose, could suggest that that would be unsuitable. If one side or the other suggested that the arbitrator should be appointed by the chairman of a body wholly inexperienced in reinsurance and that the arbitration should take place in Timbuktu, I suppose, equally clearly, it would be plain that that was not suitable.

I do not think that there is any great difficulty about construing the words 'suitable arbitration clause' in a contract of this kind. It is any form of arbitration which reasonable men in this type of business would consider suitable.

There has been a very interesting argument in this court on the topic, there has been a difference of opinion between the learned Master and the learned Judge, and, as far as I am concerned, between the learned Judge and myself. But I cannot think that any businessman — and, after all, this is a contract made by businessmen — would entertain the doubts which are apparently entertained by lawyers. I think that any insurance broker who is told that, in a contract of this kind, 'suitable arbitration clause' is completely meaningless, would, as one of the gentlemen concerned in this matter did, say: 'What is this all about?'

The parties, by clause 16, have made it quite clear that their intention is that their differences should be arbitrated. I do not think that the word 'suitable' adds to or detracts from the meaning of the clause. If the clause had read 'arbitration clause' there could have been no doubt that it would have been sufficiently precise to be given the meaning which, to my mind, any ordinary man would consider that it obviously bears. I do not think that we should be so pedantic as to suggest that the addition of the word 'suitable' makes its meaning uncertain. Any such conclusion would, in my view, make the law ridiculous in the eyes of those who enter into contracts of this kind.

I would accordingly allow the appeal.

EDMUND DAVIES LJ: [Counsel for the plaintiffs] has attractively submitted that the arbitration clause here is indeed meaningless and, accordingly, should be ignored, while still leaving the contract otherwise certain and enforceable. But, unless I misunderstood [counsel] completely he was forced to concede that, had the clause simply read 'arbitration clause', then, since it is the duty of the court to seek to attach meaning to all parts of an agreement concluded between the parties, not only would that two-word clause be capable of having a meaning attached to it, but there would be little or no difficulty in so doing. There would be involved, for example, the application of section 6 of the Arbitration Act 1950 which provides that, there being no contrary intention expressed, the arbitration should be conducted by a single arbitrator. A number of other consequences, well established in the law, would also flow therefrom, such as, for example, the power of the arbitrator to decide where the arbitration should be held.

[Counsel] says: 'That is all very well, but we are not here concerned with a two-word clause; the clause agreed upon between the parties is "suitable arbitration clause", and the inclusion of the adjective makes all the difference'. He would have this court advert to the negotiations between the parties, who had attempted a draft, clause 17 of which was in these words:

'In the event of failure to agree any part of these Heads of Agreement the parties undertake to abide by a (decision) of a single arbitrator to be nominated by the Chairman of Lloyd's for the time being'.

That draft clause was struck out and nothing resembling it was put in the final contract between the parties. In these circumstances, I do not think that it is open to either of the parties to refer to the draft at all. Nevertheless, [counsel] says that, granted that that be so strictly in law, the draft serves to illustrate that there can be differences between parties as to what is a 'suitable arbitration provision — for example, whether or not it is the Chairman of Lloyd's who is to be the person to appoint the arbitrator, and so on. There being thus room for differences between the parties, when one applies a subjective test as to what is a suitable arbitration clause, [counsel] contends that the only possible conclusion is that this clause is meaningless, although the rest of the contract remains clear and enforceable.

I share the view of my Lord that that will not do. I cannot think that the addition of the one adjective 'suitable' to the phrase 'arbitration clause' can have the catastrophic effect, as far as the business enforceability of this contract is concerned, contended for by the plaintiffs. In my judgment, having regard to the way that this matter has developed, this is a perfectly meaningful arbitration clause, and the decision of the learned Judge to the contrary is one with which I must respectfully disagree. I, accordingly, concur that the appeal be allowed.

KARMINSKI LJ: I also feel that the appeal must be allowed.

Appeal allowed

Note
The report in [1969] 2 Lloyds Rep 548 states, incorrectly, that the appeal was dismissed.

Agreements for arbitration 'in the usual way' (see LPA 2.1)

If an arbitration clause in a contract reads, in 'time-honoured' words, that arbitration is to take place in London 'in the usual way' that may be void for uncertainty unless there is evidence that there is in London a usual way of dealing with disputes on the subject matter of the contract.

Scrimaglio v Thornett and Fehr (Court of Appeal, 1924)

> On an issue as to whether an award by a single arbitrator was a valid one, evidence was given that the usual method of arbitration in the chemical trade was by two arbitrators and an umpire. The sellers not having appointed their arbitrator, the buyers' arbitrator proceeded alone as he was entitled to as under section 6(b) of the 1889 Act (now 7(b) of the 1950 Act).

BANKES LJ: This appeal raises the question whether Greer J put a right construction on a clause in a contract entered into between the parties for the purchase and sale of a quantity of soda ash. The clause in question was one which provided that any dispute arising out of this contract should be settled by arbitration in London in the usual way, the contract being one between merchants in this country and a merchant at Genoa. A dispute did arise, and thereupon the merchants in this country, the sellers, appointed an arbitrator and gave notice to the Genoa merchant to appoint his arbitrator, and that they had appointed their arbitrator. The Genoa merchant did not appoint an arbitrator, and thereupon the arbitrator appointed by the sellers proceeded to act as sole arbitrator, and he gave notices to the buyer that he was intending to proceed.... The form of action here was an action by the buyer for a balance of account which he said was owing to him. That was not disputed, but the sellers counter-claimed by claiming the amount which had been awarded to them by the sole arbitrator, amounting to over £4,000. In answer to that counter-claim, the buyer set up, in substance, two separate defences — namely (i) that the arbitrator had no jurisdiction, and (ii) that, even if he had jurisdiction and was properly acting as arbitrator, he had acted irregularly in certain matters which he specified, including the failure to give proper notices of the hearing. I think it is quite clear, on the authorities, that that class of defence is not open to the buyer....

The question, therefore, resolves itself into this, whether the learned judge was right in saying that this sole arbitrator had jurisdiction to act, and that depends on the construction which has been placed on this clause. He read it in this way:

'Any dispute arising out of this contract to be settled in London', that is to say, the place where the arbitration was to take place, and it also indicates the law by which the arbitration is to be governed as far as ordinary law applies having regard also to the further terms of the contract which provided that it was to be 'arbitration in London in the usual way'.

And the learned judge has held, and I think rightly held, that that meant in the usual way in which disputes in reference to the particular commodity or class of commodity are dealt with. The learned judge says that it does not provide that it must necessarily be the universal way, but only a usual way. These are his words: 'In the usual manner as in the chemical trade in London'. It appears to me that that means not the invariable way — the learned judge does not say 'the invariable way' — but the usual way. I think 'the usual way' is a way usually, though not always, adopted. If the learned judge is right in his construction that 'in the usual way' means in the usual way of dealing with disputes in reference to commodities such as this particular one (that is to say, in the chemical trade generally), the evidence was really all one way on the question whether or not this particular way of proceeding by appointing arbitrators, and if the one party did not appoint his arbitrator then the sole arbitrator would act under section 6(b) of the Arbitration Act 1889, was the usual way, and if the learned judge was right in saying that the contract referred to the usual way in this particular trade, then I think it follows that the judgment was correct and cannot be interfered with.

SCRUTTON LJ: An Italian gentleman resident in Genoa makes a contract with an English firm, but in the form of contract is the clause: 'Any dispute arising out of this contract to be settled by arbitration in London in the usual way'. That particular clause, in my experience, is a time-honoured clause in London and in many cases it is impossible to find out what it means because, on the evidence, there does not appear to be any usual way relating to that particular commodity. It must be settled by evidence whether there is a usual way, and one question is within what sphere is that usual way to be found. Counsel for the buyer suggests that there might be three methods. It might be the usual way of arbitrations in London without reference to any particular trade; it might be the usual way in the particular trade in which the commodity which was the subject-matter of the contract was dealt in; or it might be where a course of business is proved between the parties, the usual way between those parties, according to that course of business.

In this case, there have been no previous dealings between the parties which had involved arbitration, and I agree with the view of the learned judge that, in such a case, it means the usual way in the trade which embraces the particular article which is to be bought or sold. In some cases it is difficult to ascertain even this usual way because the ways of arbitration in the trade vary so much. Commercial men know their own business best, but I think it is a pity they keep to this form instead of stating in two or three lines, as they might do, what form of arbitration they mean. But they keep on using this form and when they do use this form the court has to find evidence whether there is or is not a usual way in that trade. I agree with Greer J that that does not mean the invariable way. It means the way so frequently used in relation to the number of arbitrations that it may properly be described as the usual way — not a usual way, because there may be two or three — but the usual way in the trade. If that is the proper meaning of the clause, then the evidence in this case was practically all one way, namely, that the usual way was to have an arbitration conducted by two arbitrators who may appoint an umpire. As to the procedure in the arbitration, when once one has the arbitration, I do not think this means that one has to find out what is the usual way in the trade in which arbitrations are conducted. I think that would generally be a hopeless attempt. What it means is this: once one has the arbitrators appointed, they have to deal with the matter according to the law of England and the conditions laid down in the Arbitration Act 1889....

SARGANT LJ: I am of the same opinion. I would only add what I think is the construction of this short phrase 'by arbitration in London in the usual way'. In the first place, I think 'in London' denotes primarily the locality where the arbitration is to be held. That may not exhaust its meaning, because the locality may have some influence on the character of the arbitration, and that is made plain by the subsequent words 'in the usual way'. I think those words must show that some comparatively definite subject-matter is being considered, because it is hardly possible to use that phrase 'in the usual way' if anything in the world, in any place, is to be considered. In my judgment, the words 'in the usual way' mean this: in the way usual in arbitrations there, that is in London, with reference to the subject-matter of the contract.

Appeal dismissed

Note
See also *Naumann v Nathan* (1930) in Part V for a further discussion of the expression 'in the usual way'.

Agreements annexed by reference (see LPA 2.3)

There may be an arbitration agreement in writing, subject to the 1950 Act, even though it is only in the form of a document annexed by reference.

Modern Buildings Wales Ltd v Limmer and Trinidad Co Ltd (Court of Appeal, 1975)

BUCKLEY LJ: This is an appeal from an order of Kerr J in chambers of the 20 November 1974 by which he refused a stay of further proceedings in this action pending arbitration. We have not got the advantage of any written note of the learned judge's reasons for so doing, but we are told that the ground on which he made his order was that he considered that there was a doubt whether the contractual document with which we are concerned, which is a written order dated 18 December 1968 for the supply of certain labour, plant and machinery, imported by reference a form of contract between a contractor and a sub-contractor which has in it an arbitration clause, and possibly that there was further doubt that if that form of contract was by reference imported into the contract between the parties at all, that part of it which contained the arbitration clause was a part which was so imported. Our attention has been drawn to a passage in Russell on Arbitration [18th edition, 1970], which reads as follows:

'Any doubt about the written submission being quite clearly established is...a sufficient reason for the judge's exercising his discretion against a stay'.

The relevant statutory provision is section 4(1) of the Arbitration Act 1950, which provides:

'If any party to an arbitration agreement, or any person claiming through or under him, commences any legal proceedings in any court against any other party to the agreement, or any person claiming through or under him, in respect of any matter agreed to be referred, any party to those legal proceedings may at any time after appearance, and before delivering any pleadings or taking any other steps in the proceedings, apply to that court to stay the proceedings, and that court or a judge thereof, if satisfied that there is no sufficient reason why the matter should not be referred in accordance with the agreement, and that the applicant was, at the time when the proceedings were commenced, and still remains, ready and willing to do all things necessary to the proper conduct of the arbitration, may make an order staying the proceedings.'

The expression 'arbitration agreement' is defined in section 32 of the 1950 Act in these terms:

'In this Part of this Act, unless the context otherwise requires, the expression "arbitration agreement" means a written agreement to submit present or future differences to arbitration, whether an arbitrator is named therein or not.'

The situation in this case is that the plaintiffs are head contractors under a contract with the Taf Fechan Water Board for the construction of a building at Nelson in Glamorgan. On 4 September 1968 the defendants, who were nominated sub-contractors for the purpose of putting in some suspended ceilings in the building, delivered a quotation to the architect for that work in the sum of £5018 7s 6d. The only terms specified in that document that I need mention are:

'TERMS: — Less 2½% discount to Main Contractor. Payment of 90% of the value of the work executed to be made monthly as the work proceeds and the balance one month from date of invoice.'

On 18 December 1968 the plaintiffs placed an order, referring to that quotation explicitly:

'To supply adequate labour, plant and machinery to carry out and complete ventilated and non-ventilated ceilings at the above Contract, within the period stipulated in the Programme of Work and in full accordance with the appropriate form for nominated Sub-Contractors (RIBA 1965 Edition). All work to be carried out to the complete satisfaction of the Architect and in full accordance with our detailed programme which can be inspected on site or at this office. All as your quotation (and then it gives the reference to the quotation of 4 September to which I have referred)'.

It is common ground that the effect of this document was to constitute a contract between the plaintiffs and the defendants as contractors and sub-contractors respectively in respect of the work detailed in the quotation. It transpires that in fact the RIBA do not have a form of contract between a contractor and a nominated sub-contractor, nor, indeed, do they have any form of contract which exists in a 1965 edition. So the words in brackets in the order are inappropriate.

The head contract in this case was in a form issued under the sanction of the RIBA and various other bodies. There is in existence a form of contract intended to be used by contractors and nominated sub-contractors when contracting *inter se,* but that is a form which is not put out under the authority of the RIBA, but of the National Federation of Building Trades Employers and the Federation of Associations of Specialists and Sub-Contractors, and is approved by the Committee of Associations of Specialist Engineering Contractors. That form of contract has been referred to in the argument as 'the green form', and it is convenient to use that term to identify it.

The plaintiffs issued a writ on a date which I do not know claiming damages for breach of the contract between themselves and the defendants. Initially that was framed in a very terse manner, but the endorsement on the writ has been amended, and the claim for damages is now set out in considerable detail and amounts in total to a sum of £10284.52, and it is mainly, if not entirely, based on the contention that the defendants failed to do the work which they were obliged to do in due time.

The plaintiffs launched an application under Rules of the Supreme Court Order 14 for summary judgment. That was countered by the defendants with an application for a stay of the action on the ground that the written order incorporated the green form of contract, and that the green form of contract contains an arbitration clause. The application was for a stay of the proceedings in the action pending the dispute between the parties being referred to arbitration. The defendants put in an affidavit in support of that application in which they stated that they denied that they were in breach of the contract, without further specifying the grounds on which they denied liability. The reason that that was done was that they were anxious to avoid any possibility of its being said that they had put in an affidavit on the merits in response to the RSC Ord 14 summons, thereby taking a step in the action, something which they could not do if they wished to apply for a stay of proceedings under section 4 of the 1950 Act.

The application was further supported by an affidavit of Mr Atkins, who is the contracts administrator of a company which is a wholly-owned subsidiary of Tarmac Ltd, which is the parent company also of the defendants. It does not appear that Mr Atkins is an employee or an officer of the defendant company, but he gives the evidence which he does give as one who is an expert in the field of contracts of this nature. He says that he has been specialising in sub-contract work in the building industry for 41 years, and his evidence can be accepted as that of an expert on the subject. What he says is this:

'I have no doubt that anyone in the industry would understand, as I understand, the words "in full accordance with the appropriate form of nominated Sub-Contractors (RIBA 1965 Edition)" appearing on the Plaintiffs' order of 18 December 1968 being Document 1 in Exhibit MEB 1 to refer to what is known as "The Green Form" and is in fact the Sub-Contract being the third Document in the bundle MEB 1'.

He draws attention to the fact that the green form is headed: 'For use where the Sub-Contractor is nominated under the 1963 edition of the RIBA form of Main Contract.' Then he says that it is correct that there is no 1965 edition, but only a 1963 edition, of the green form, and he would understand that that was the document intended to be referred to. Since that affidavit was sworn on 16 July 1974, evidence has been put in in affidavit form by the plaintiffs, an affidavit of a Mr Parry, but he does not deal with Mr Atkins's affidavit in any way.

The question that we have to decide is whether this is a case in which there is an arbitration agreement between the parties, in which case the action should be stayed pending arbitration, or whether it is not. It has been argued by counsel for the plaintiffs that here there is a doubt whether the green form is or is not imported; and he says that where a doubt exists there is good ground for the judge exercising his discretion under section 4 of the 1950 Act in such a way as to allow the action to go on. For that purpose he relies on the decision of this court in *London Sack and Bag Co Ltd v Dixon and Lugton Ltd* (1943). There the plaintiff company bought from the defendant company 5000 used cotton flour bags, and on delivery complained that the goods were not up to description and claime'd repayment, with interest and damages. There was no arbitration clause in the written contract, but the point was taken that both the parties were members of a company called United Kingdon Jute Goods Association Ltd, the articles of association of which provided that 'all disputes arising out of transactions connected with the trade (which the court treated as referring to the jute trade) shall be referred to arbitration'. It was said that the dispute was a question concerned with the jute trade, and that, as a result of the provisions of section 20 of the Companies Act 1929, the articles of association formed a written agreement between all the members and in that way there was an arbitration agreement there in force. Scott LJ said:

'The arbitration clause must be in the written submission. It cannot be said that there is a written agreement to arbitrate unless there is a clear reference in the written contract between the parties to the alleged arbitration clause and that reference must amount to an incorporation of it.'

Then he went on to refer to the point under section 20 of the 1929 Act and said:

'The importance of that paragraph (that is a reference to a paragraph in Halsbury's *Laws of England*) is that any doubt about the written submission being quite clearly established is, in my view, a sufficient reason for the judge's exercising his discretion against a stay: and *a fortiori* a reason for our not disagreeing with him.'

Scott LJ had already expressed the view that he was not satisfied that the effect of section 20 of the 1929 Act, in the circumstances of that case, was to constitute any written agreement between the parties to the action that the dispute with which the case was concerned should be referred to arbitration. He went on to deal with quite a different point, which he said was a conclusive ground for dismissing the appeal, and he said that that rendered consideration of the other point — by which I understand him to have been referring back to the point about uncertainty — superfluous.

When one comes to look at the judgments of Mackinnon and Du Parcq LJJ, the other two members of the court on that occasion, in my view it is clear that what the court was there deciding was that it was not established that there was any contract containing an arbitration clause between the two parties in the action. Mackinnon LJ said:

'To establish that in these rules there is a submission or agreement to arbitrate any dispute arising out of the contract sued on by the plaintiffs, the defendants must prove (i) that the plaintiffs and defendants made a binding contract with each other to abide by and be subject to these rules, and

(ii) that the dispute involved in this action arises out of a "transaction connected with the jute goods trade". In my opinion, they failed to prove either of these propositions.'

Then he says that reliance was placed on a certain article in the articles of association and on section 20 of the Companies Act 1929 and he says:

'But I think it is impossible to contend that, by reason of these articles, the plaintiff company and the defendant company have made a contract to submit disputes to arbitration because each has a director who is a shareholder and the companies have been admitted to the association — whatever that may mean.'

Du Parcq LJ said:

'The evidence which was advanced before this court and before the judge has not satisfied me that the parties ever agreed to refer to arbitration the matter in dispute in the action.'

In my judgment, that authority is not authority for anything further than that, in a case in which the party who seeks a stay fails to prove that there is an arbitration agreement in force between the parties, he cannot get a stay. That seems to me, with due respect to the argument of counsel for the plaintiffs founded on that case, to be a fairly obvious proposition, and I think that the way in which it is stated in Russell is misleading. It is not sufficient, in my judgment, for the party who resists a stay merely to say: 'Well, there is some doubt as to how the contract between the parties should be construed and, therefore, it is proper for the court in the exercise of its discretion to refuse a stay.' On the contrary, in my judgment, when an application is made by one party for a stay on the ground that there is in operation an arbitration agreement, it is incumbent on the court to discover whether or not there is such an agreement in force; and if that involves determining a question of construction, that question of construction must be decided there and then.

Counsel for the plaintiffs says that it is unsatisfactory that a question of this nature should be decided on an interlocutory basis, by which I understand him to mean in proceedings in chambers on affidavit evidence. But, in my judgment, it is the duty of the court to decide whether or not there is an arbitration agreement in force, and it has to be decided at an interlocutory stage in the action, because it has to be decided before the defendants take any other steps.

We were also referred in support of this same point to *The Elizabeth H* (1962). That was a case in which a ship was chartered under a charter which contained a clause in these terms:

'Any dispute arising from the making, performance or termination of this Charter Party shall be settled in New York, Owner and Charterer each appointing an arbitrator, who shall be a merchant, broker or individual experienced in the shipping business....'

Some lard was to be shipped on the ship operating under the charter, and the bills of lading in respect of that lard provided, amongst other things, as follows:

> '....All the terms whatsoever of the said charter except the rate and payment of freight specified therein apply to and govern the rights of the parties concerned in this shipment.'

It was suggested that that language was apt to introduce into the contract of carriage the arbitration clause in the charterparty. But it is to be observed that all that was to be arbitrated under the arbitration clause was: 'Any dispute arising from the making, performance or termination of this Charter Party....' Therefore, it would seem to me that that clause would have been wholly inappropriate to any dispute between the owners of cargo and the charterers. Hewson J said:

> 'Because I am left in a state of considerable doubt as to how far the full clause of the charter-party was considered in the *Sun* case [*Sun Shipping Co Inc v De Fosse & Tanghe* (1952)] (he is there referring to another case which had been cited to him) I am not prepared to find that there was a clear agreement to arbitrate between the cargo-owners and the shipowners'.

In that case, once again, in my judgment, the court refused a stay on the ground that the defendants had not established that there was in fact any arbitration agreement in force between the plaintiff and the defendant.

I think we have to consider whether, on the language of the order of 18 December, the arbitration clause in the green form was or was not imported into the contract between the parties in the present case. Counsel for the plaintiffs has said that there are various ways in which that order can be construed which would result in its being held that the arbitration clause was not so imported. First of all, he says that the words within the brackets, '(RIBA 1965 edition)', are really nonsensical, and the whole of the importation clause in the order form, if I can so describe it, is therefore of no effect at all, on the basis, I think, that it must be read as a whole, and if it purports to import a non-existent form of contract, then it has no effect. In my judgment, the answer to that argument is this: that this is a clear case of *falsa demonstratio*. The words, 'the appropriate form for nominated Sub-Contractors', if read in the light of the evidence of Mr Atkins, are clearly capable of identifying the document that was intended to be referred to, and, as I have said, Mr Atkins's evidence has not been answered or attacked in any way, and I think we must accept it at its face value. There is language perfectly appropriate to describe the green form. What follows in brackets is inappropriate to fit with identification of the green form. It is not language which ought to be read as intended to cut down and restrict the identifying operation of the preceding words. It is just an added description which on investigation turns out to be factually inaccurate. In those circumstances, in accordance with the ordinary practice of the courts in cases where there is some misdescription of this character, the court disregards what is inaccurate and inapplicable and proceeds on that which is appropriate and intelligible and what are evidently intended to be the governing words of definition. Accordingly, I think the right way to construe this order form is to ignore the words in brackets altogether as being a *falsa demonstratio,* and to accept that the reference to the appropriate form for sub-contractors is a reference to the green form, that being the only form to which it is suggested that those words could apply and the form to which it is said that anybody in the trade would understand them as applying.

Then it is said that endorsed on the form of order there are certain conditions, condition 7 of which is in these terms: 'FORM OF CONTRACT — All Sub-Contractors may be required to enter into a form of contract.' This is said to indicate that the parties have not shown a concluded intention in the written order to incorporate the green form, but merely to indicate that the defendants might be required to enter into a contract in the green form. In fact, they never were asked to sign any formal agreement in that or in any other form. Therefore, it is said that, reading the document as a whole the parties have not shown a firm intention that the green form should be imported into the contract. I do not feel able to accept that argument. Condition 7 does not seem to me in any way to detract from the force of the words 'in full accordance with', and so forth, in the written order. Condition 7 could not, I think, in any way affect the question whether the green form was intended to be imported into the contract or not, but merely indicates that the plaintiffs may or may not require the sub-contractor to sign a further and more formal contractual document than that constituted by the quotation and the order based on it. Accordingly, I do not think that condition 7 affords a reason for saying that the order does not import the green form.

Then counsel for the plaintiffs has submitted that the language is only appropriate to incorporate those clauses of the green form which can be said to relate to the supply of labour, plant and machinery; for, he says, you cannot supply labour under an arbitration clause or in accordance with an arbitration clause; and you cannot, similarly, supply plant or machinery, or carry out works, in accordance with an arbitration clause. But the dispute which has here arisen is a dispute relating to the carrying out of the works by the sub-contractors, the defendants, and I think it is a dispute relating to the supply of labour, plant and machinery and the carrying out of the works, and the words, 'in full accordance with the appropriate form for nominated Sub-Contractors', appear to me to be fully wide enough to introduce into the contract between the parties all the terms of the green form which relate to the supply of labour, and so forth, and the carrying out of the works, including the arbitration clause, which is itself a clause relating to those matters. Accordingly, I do not feel that there is substance in that submission.

Counsel for the plaintiffs has suggested that the written contract contains insufficient indication how various matters that are left in blank in the green form contract, and in particular in the appendix to the contract, which relates to such matters as the completion period, the retention money and so forth, should be filled in. Where parties by an agreement import the terms of some other document as part of their agreement those terms must be imported in their entirety, in my judgment, but subject to this: that if any of the imported terms in any way conflicts with the expressly agreed terms, the latter must prevail over what would otherwise be imported. Here it is not disputed that the written contract between the parties, consisting of the quotation, and the order, contains all the essential terms of the contract, and, in my judgment, the green form of contract must be treated as forming part of the written contract, subject to any modifications that may be necessary to make the clauses in the green form accord in all respects with the express terms agreed between the parties.

For these reasons, I reach the conclusion that this is a case in which there is a written arbitration agreement between the parties which is applicable to any dispute or difference in regard to any matter or thing of whatever nature arising out of the sub-contract or in connection with it.... in my judgment, this is a case in which the action ought to be stayed under the section.

The learned judge refused leave to appeal. The appellants here seek leave to appeal. I would grant leave to appeal, and I would allow the appeal for the reasons that I have indicated.

ORMROD LJ agreed.

Leave to appeal granted:
appeal allowed

The law applicable to an arbitration (See LPA 2.1)

The law of procedure for arbitration may be different from 'the proper law' of a contract. If the parties fail to indicate clearly in their agreement which law should apply to the arbitration, the proceedings should be governed by the law of the country in which the arbitration is held because that is the country most closely connected with the proceedings.

James Miller & Partners Ltd v Whitworth Street Estates (Manchester) Ltd (House of Lords, 1970)

> A Scottish company made an agreement on the standard JCT (Joint Contracts Tribunal) contract form (or RIBA standard form, as it was formerly known) with an English company for building work to be done at the English company's Scottish factory. There was at the time no separate JCT form for Scotland. Differences having arisen, the President of the RIBA appointed a Scottish arbiter and the arbitration was held in Scotland in the Scottish form. The English company asked for a case stated on a point of law under the Arbitration Act 1950 (which does not apply to Scotland) and at a time when there was no procedure for special cases in Scotland.
>
> On an application to a master of the English High Court, he ordered the arbiter to state his award in the form of a special case. A judge reversed this and rescinded the order. The Court of Appeal reversed the judgment and reinstated the order. The House of Lords, in this judgment, allowed the appeal and again rescinded the order. A majority (Lords Hodson, Guest, Dilhorne) held that the 'proper' law of the contract was English, notwithstanding that the work took place in Scotland, because the use of the RIBA printed form showed that to be the intention of the parties. Lords Reid and Wilberforce dissented and thought the proper law of the contract was Scottish.
>
> The whole court was agreed however that the conduct of the parties after the appointment of the arbiter showed that they intended the curial law (ie, that of the tribunal) to be Scottish law and under that there could be no case stated.

LORD REID: The question in this appeal is whether this was a Scottish or an English arbitration. If it was governed by the law of Scotland the arbiter acted correctly. Under Scots law an arbiter is the final judge both of fact and law, and (the arbiter in question) was entitled and, indeed, bound to issue his final award. But if the arbitration was governed by the law of England he was bound to state a case in order that questions of law which had arisen might be decided by the English court.

Two questions were argued: first, whether the proper law of the parties' original contract was Scots or English law, and secondly, if the proper law was English law, was the arbitration nevertheless governed by the law of Scotland? I shall first consider what was the proper law of the contract.

The general principle is not in doubt. Parties are entitled to agree what is to be the proper law of their contract, and if they do not make any such agreement then the law will determine what is the proper law. There have been from time to time suggestions that parties ought not to be so entitled, but in my view there is no doubt that they are entitled to make such an agreement, and I see no good reason why, subject it may be to some limitations, they should not be so entitled. But it must be a contractual agreement. It need not be in express words. Like any other agreement it may be inferred from reading their contract as a whole in light of relevant circumstances known to both parties when they made their contract. The question is not what the parties thought or intended but what they agreed. ...

[After discussion of various factors, his Lordship concluded]:

It therefore appears to me that the weight to be attached to the place of performance being in Scotland is considerably greater than the weight to be attached to such connections as there are between the form of the contract and the law of England and so I would hold that the law of Scotland is the proper law of this contract.

If that is right the second question does not arise. But if the proper law of the contract is the law of England, I think that the actings of the parties after the appointment of (the arbiter) sufficiently show an agreement that the arbitration proceedings should be governed by the law of Scotland.

I would allow the appeal.

LORD HODSON held the proper law of the contract to be English law but continued:

I am satisfied, however, that, whether the proper law of the contract is English or Scottish, the arbitration being admittedly a matter of procedure as opposed to being a matter of substantive law is on principle and authority to be governed by the *lex fori*, in this case Scottish law. Furthermore, the parties have, in my judgment, plainly submitted to the Scottish arbitration on the footing that Scottish procedure was to govern.

The leading case of *Don v Lippmann* (1837), a Scottish appeal to your Lordships' House, was concerned with the law of prescription and it was held that the sexennial period according to the *lex fori* prevailed over the *lex contractus*. Lord Brougham held that there is this distinction between the contract and the remedy: that whatever relates to the remedy is to be governed by the *lex fori*, the law of the country to whose courts application is made for performance. I see no reason why this principle should not be applied to arbitration proceedings. It appears from *Norske Atlas Insurance Co Ltd v London General Insurance Co Ltd* (1927) that Mackinnon J was of this opinion. An opinion to the same effect is to be found in Dicey and Morris, *Conflict of Laws* (8th edition 1967), where the editors submit, at page 1048.

'Where the parties have failed to choose the law governing the arbitration proceedings, those proceedings must be considered, at any rate *prima facie*, as being governed by the law of the country in which the arbitration is held, on the ground that it is the country most closely connected with the proceedings.'

I agree with this submission.

Here the parties did not, in the first place, choose the law which should govern the arbitration proceedings but they subsequently accepted a Scottish arbiter in Scottish arbitration proceedings. This agreement involved no variation of the original contract for it is not inconsistent with the terms of that agreement that arbitration, if any, should take place in Scotland and be governed by Scottish procedure. That Scottish arbitration procedure was to be followed was accepted by the parties as is shown by the correspondence which took place following the appointment of the arbiter in Glasgow. The arbiter himself made the position abundantly clear by appointing as his clerk a Glasgow solicitor. Scottish procedure was followed throughout without objection until the application was made for a case to be stated. Then for the first time, when it was realised that this procedure was not available in Scotland, was any attempt made to depart from what had previously been agreed. The respondents submit that in agreeing to Scottish procedure they were not contemplating the case stated process which is used in England but not in Scotland. This will not avail them since, as was admitted, stating a case is a procedural matter and the respondents cannot pick and choose from the various operations involved in Scottish procedure. The form of the application made by the appellants for the appointment of an arbitrator does not avail the respondents — merely because of the use of the form of words 'where there is a submission to arbitration, within the meaning of the Arbitration Act 1950'. There was in truth a submission within the meaning of the English Act, which does not apply to Scotland, but this does not lead to the conclusion that the English Act was to govern the Scottish arbitration proceedings.

I would allow the appeal.

LORD GUEST held the proper law of the contract was English but continued:
I now turn to the crucial question: what is the curial law of the arbitration? It is said that there is no case where it has been held that the law of the arbitration was different from the law of the contract. I am not impressed by this argument when it is conceded, as it was by (counsel) for the respondents, that this could be the position. This concession could not have been withheld in view of the observations in *Don v Lippmann (supra)* and *Hamlyn & Co v Talisker Distillery* (1894).

No question arises as to any split in the proper law of the contract or any variation of the proper law. When the stage of an arbitration is reached, there must arise, apart from a particular term in the contract or some agreement between the parties, the question what procedural law is to be adopted by the arbiter. This question must be: what procedural law did the conduct of the parties evince their intention to adopt?

In the present case the parties did not agree upon an arbiter and it therefore became necessary for the president of the Royal Institute of British Architects to appoint an arbiter. It may be that the appellants thought that if they did not agree to the respondents' nominee, the president .... would probably appoint a Scots arbiter. However that may be, the president did in fact appoint an architect practising in Scotland as arbiter. In the application by the appellants for the appointment made to the president of the Royal Institute of British Architects there occurs a reference to a 'submission to arbitration, within the meaning of the Arbitration Act 1950'. It was argued for the respondents that this was conclusive of the matter and amounted to a consent by the appellants to an arbitration under the English Arbitration Act 1950, and an acceptance by the arbiter of the jurisdiction of the English High Court under that Act. In my view, far too great an emphasis has been laid on this expression. The expression 'submission to arbitration' only occurs in section 4(2) of the Act of 1950 in reference to foreign arbitrations and the reference in the application only imports what the law would in any case imply. The arbiter's power and jurisdiction stem not from this application and his acceptance of office, but from the arbitration clause in the contract. This form was merely the machinery for the appointment of the particular arbiter in view of the failure to agree upon an arbiter.

At this stage of the appointment of an arbiter I am satisfied that neither party applied his mind to what procedural law should be adopted. But as soon as the arbiter was in the saddle matters took a more definite turn. The arbiter appointed a Scottish solicitor as his clerk. He made it clear to the parties that he was adopting Scots procedure. The respondents instructed Scots solicitors and Scots counsel as did the appellants. The pleadings took Scottish form and the respondents tabled pleas to the relevancy in Scots form and used Scots terminology for the remedies which they sought on the counterclaim, namely 'decree arbitral'. The form of order by the arbiter was a Scots interlocuter. The seat of the arbitration continued to be in Scotland. With all these proceedings the respondents acquiesced and took not a single objection.

Apart from the contract itself there was not a single factor in the parties' conduct which suggested that any other procedural law was being adopted but Scots law. I have little doubt that, until the critical question arose as to the form of the award, neither party had any doubt that it was the Scots form of procedure which was being adopted. That was certainly the view of the arbiter and I feel certain that it would have been the view of 'the officious bystander' to the proceedings.

It has been suggested that the seat of the arbitration is unimportant and that an arbiter might decide to sit in several different places and that no party would restrain him for so doing. That may be so. However, the provisions of Rules of the Supreme Court, Order 73, rule 7 do indicate that the territorial nature of the arbitration is important: see also the passage in *Dicey and Morris*, op cit, page 1048.

Where all the proceedings take Scots form and the arbiter plainly indicates that he is following Scots procedure, then, in the absence of any protest, the parties will, in my opinion, be taken to have agreed that the arbitration will be governed by the curial rules of Scotland.

As a pure matter of convenience I should have thought it extremely unlikely that a Scottish architect, advised by a Scots solicitor, before whom Scots counsel instructed by a Scots solicitor appeared, would think for one moment of applying the English rules of procedure. The view of respondents' counsel at any rate was that the respondents had consented to the arbitration taking place in Scotland 'under Scottish procedure' (see reason 8 in the respondents' case).

[Counsel] for the respondents conceded that the application for the arbiter to state his award in the form of a special case under section 21 of the Arbitration Act 1950 was a question of procedure. If the Scots law of procedure is applicable to the arbitration, then as the Arbitration Act 1950 does not apply to Scotland the respondents must fail to obtain this remedy or, indeed, any other remedy under the Act of 1950.

I would allow the appeal and restore the order of Eveleigh J.

LORD DILHORNE held the proper law of the contract was English law but continued:

The inference to be drawn from the appointment of a Scottish solicitor as clerk and the reference to 'our procedure' was that Scottish procedure would be followed.

On 24 May 1967 the matter was put beyond all doubt. The clerk to the arbiter then wrote to the respondents' solicitors telling them that procedure proposed by them 'was not in accordance with Scottish arbitration procedure'.

The respondents appointed Scottish solicitors to act for them in the arbitration. The pleadings were in Scottish form and the procedure followed at the hearing was Scottish.

It was not until towards the end of the hearing after all the evidence had been given that any question arose as to the law applicable to the arbitration. Counsel for the respondents then asked for a case to be stated. In the course of his address he said that he had never conceded that Scots law applied. The arbitrator said that he had never been in doubt 'and that is why I am astonished that it is raised now'.

In the light of these facts I cannot escape from the conclusion that the respondents accepted that the arbitration was subject to Scottish procedure and so, too, to Scottish law.

It is not, in my opinion, necessary to consider whether their acceptance of this amounted to a variation of the contract or filled a gap in that contract. Having followed that procedure in an arbitration held in Scotland from the inception of the arbitration, the hearing of which occupied eleven days, their contention that English law governed the procedure at the arbitration in my view fails. It was conceded by [counsel for the respondents] in the course of his able argument that stating a case is part of the procedural law, and it was common ground that, unless the procedural law was English, the arbitrator could not be required to state a case.

In my opinion, the order of Eveleigh J was right and should be restored.

I would allow the appeal.

LORD WILBERFORCE held that the proper law of the contract was Scottish law and continued:

I turn to the second question: what law is to govern the arbitration procedure? If the proper law of the contract is Scottish there could be no argument in favour of the intrusion of English law into the arbitration. But if the proper law is English, an interesting question arises. One must ask first whether, in principle, it is possible for the law governing the arbitral procedure to differ from that governing the substance of the contract. No authority was cited to us which explicitly answers this question one way or the other, but I have no doubt as to the answer. It is a matter of experience that numerous arbitrations are conducted by English arbitrators in England on matters governed by contracts whose proper law is or may be that of another country, and I should be surprised if it had ever been held that such arbitrations were not governed by the English Arbitration Act in procedural matters, including the right to apply for a case to be stated. (I leave aside as a special case arbitrations conducted under the rules of the International Chamber of Commerce, though even these may be governed by the law of the place of arbitration. See also *International Tank and Pipe SAK v Kuwait Aviation Fueling Co KSC* (1974).) The principle must surely be the same as that which applies to court proceedings brought in one country concerning a contract governed by the law of another, and that such proceedings as regards all matters which the law regards as procedural are governed by the *lex fori* has been accepted at least since Lord Brougham's judgment in *Don v Lippmann (supra)*. In my opinion, the law is correctly stated by Professor Kahn-Freund and Dr Morris in *Dicey and Morris* op cit, page 1048, where they say:

> 'It cannot however be doubted that the courts would give effect to the choice of a law other than the proper law of the contract. Thus, if parties agreed on an arbitration clause expressed to be governed by English law but providing for arbitration in Switzerland, it may be held that, whereas English law governs the validity, interpretation and effect of the arbitration clause as such (including the scope of the arbitrators' jurisdiction), the proceedings are governed by Swiss law. It is also submitted that where the parties have failed to choose the law governing the arbitration proceedings, those proceedings must be considered, at any rate *prima facie*, as being governed by the law of the country in which the arbitration is held, on the ground that it is the country most closely connected with the proceedings.'

The first part of this is well supported by *Hamlyn & Co v Talisker Distillery* (1894) per Lord Herschell LC and Lord Watson and also by *N.V. Kwik Hoo Tong Handel Maatschappij v James Finlay & Co Ltd* (1927), and both parts rest solidly on common-sense.

Appeal allowed

See also *International Tank and Pipe SAK v Kuwait Aviation Fuelling Co KSC* (1974) in Part II and *Frota Nacional de Petroleiros v Skibsaktieselskapet Thorsholm* (1957) in Part III.

Arbitration as a condition precedent (see LPA 2.2)

Where parties have contracted that arbitration shall be a condition precedent to an action at law, no action can be heard until the arbitration has taken place.

Scott v Avery and others (House of Lords, 1856)

> The plaintiff brought an action on a shipping insurance policy which included the words:

>> 'Provided always, and it is hereby expressly declared to be part of the contract of insurance between the members of the association, that no member who refuses to accept the amount of any loss as settled by the committee in manner hereinbefore specified, in full satisfaction of such loss, shall be entitled to maintain any action at law or suit in equity on his policy, until the matters in dispute shall have been referred to and decided by arbitrators appointed as hereinbefore specified, and then only for such sum as the said arbitrators shall award; and the obtaining the decision of such arbitrators on the matters and claims in dispute is hereby declared to be a condition precedent to the right of any member to maintain any such action or suit.'

> The Court of Exchequer found for the plaintiff but the Court of Exchequer Chamber reversed this by a four to three majority. The plaintiff appealed to the House of Lords.

> LORD CRANWORTH LC: The question appears to me to be one merely of construction of the policy in question. For there is no doubt of the general principle, which was argued at your Lordships' Bar, that parties cannot by contract oust the ordinary courts of their jurisdiction.
> That has been decided in many cases. Perhaps the first case I need refer to was a case decided about a century ago, *Kill v Hollister* (1746). That was an action on a policy in which there was a clause that in case of any loss or dispute it should be referred to arbitration. It was decided there that an action would lie, although no reference had been made to arbitration. After a lapse of about half a century, occurred a case before Lord Kenyon — and probably many other cases, from the language that fell from that learned judge, had been decided which are not reported — but in the time of Lord Kenyon occurred a case which is considered the leading case upon this subject, *Thompson v Charnock* (1799). That was an action upon a charter-party in which there was a stipulation that if any difference should arise it should be referred to arbitration. That clause was pleaded in bar to the action which

had been brought upon a breach of the covenant with an averment that the defendant had been and always was ready to refer the matter to arbitration. That was held to be a bad plea upon the ground that a right of action had accrued, and that the fact that the parties had agreed that the matter should be settled by arbitration did not oust the jurisdiction of the courts. Just about the same time occurred a case in the Court of Common Pleas, when that court was presided over by Lord Eldon — *Tattersall v Groote* (1800). That was an action by the administratrix of a deceased partner against a surviving partner for not naming an arbitrator pursuant to a covenant in the deed of partnership. To that action there was a demurrer, and the demurrer was allowed. But that case I think can afford very little authority in the present action, or in actions similar to the present, because there the covenant was only that, if any dispute arose between the partners, they should name an arbitrator. One of the partners died, and his administratrix brought an action, and Lord Eldon pointed out that the covenant did not apply to a case where one of the partners was dead and an action was brought by his representative. Therefore, in truth, that amounts to no decision whatever upon the general question. There was a case before Lord Kenyon at the Rolls, *Halfhide v Fenning* (1788) in which he held a different doctrine. That was a bill for an account of partnership transactions. The plea to that bill was that the articles contained an agreement that any differences which should arise should be settled by arbitration; and Lord Kenyon allowed that plea. But I think that case cannot be relied upon, and it has been universally treated as having proceeded upon an erroneous principle, because, no doubt, where a right of action has accrued, parties cannot by contract say that there shall not be jurisdiction to enforce damages for a breach of that contract.

This doctrine depends upon the general policy of the law, that parties cannot enter into a contract which gives rise to a right of action for the breach of it, and then withdraw the jurisdiction on such a case from the ordinary tribunals. But surely there can be no principle or policy of the law which prevents parties from entering into such a contract as that no breach shall occur until after a reference has been made to arbitration. It appears to me that in such cases as that the policy of the law is left untouched; and that, I take it, is what was alluded to by Lord Hardwicke in *Wellington v Mackintosh* (1743) which was this. The articles of partnership in that case contained a covenant that any dispute should be referred. A bill was filed by one of the partners, and a plea set up that covenant to refer as a bar to the bill. Lord Hardwicke overruled the plea, but said that the parties might have so framed the deed as to oust the jurisdiction of the court. I take it that what Lord Hardwicke meant was, that the parties might have so framed the stipulation among themselves that no right of action or right of suit should arise until a reference had been previously made to arbitration. I think it may be illustrated thus. If I covenant with A to do particular acts, and it is also covenanted between us that any question that may arise as to the breach of the covenant shall be referred to arbitration, that latter covenant does not prevent the covenantee from bringing an action. A right of action has accrued, and it would be against the policy of the law to give effect to an agreement that such a right should not be enforced through the medium of the ordinary tribunals, but if I covenant with AB that if I do or omit to do a certain act, then I will pay to him such a sum as IS shall award as the amount of damage sustained by him, then, until IS has made his award and I have omitted to pay the sum awarded, my covenant has not been broken and no right of action has arisen.

The policy of the law does not prevent parties from so contracting, and the question is here: what is the contract? Does any right of action exist until the amount of damage has been ascertained in the specified mode? I think, clearly not. The stipulation is that the sum to be paid to the suffering member shall be settled by the committee. If he does not agree with the committee as to what the amount is, then the committee shall name one arbitrator and he shall name another, and these two arbitrators shall name an umpire, and they shall determine what the amount is, and that shall be the amount recovered. There is the express stipulation that the obtaining of the decision of the arbitrators on the matters and claims in dispute is hereby declared to be a condition precedent to the right of any member to maintain any such action or suit. That the meaning of the parties, therefore, was that the sum to be recovered should be only such a sum as, if not agreed upon in the first instance between the committee and the suffering member, should be decided by arbitration, and that the sum so ascertained by arbitration, and no other, should be the sum to be recovered, appears to me to be clear beyond all possibility of controversy; and, if that was their meaning, the circumstance that they have not stated that meaning in the clearest terms or in the most artistic manner is a matter utterly unimportant. What the court below had to do was to ascertain what was the meaning of the parties as deduced from the language they have used. It appears to me perfectly clear that the language used indicated this to have been their intention — that, supposing there was a difference between the person who had suffered loss or damage and the committee as to what amount he should recover, that was to be ascertained in a particular mode, and, until that mode had been adopted and the amount ascertained according to that mode, no right of action should exist — in other words, that the right of action should be, not for what a jury should say was the amount of the loss, but for what the persons designated in that particular form of agreement should so say.

It was argued that here the arbiters were to decide, not the mere amount, but other matters, as, for instance, what average was to be allowed, whether there had been a loss, and a variety of other matters, which were ingeniously argued at your Lordships' Bar. In the first place, if that were so, it would not necessarily change my view of the case. I am not at all clear that it is not so. I observe the learned judges differed about that. I do not think it necessary to go into that, because I am quite prepared to say that, in my view of the case, that makes no difference at all. If, in consideration of a sum of money paid to me by AB, I agree with him that, in case IS should decide that he, AB, had fulfilled certain conditions and had sustained certain damage, and IS should make his award accordingly, I would pay to AB the sum so ascertained and awarded, no right of action would exist until IS had made his award. I do not go into the question, therefore, whether in this case, according to the true construction of the contract, the amount of damage alone is to be ascertained, because, in my view of the case, the principle goes much farther.

It appears to me perfectly clear that, until the award was made, no right of action accrued, and consequently the judgment of the court below, reversing the judgment of the Court of Exchequer and allowing the plea, was a perfectly correct judgment. Your Lordships have had the benefit of having this case argued before the learned judges. The learned judges differed in their opinion. There was a majority, but a bare majority, in favour of the view which I have taken of this case. Whichever way the preponderance of opinion among the learned judges may be, and however great it may be either way, the ultimate decision rests with your Lordships, but it is always satisfactory to know that the view taken by your Lordships is in concurrence with the opinion of the learned judges. Here it is in concurrence with the opinion of a majority, though by a slender majority, of those learned judges. I, therefore, humbly move your Lordships that the judgment below be affirmed, and that judgment be given for the respondents, with costs.

LORD CAMPBELL: After a very deliberate and dispassionate consideration of the case, I have come to the same conclusion as my noble and learned friend on the Woolsack. It appears to me, I confess, to be very clear (with great deference to the dissenting judges) that, upon principle, and without overturning any authority, your Lordships ought to affirm the judgment of the Exchequer Chamber. In the first place, I think that the contract between the shipowner and the underwriters in this case is quite clear — as clear as the English language could make it — that no action should be brought against the insurers until the arbitrators had disposed of any dispute that might arise between them. It is declared to be a condition precedent to the bringing of any action. There is no doubt that such was the intention of the parties; and, upon a deliberate view of the condition of the policy, I am of opinion that it embraces not only the assessment of damages, the computation of quantum, but also any dispute that might arise between the underwriters and the insured respecting the liability of the insurers as well as the amount to be paid. If there had been any question about want of seaworthiness, or deviation, or a breach of blockade had been committed, I am clearly of opinion that upon a just construction of this instrument, until those questions had been determined by the arbitrators, no right of action could have accrued to the insured.

That being the intention of the parties, about which I believe there is no dispute, is the contract illegal? There is an express undertaking that no action shall be brought until the arbitrators have decided, and there is abundant consideration for that in the mutual contract into which the parties have entered. Therefore, unless there be some illegality in the contract, the courts are bound to give it effect. There is no statute against such a contract. Then on what ground is it to be declared to be illegal? It is contended that it is contrary to public policy. That is rather a dangerous ground to go upon. I say it with great deference before your Lordships after the view that was taken in a very important case lately decided in this House [*Egerton v Earl Brownlow* 1853: Ed]. But what pretence can there be for saying that there is anything contrary to public policy in allowing parties to contract that they shall not be liable to any action until their liability has been ascertained by a domestic and private tribunal upon which they themselves agree? Can the public be injured by it? It seems to me that it would be a most inexpedient encroachment upon the liberty of the subject, if he were not allowed to enter into such a contract. Take the case of an insurance club, of which there are many in the north of England. Is there anything contrary to public policy in saying that the company shall not be harassed by actions to be brought against them, the costs of which might be ruinous, but that any dispute that arises shall be referred to a domestic tribunal, which may speedily and economically determine the dispute? I can see not the slightest ill consequence that can flow from such a liberty, and I see great advantage that may arise from it. Public policy, therefore, seems to me to require that effect should be given to the contract.

When we come to the decided cases, if there were any decision that had not been reviewed by your Lordships which adjudged such a contract to be illegal, I should ask your Lordships to reverse it, for it would seem to me really to stand on no principle whatsoever. I know that there has been a very great inclination in the courts for a good many years to throw obstacles in the way of arbitration. I wish to speak with great respect of my predecessors the judges; but I must just let your Lordships into the secret of that tendency. There is no disguising the fact that as formerly the emoluments of the judges depended mainly or almost entirely upon fees and they had no fixed salary, there was great competition to get as much as possible of litigation into Westminster Hall, and a great scramble in Westminster Hall for the division of the spoil, ·and hence the disputes between the different courts about the effect of a *latitat*, a *capias*, and a *quo minus* — the *latitat* bringing business into the Court of Queen's Bench, the *capias* into the Common Pleas, and the *quo minus* into the Exchequer. They had great jealousy of arbitrations, whereby Westminster Hall was robbed of those cases which came neither into the Queen's Bench, nor the Common Pleas, nor the Exchequer. Therefore, they said that the courts ought not to be ousted of their jurisdiction, and that it was contrary to the policy of the law. But, my Lords, that really grew up only subsequently to the time of Lord Coke, whose memory I revere, and whose authority I am always anxious to support where I can. There is a saying of Lord Coke's which is the original foundation of this doctrine. It is this:

'If a man make a lease for life, and by deed grant that if any waste or destruction be done it shall be redressed by neighbours, and not by suit or plea, notwithstanding an action of waste shall lie, for the place wasted cannot be recovered without a verdict of the neighbour being first had and obtained.'

Where an action is indispensable you cannot oust the court of its jurisdiction over the subject, because justice cannot be done without a plea. This is the foundation of the doctrine that the courts are not to be ousted of their jurisdiction.

I am glad to think that there is no case that I am aware of that will be overturned by your Lordships affirming the judgment now in dispute. Because all that has been hitherto decided in *Thompson v Charnock (supra)* and the other cases referred to is this — that if the contract between the parties simply contains a clause or covenant to refer to arbitration, and goes no further, then an action may be brought in spite of that clause, although there has been no arbitration. But there is no case that goes the length of saying that where the contract is, as it is here, that no right of action shall accrue until there has been an arbitration, then an action may be brought, although there has been no arbitration. In this contract of insurance, it is stipulated in the most express terms that, until the arbitrators have determined, no action shall lie in any court whatsoever. That is not ousting the courts of their jurisdiction, because they have no jursidiction whatsoever, and no cause of action accrues until the arbitrators have determined. Therefore, without overturning *Thompson v Charnock (supra)*, and the other cases to the same effect, your Lordships may hold that in this case, where it is expressly, directly, and unequivocally agreed upon between the parties that there shall be no right of action whatever till the arbitrators have decided, it is a bar to the action that there has been no such arbitration.

It gives me great satisfaction to know that while this case has been pending, there has been a decision bearing on this question in the Court of Exchequer, in which this case arose. That case is expressly in point, and it seems to me further to show that this judgment of the Court of Exchequer Chamber ought to be affirmed. That case was decided in Hilary Term of the present year. It is *Brown v Overbury* (1865). It was an action on a horse-race. The winner, who had contributed to the sweepstakes, said that his horse had won, and he brought an action against the stakeholder to recover the stakes. But it was a condition in the race that if any dispute arose the stewards should decide. He first attempted to say that the stewards had decided, but it turned out that the stewards had not decided, for they differed in opinion. Then he attempted to show that his horse had won, but the judge held that he could not go into that even if the horse could clearly be shown to have won, because the action had not accrued till the arbitrators, the stewards, had determined, and so the plaintiff was nonsuited. The case was brought before the Court of Exchequer, and they unanimously concurred in the ruling of the judge at *nisi prius*, and upon the very reason that it was part of the contract that the stewards should decide and not a jury, and that it could not be brought before a jury till the stewards had determined, and they would not allow the plaintiff to recover either the sweepstakes or his own contribution: and the nonsuit was confirmed. I cannot distinguish that case in principle from the present. Substitute stewards for arbitrators, and it is the same question, whether it is a contract of insurance or a contract upon a horse-race (which by Act of Parliament is legal). The Court of Exchequer held that in that case the action could not be maintained until the stewards had decided, and that, therefore, it was a good defence to the action that the stewards had not decided. Here the plea is that the arbitrators recovered and, therefore, an action will not lie. That seems to me to be a strong authority in point, and calculated to remove any scruples that any of your Lordships may have in maintaining the judgment of the Court of Exchequer Chamber, which reversed the judgment of the Court of Exchequer.

For these reasons I am happy to say that I entirely concur in the view of this case taken by my noble and learned friend, the Lord Chancellor, and I think that the judgment ought to be affirmed.

LORD CRANWORTH LC: I have communicated with LORD BROUGHAM, who is absent in consequence of illness, and he authorises me to say that he entirely concurs in the view which myself and my noble and learned friend have taken of this case.

Appeal dismissed

Where the parties have agreed that a claim shall be barred if arbitration is not started within a certain time, this is effective, subject to the provisions of section 27 of the Arbitration Act 1950 (see page 94 where section 27 is given in full) and the power thereby conferred on the court to extend the period of time.

Atlantic Shipping & Trading Co v Louis Dreyfus & Co (House of Lords, 1922)

A charter party including the clause:

> 39: All disputes from time to time arising out of this contract shall, unless the parties agree forthwith on a single arbitrator, be referred to the final arbitrament of two arbitrators carrying on business in London, who shall be members of the Baltic and engaged in the shipping and/or grain trades, one to be appointed by each of the parties, with power to such arbitrators to appoint an umpire. Any claim must be made in writing and claimant's arbitrator appointed within three months of final discharge, and, where this provision is complied with, the claim shall be deemed to be waived and absolutely barred.

The case is here reported only on the first point, the validity of such time clauses.

LORD DUNEDIN: Under the old law an agreement to refer disputes arising under a contract to arbitration was often asserted to be bad as an ousting of the jurisdiction of the courts, but that position was finally abandoned in *Scott v Avery* (1856). As I read that case it can no longer be said that the jurisdiction of the court is ousted by such an agreement, on the contrary, the jurisdiction of the court is invoked in order to enforce it, and there is nothing wrong in persons agreeing that their disputes should be decided by arbitration. It follows that the clause here is not obnoxious in so far as it provides for arbitration. It goes on, however, to say that if the claim is not made and the arbitration started within a certain time the claim is to be held to be departed from. Now, if it were illegal to arrange that a claim should not be good unless made within a certain time I should understand the argument, but as it is admitted that it is perfectly legal to make such a stipulation — it is done, for example, every day in insurance policies — then why should it be bad because it is tacked on to a provision for arbitration instead of to an action at law? All it comes to is this. I stipulate that you shall settle your differences with me by arbitration and not by action at law, and I stipulate that you shall state your differences and start your arbitration within a certain time or you shall be held to have waived your claim. For these reasons, I do not think the judgment of the Court of Appeal can be supported....

LORD SUMNER: This case turns upon clause 39 of the charter. The first question is whether it means that, if the charterer does not make a claim or name an arbitrator within three months of the final discharge, he agrees that he is not in any way or in any circumstances to have any access to His Majesty's courts for the purpose of raising his claim. The Court of Appeal thought that it does. With great respect, I am unable to agree. The clause does not mean that in no circumstances shall a claimant be allowed to enter His Majesty's courts at all, but that the cause of action shall not be complete and, therefore, cannot be made the subject of proceedings, unless the specified conditions have first been satisfied. The point, however, hardly admits of discussion; a view is formed of it, one way or the other, simply on the perusal of the words, for the question is purely one of interpretation. I think the words do not exclude the cargo-owner from such recourse to the courts as is always open, by virtue of the provisions of the Arbitration Act, to a party who has agreed to arbitrate. If so, as of course the Court of Appeal would have been the first to recognise, the jurisdiction of the courts is not ousted so as to make this arbitration clause bad altogether. Its terms can be enforced.

Appeal allowed

Liberian Shipping Corporation v A. King & Sons Ltd (Court of Appeal, 1967)

DENNING MR: The owners' solicitors applied to the court for an extension of time under section 27 of the Arbitration Act 1950. It was heard by Master Lawrence on 27 July 1966. He extended the time. The charterers appealed to Mr Justice Donaldson, who is very experienced in commercial matters. He considered the authorities, and held that owing to the restricted manner in which the courts have interpreted section 27 (about undue hardship), the time should not be extended. He said: 'I accept that there is hardship but within the narrow meaning of undue hardship this case does not come within a mile of it'.

If his judgment stands, it means that the claim is absolutely barred because the owners were nine days out of time....

We have been referred to the cases on this subject. The courts have on occasion given a narrow meaning to 'undue hardship'. Thus in *G. Sigalas Sons v Man Mohan Singh & Co* (1958), Lord Parker CJ said: 'The powers of this court to extend the time, though discretionary, are only exercised in very restricted cases'.

In that case the owners were only two days late, but the Court did not extend the time.

Mr Davenport, in his excellent argument, supported these cases by saying that commercial men must know where they stand; and that, as soon as the three months are up, they are entitled to consider that all claims are barred save in very exceptional circumstances. He said exceptional circumstances would exist when the claimant was not at fault at all, as, for instance, where the claimant did not know he had a claim within three months and could not reasonably be expected to know: such as goods afterwards discovered not to be up to sample, or late claims by third parties. But if the claimant was at fault himself in not reading the clause, or forgetting about it, or overlooking it, the time should not be extended.

It does appear that in the past the courts have been inclined to use this argument: the words used in the statute are 'undue hardship'. A 'hardship' by itself is something severe which is hard to ensure. It is always a 'hardship' to be barred by a time limit. If a man does not read the contract and is a day or two late, it is a 'hardship', but it is not an 'undue hardship', because it is his own fault.

I cannot accept this narrow interpretation of the statute. These time-limit clauses used to operate most unjustly. Claimants used to find their claims barred when, by some oversight, they were only a day or two late. In order to avoid that injustice, the legislature intervened so as to enable the courts to extend the time whenever 'in the circumstances of the case undue hardship would otherwise be caused'. 'Undue' there simply means excessive. That is, greater hardship than the circumstances warrant. Even though a claimant has been at fault himself, it is an undue hardship on him if the consequences are out of proportion to his fault.

Applying this test, it seems to me that if a claimant makes a mistake which is excusable, and is in consequence a few days out of time, then if there is no prejudice to the other side, it would be altogether too harsh to deprive him of all chance for ever of coming and making his claim. All the more so if the mistake is contributed to or shared by the other side. That indeed is this very case... They were both under a misapprehension. Neither of them realised that the time had already expired. But it is pretty plain that the conduct of the charterers put the owners off their guard. The owners would not contemplate that they would be barred while negotiations were still going on. As soon as they realised that the negotiations were not going to be fruitful, they at once took the necessary steps. They were only nine days late. In these circumstances it seems to me it would be undue hardship to hold that the owners are barred absolutely. The case has a resemblance to *Thomas Hughes v Directors, etc of the Metropolitan Railway Company* (1877), where there were negotiations for a settlement and it was held that pending those negotiations, the strict rights of the parties did not apply.

It was said that this was a matter for the judge's discretion. True enough. But we have said time and again that we will interfere with a judge's discretion if satisfied that the discretion was wrongly exercised. In any case, the judge was not exercising an unfettered discretion. He felt himself fettered by the trend of the authorities to give the words 'undue hardship' a narrow meaning. I think we should reverse that trend and give the words their ordinary meaning, as Parliament intended.

It would be 'undue hardship' on the owners to hold them barred by the clause. I would allow the appeal, and restore the order of the Master.

SALMON LJ: I entirely agree with Lord Justice Harman that everything in this appeal turns upon the true construction of the words 'undue hardship'. I further agree that it is not enough for the appellants to show mere hardship. They must show undue hardship. I am, however, unable to accept Lord Justice Harman's construction of section 27 of the Arbitration Act 1950: nor that which has been placed upon it in several cases by the Divisional Court....

That section seems to me to state quite plainly that if, having considered all the circumstances of the case, the court comes to the conclusion that the hardship imposed by the form of the arbitration clause upon the claimant is greater than that which, in justice, he should be called upon to bear, the time within which to appoint an arbitrator may be extended by the court. I do not believe that the courts are entitled to read words into this section which are not there and which would have the effect of cutting down the power given to the courts by the plain language of the section itself.

Prior to this enactment, which was first introduced into the law in 1934, the commercial community — and not only the commercial community but those who practised and administered commercial law — were shackled by the form, sometimes the printed form, of this type of arbitration clause. It put it out of the power of the court to grant any relief to a claimant who had allowed perhaps a day or two to run beyond the period (sometimes only ten days) specified in the clause, even although the delay could have caused no conceivable harm to the other side. Commercial men and those who practised and administered the commercial law had spent their working lives with the law in this state. They had no doubt experienced many cases in which a man, with a perfectly good claim for thousands of pounds' worth of damage for breach of contract, inadvertently allowed a day or two to go by and was thereby deprived of the right to be compensated for the loss he had suffered. The other party, who had not been in any way affected by this slight delay and who perhaps had been guilty of a deliberate breach of contract, was relieved from liability to pay compensation for the heavy loss which he had caused.

It was no doubt to remedy this hardship and injustice that the legislature intervened to alter the law. This enactment was a beneficent reform, liberalising the law in an admittedly narrow sector of the commercial field. I have heard it said that when people have spent their lives in chains and the shackles are eventually struck off, they cannot believe that their chains are not still there. They still feel bound by the shackles to which they have so long been accustomed. To my mind, that factor may explain the court's approach in some of the cases to the problem with which we are now faced.

In the present case I, for my part, agree that it cannot be said that the respondents contributed to the delay. The delay was caused by what I regard as a very minor piece of inadvertence by the claimants. It is quite obvious from the letters, which the Master of the Rolls has read, that although both sides were breathing fire in the correspondence, they were both also expressing a willingness to meet and see whether, as ordinary sensible businessmen, they could not compose their differences. Indeed, on two occasions the respondents proposed a meeting in London for this purpose. It is obvious from the fact that the respondents suggested 27 June as the day on which the conference should take place in London, that the respondents were quite unaware that time expired on 26 June. [Counsel for the respondents] says, and I naturally accept, that they had no idea that time expired on that day.

It would appear that the reason why they did not know that the time had expired was because they, too, had not looked at the arbitration clause. They apparently did not do so until the delay had been pointed out to them in a telephone conversation on 6 July by the claimants' representative, when he asked for an extension of time. The importance of that fact is that it shows conclusively that these respondents did not do anything or fail to do anything as a result of the time for appointing an arbitrator having expired. They had not appreciated that the time for appointing an arbitrator had gone by, and indeed it has not been suggested and it could not be suggested that they have been in any way prejudiced by the delay. I cannot find anything in section 27 which in these circumstances compels me to say that it would not impose undue hardship on the claimants to hold they must forfeit their claim to some £33,000 because of this small delay which has had no effect at all upon the respondents.

It is said rightly that commercial men enter into contracts such as the present on the basis of the arbitration clause. They must be presumed, however, to read it in the light of section 27. I have no doubt at all that, if two ordinary businessmen entering into this contract had been asked if it would cause undue hardship to refuse to extend the time should circumstances such as the present occur, they would both unhesitatingly have answered 'yes'. I am not prepared to hold that the court's powers under the section should be very rarely exercised. Still less that they should be exercised freely. The question as to whether or not those powers should be exercised must turn exclusively on the particular facts of each case in which the question arises.

In considering this question the court must take all the relevant circumstances of the case into account, the degree of blameworthiness of the claimants in failing to appoint an arbitrator within the time, the amount of the delay, whether the claimants have been misled, whether through some circumstances beyond their control it was impossible for them to appoint an arbitrator in time. In the last two circumstances I have mentioned, which do not arise here, it is obvious that normally the power would be exercised. But those are not the only circumstances and they are not, to my mind, necessary circumstances for the exercise of the power to extend time. I do not intend to catalogue the circumstances to be taken into account, but one very important circumstance is whether there is any possibility of the other side having been prejudiced by the delay. Of course, if there is such a possibility, it might be said that it is no undue hardship upon the claimants to refuse an extension of time because if the hardship is lifted from their shoulders, some hardship will fall on the shoulders of the respondents and, after all, the delay is the claimants' fault.

But there is no such possibility in this case. This is a simple case of a few days' delay, caused by an excusable piece of inadvertence which has done the respondents no conceivable harm and which, unless we exercise the powers which in my view we undoubtedly have, will deprive these claimants of what may turn out to be a valid claim for £33,000 and lift the liability off the shoulders of the respondents. I have no doubt but that this would cause the claimants undue hardship. There is nothing in this Act which obliges me to come to the conclusion that in these circumstances time should not be extended. Nor do I believe that I am bound by any of the cases to reach such a conclusion. The learned judge thought rightly that he was so bound and accordingly refused to extend the time.

I would allow the appeal.

HARMAN LJ dissented.

Appeal allowed

Note.
The cases which were referred to and which must now be taken as over-
ruled on this point are:
F. E. Hookway & Co Ltd v W. H. Hooper & Co (1950)
Jajasan Urusan Bahan Makanan v Comparia de Navegacion Geamur
Sociedade de Responsabilidad Limitada (1953)
Watney Compe Reid & Co Ltd v E. M. Dower & Co Ltd (1956)
G. Sigazas Sons v Man Mohan Singh & Co (1958)
The Leise Maersk (1958)

Section 27 of the Arbitration Act 1950 applies even though neither party is within English jurisdiction, and the arbitration may be subject to a foreign procedure, provided they have made English law the proper law of the contract.

Section 27 states: 'Where the terms of an agreement to refer future disputes to arbitration provide that any claims to which the agreement applies shall be barred unless notice to appoint an arbitrator is given or an arbitrator is appointed or some other step to commence arbitration proceedings is taken within a time fixed by the agreement, and a dispute arises to which the agreement applies, the High Court, if it is of opinion that in the circumstances of the case undue hardship would otherwise be caused, and not withstanding that the time so fixed has expired, may, on such terms, if any, as the justice of the case may require, but without prejudice to the provisions of any enactment limiting the time for the commencement of arbitration proceedings, extend the time for such period as it thinks proper.'

International Tank and Pipe SAK v Kuwait Aviation Fueling Co KSC
(Court of Appeal, 1974)

A contract between the parties, both Kuwait companies, was in the standard FIDIC form, but amended and with an additional clause 75:

'Construction of contract: This contract shall in all respects be construed and operated in conformity with the laws of England and the respective rights and liabilities of the parties shall be in accordance with the laws for the time being'.

The standard clause 67 provides that disputes shall be referred in the first place to the engineer but if either of the parties is dissatisfied with the engineer's decision, they can go to arbitration under the Rules of the Conciliation and Arbitration of the International Chamber of Commerce. Those rules provided that an arbitration should be governed by 'the law of procedure chosen by the parties or, failing such choice, those of the law of the country in which the arbitrator holds the proceedings'.

LORD DENNING MR: This submission raises this important point of jurisdiction. Can section 27 of the 1950 Act be invoked here? This depends on what is the law to be applied. Is it English law or some other law? The contract itself is to be construed by English law. But the arbitration is to be governed by the law of Kuwait or some other country. I say this because the arbitration is governed by the rules of the International Chamber of Commerce. And the Rules of the International Chamber of Commerce say in article 16 that the arbitration is governed by the rules:

> 'of the law of procedure chosen by the parties or, failing such choice, those of the law of the country in which the arbitrator holds the proceedings.'

Thus the parties may choose that the arbitration procedure is to be governed by the law of some country other than England. If they do not so choose, the procedure will be governed by the law where the arbitrator sits. That may be in Kuwait.

We reach, therefore, this point. English law governs the interpretation and effect of the contract. But the Kuwait law, or some other law, governs the arbitration procedure. This sort of difference is well known. It is recognised by the decision of the House of Lords in *James Miller and Partners Ltd v Whitworth Street Estates (Manchester) Ltd* (1970). Lord Dilhorne and Lord Wilberforce expressed the opinion that the law is correctly stated in *Dicey and Morris*:

> 'It cannot however be doubted that the courts would give effect to the choice of a (procedural) law other than the proper law of the contract. Thus, if parties agreed on an arbitration clause expressed to be governed by English law but providing for arbitration in Switzerland, it may be held that, whereas English law governs the validity, interpretation and effect of the arbitration clause as such (including the scope of the arbitrators' jurisdiction), the proceedings are governed by Swiss law.' (Dicey and Morris, *Conflict of Laws* (8th edition 1967, page 1048.)

In these circumstances the question is whether English law applies so as to enable the contractors to invoke section 27 of the Arbitration Act 1950? The learned judge held that it did. He said that the rules of the International Chamber of Commerce had not come into operation. Article 16 had not come into force because the parties had not chosen what country was to govern the procedure; and no decision had been taken as to where the arbitration should take place. So the judge thought that the only law which could govern the matter was the proper law of the contract itself, which was English law. The judge may be right about this; but I should prefer to put it differently. It seems to me that English law governs a great deal of the arbitration clause. Take the interpretation of it. Suppose the arbitration clause had said the claim had to be made within three months, and then there was an argument as to whether 'months' meant lunar months or calendar months. That dispute would have to be solved according to English law. Take next the very question here, that is, whether a sufficient 'communication' had been made to the engineer within 90 days. That, too, would have to be decided by English law. Similarly it seems to me that it is for English law to say whether or not section 27 of the 1950 Act can be invoked. That section says that when the terms of the agreement contain a time-bar:

'the High Court, if it is of opinion that in the circumstances of the case undue hardship would otherwise be caused...may, on such terms, if any as the justice of the case may require...extend the time for such period as it thinks proper'.

I look on section 27 as being, in effect, an additional statutory term written into the arbitration clause. As such, its interpretation, its application and effect are to be governed by English law. It may be that some other law will govern the procedure in the arbitration itself. It may be Kuwait law, or some other law. But that procedural law does not take effect until the arbitration has actually started, that is to say, not until the arbitrator has been properly appointed and is able to rule on the procedure to be adopted in the arbitration.

Counsel for the employers drew our attention to *Ch E Rolimpex Ltd v Avra Shipping Co Ltd (The Angeliki)* (1973). In that case Kerr J said that, when there was a time limit under the Hague Rules, it would be very rare for our courts to exercise their power under section 27 of the 1950 Act to extend the time. Counsel submitted that, when parties contracted on the form of an international agreement, the time ought not to be capable of extension by the fortuitous circumstance that the determination of the matter might arise in England. I cannot accept this submission. It may be that other countries have provisions similar to section 27. In any case the parties have agreed that the contract shall be interpreted and operated in conformity with the laws of England. This means reading into it section 27 of the 1950 Act. In my opinion, therefore, the High Court has jurisdiction under section 27 to extend the time.

The next question is whether the judge was right in the circumstances to extend the time. I think he was. The contractors thought that their letter of 19 April 1973 was sufficient claim to arbitration within the 90 days. Thereafter discussions for a settlement continued. It was only on 8 September 1973 that the employers took the point that the 90 days requisite had not been fulfilled. The employers knew perfectly well that the contractors were reserving their rights in regard to arbitration. The employers suffered no prejudice whatever. On 3 December 1973 the contractors applied for an extension of time under section 27. The judge, applying *Liberian Shipping Corporation v A. King and Sons Ltd* (1967), thought that in all the circumstances undue hardship would be caused to the contractors unless the time was extended. I agree with him. He extended the time for six weeks. It may be it will have to be extended further in view of the appeal. I would dismiss the appeal.

ORR LJ agreed.

BROWNE LJ: I also agree that the appeal should be dismissed for the reasons given by Lord Denning MR. I only add a few words on the question of jurisdiction. It is common ground that the proper law of a contract and the law governing the procedure in an arbitration arising from that contract may be different. In this case the law to be applied to the problem we have to decide is in my view the proper law of the contract, that is, English law, in accordance with clause 75 of the contract. The question is whether the plaintiffs are entitled to require the defendants to go to arbitration. If they have a right to go to arbitration, this is (and can only be) a right arising from the contract. The first question, as Lord Denning MR has said, is whether the plaintiffs' letter of 19 April 1973 was an effective claim or demand for arbitration under clause 67 of the contract. In my view that is clearly a question of the construction or operation of the contract within clause 75 and will have to be decided according to English law. For the purposes of this appeal, we are assuming that that letter was not an effective claim or demand. The effect of granting an extension under section 27 of the Arbitration Act 1950 is that the plaintiffs will be entitled to exercise their right under clause 67 to claim arbitration, although they are out of time and their right to claim arbitration would otherwise be barred. The effect of granting an extension under section 27 is that the engineer's decision is no longer final and binding within clause 67. In my view this is not a matter of procedure in the arbitration, which in fact does not yet exist, but a matter of the operation of the contract. In my view, it is a question of the effect of the arbitration clause, which is stated in the passage from *Dicey and Morris* which Lord Denning MR has already quoted and which was approved by Lord Wilberforce in the House of Lords, in *James Miller and Partners Ltd v Whitworth Street Estates (Manchester) Ltd (supra)* to be a question to be decided in accordance with English law, in the circumstances of this case. In my view therefore English law applies to this problem in accordance with clause 75 and the English courts have jurisdiction to grant an extension of time under section 27 of the Arbitration Act 1950. For this reason, in addition to those given by Lord Denning MR, I agree that this appeal should be dismissed.

Appeal dismissed

See also *James Miller & Partners Ltd and Whitworth Street Estates (Manchester) Ltd* (1970) in Part II and *Frota Nacional de Petroleiros v Skibsaktieselskapet Thorsholm* (1957) in Part III.

The effect of repudiation and frustration of contract (see LPA 2.3)

If one party has repudiated the whole of a contract, and the repudiation has been accepted by the other, an arbitration clause will still be binding.

Heyman and another v Darwins Ltd (House of Lords, 1942)

VISCOUNT SIMON LC: My Lords, by a written contract dated 19 February 1938, the respondents, who are manufacturers of steel in Sheffield, as principals appointed the appellants, whose business address is in New York, to be sole selling agents of their tool steels in a wide area of territories, including the western hemisphere (excluding USA and Argentine), Australia, New Zealand and India... The agreement contained an arbitration clause in the following terms:

'If any dispute shall arise between the parties hereto in respect of this agreement or any of the provisions herein contained or anything arising hereout the same shall be referred for arbitration in accordance with the provisions of the Arbitration Act 1889, or any then subsisting statutory modification thereof'.

The question to be decided in this appeal is whether an action started in the King's Bench Division by the appellants against the respondents should, on the application of the latter, be stayed pursuant to the Arbitration Act 1889, section 4, in order that the matters in dispute between the parties may be dealt with under the arbitration clause.

The appellants contend that the dispute does not fall within the arbitration clause at all, and alternatively that, if it does, the judge in chambers, Cassels J, rightly exercised his discretion in refusing to stay the action. The Court of Appeal (Scott, MacKinnon and Luxmoore LJJ) took a contrary view and held that the arbitration clause clearly applied, and that the judge made a wrong use of his discretion in refusing the stay. The Court of Appeal refused leave to appeal further, considering that the case was 'a very simple one', but the appeal committee of this House, largely, I think, because of the uncertainty said to result from certain pronouncements in previous cases decided in the House of Lords and the Judicial Committee, gave leave.

The answer to the question whether a dispute falls within an arbitration clause in a contract must depend on (a) what is the dispute, and (b) what disputes the arbitration clause covers. To take (b) first, the language of the arbitration clause in this agreement is as broad as can well be imagined. It embraces any dispute between the parties 'in respect of' the agreement or in respect of any provision in the agreement or in respect of anything arising out of it.... Ordinarily speaking, there seems no reason at all why a widely drawn arbitration clause should not embrace a dispute as to whether a party is discharged from future performance by frustration, whether the time for performance has already arrived or not.

My Lords, it is of much practical importance that the law should be quite plain as to the scope of an arbitration clause in a contract where the clause is framed in wide and general terms such as this, and I trust that the decision of the House in this appeal may be useful for this purpose and will remove any misunderstanding which may have grown up out of certain phrases in some of the previous decisions to which I have referred. At the risk of some repetition, I would summarise what I conceive to be the correct view on the matter as follows.

An arbitration clause is a written submission, agreed to by the parties to the contract, and, like other written submissions to arbitration, must be construed according to its language and in the light of the circumstances in which it is made. If the dispute is as to whether the contract which contains the clause has ever been entered into at all, that issue cannot go to arbitration under the clause, for the party who denies that he has ever entered into the contract is thereby denying that he has ever joined in the submission. Similarly, if one party to the alleged contract is contending that it is void *ab initio* (because, for example, the making of such a contract is illegal), the arbitration clause cannot operate, for on this view this clause itself is also void.

If, however, the parties are at one in asserting that they entered into a binding contract, but a difference has arisen between them as to whether there has been a breach by one side or the other, or as to whether circumstances have arisen which have discharged one or both parties from further performance, such differences should be regarded as differences which have arisen 'in respect of', or 'with regard to' or 'under' the contract, and an arbitration clause which uses these, or similar, expressions should be construed accordingly. By the law of England (though not, as I understand, by the law of Scotland), such an arbitration clause would also confer authority to assess damages for breach, even though it does not confer upon the arbitral body express power to do so.

I do not agree that an arbitration clause expressed in such terms as above ceases to have any possible application merely because the contract has 'come to an end', as, for example, by frustration. In such cases it is the performance of the contract that has come to an end.... There is a previous decision of this House which establishes this precise proposition. I refer to *Scott & Sons v Del Sel* (1923), where sellers of jute contended that a contract to export from Calcutta 2,800 bales to Buenos Aires was brought to an end, after a portion has been despatched, by a government prohibition of further export, notwithstanding that the contract contained an express term exempting the sellers from liability for late delivery due to unforeseen circumstances. The arbitration clause ran:

> 'Any dispute that may arise under this contract to be settled by arbitration'.

The sellers argued that the dispute as to frustration was not a dispute under the contract, but a dispute as to the existence of the contract. This contention was unanimously rejected.

I can see no reason why an arbitration clause framed on the above lines should not equally apply, if the supervening event which is alleged by one side to have effected discharge by frustration occurs after the contract has been entered into, but before the time has come for anything to be done under the contract. It is, in my opinion, fallacious to say that, because the contract has 'come to an end' before performance begins, the situation, so far as the arbitration clause is concerned, is the same as though the contract had never been made. In such cases a binding contract was entered into, with a valid submission to arbitration contained in its arbitration clause, and, unless the language of the arbitration clause is such as to exclude its application until performance has begun, there seems no reason why the arbitrator's jurisdiction should not cover the one case as much as the other.

In this summary it is not necessary to deal with the situation which arises when a contract stipulates that the arbitration must take place before an action can be brought, as in *Scott v Avery* (1856) or with the difficult question whether an arbitration clause covers a dispute as to the ambit of the submission: see the observations of Lord Parker in the *Produce Brokers' Co* case (1916).

Two further observations must be made in conclusion. The first is that, notwithstanding the general validity of the above observations, the governing consideration in every case must be the precise terms of the language in which the arbitration clause is framed. Its terms may, of course, be such as will either expressly or by implication reduce what would otherwise be the full ambit of the clause, or again, will extend it yet further. Secondly, what I have endeavoured to formulate in this summary is concerned solely with the question whether or not an arbitration clause applies. It has nothing to do with the further and quite distant question whether, where an action is started in the English courts about a dispute which is within the scope of an arbitration clause, the action should be stayed at its inception under the Arbitration Act 1889, section 4. The principles which should govern the exercise of judicial discretion on this matter have often been laid down and are well understood, and the extent to which appellate authority may interfere was last stated in this House in *Ostenton & Co v Johnston* (1942). I think the Court of Appeal was right in reversing the decision of Cassels J on this head. Even if the judge were right in regarding the issue as one in which nothing but a question of law is involved, that circumstance would not necessarily, and in all cases, make it right to refuse a stay.... Moreover, in the present case questions of fact may well have to be determined and the dispute as a whole is of a class which is constantly dealt with by an arbitrator. There is no sufficient reason why the matter should not be referred, and therefore, by the express language of the Arbitration Act 1889, section 4, there must be a stay.

In my opinion, this appeal fails on all points, and I move that it be dismissed with costs.

LORD MACMILLAN, LORD RUSSELL OF KILLOWEN, LORD WRIGHT and LORD PORTER agreed.

Appeal dismissed

Even if the contract be frustrated by supervening impossibility of performance, an arbitration clause dealing with disputes 'in relation to any thing or matter arising out of or under this agreement' is wide enough to cover issues arising out of that frustration even though the rest of the contract has ceased to have any legal effect.

Government of Gibraltar v Kenney and another (Queen's Bench Division, 1956)

SELLERS J: The plaintiffs bring these proceedings against the first defendant, who is a quantity surveyor and who had an agreement with them for some work in his professional capacity, and also against the second defendant, who, at the moment, is an arbitrator who has been appointed in accordance with an arbitration clause in the contract under which the first defendant was doing the work for the plaintiffs. The action asks for a declaration relevant to that arbitration to this effect: 'That the second defendant has no jurisdiction to hear or determine the claims by the first defendant set out in' certain paragraphs of the claim in the arbitration between the plaintiffs and the first defendant. They also ask for an order against the arbitrator restraining him from hearing or purporting to hear the matters against which complaint has been made.

As soon as these proceedings were launched, the arbitrator took the very proper course of notifying the plaintiffs that he would take no part in the proceedings but would abide by any order which the court might made. As a consequence, counsel for the plaintiffs asks for no further order against the arbitrator. The proceedings have been pursued against the first defendant for the declaration asked.

The contract in question, which contains the arbitration clause, was entered into on 25 April 1946 and was made between the Crown Agents for the Colonies, acting on behalf of the plaintiffs, and the first defendant, retaining his services as a quantity surveyor in connection with a scheme of works consisting of the construction of blocks of flats and other ancillary works at Alameda Gardens, Gibraltar. In that agreement clause 9 provided as follows:

> 'If any dispute or difference shall arise or occur between the parties hereto in relation to any thing or matter arising out of or under this agreement the same shall be referred to some person nominated as single arbitrator by the President for the time being of the Chartered Surveyors' Institution and this agreement shall be deemed to be a reference to arbitration within the meaning of the Arbitration Acts 1889 to 1934, or any statutory modification or re-enactment thereof'.

The second defendant was appointed as arbitrator under that clause by the President for the time being of the Chartered Surveyors' Institution, the plaintiffs in this action simply letting the clause be invoked by the first defendant.

In that arbitration points of claim were put in and amended, and the amended points of claim set out in detail, with particulars, the claim which the first defendant was making against the plaintiffs to this suit. No defence was put in, but reference was made before the arbitrator to the claim and it was submitted to him by counsel that he had no jurisdiction to try some of the matters which were the subject of the claim. The arbitrator heard counsel and expressed the view that he had jurisdiction and was prepared to undertake the arbitration of those issues, and it is that course which the arbitrator indicated it was his intention to take that has given rise to this action in the High Court.

The plaintiffs do not seek to say that the arbitrator had no jurisdiction at all on any of the matters claimed in the points of claim, but they allege that three matters in particular do not fall within the submission arising under clause 9 of the contract. The issues in the points of claim as delivered in the arbitration by the first defendant and not yet defined by any points of defence by the plaintiffs can be placed in five classes. There is a claim under the contract based on the express terms of the contract leaving a sum of money still outstanding which will call for consideration and also an allegation that there has been a breach of the agreement in various matters and that damages flow from that breach which are recoverable. In so far as the claim is referable to those matters, no complaint is made that they are not properly the subject of the arbitration; but there are three other matters which, it is said, are not appropriate to the arbitration and are outside its scope. They can be briefly summarised thus: first, that there is a claim, not under the contract at all but for a *quantum meruit*, for no less than £107,000 odd, which is to be compared with remuneration under the contract of something like £25,000. The claim for the *quantum meruit* is based on allegations that the agreement ceased to have any application to the services rendered by the first defendant as quantity surveyor or that it was frustrated. Then there is an alternative claim that the first defendant is entitled to recover part of the sum which represents remuneration for his services under the contract on the basis of the frustration of the contract by reason of the benefit for work done under the Law Reform (Frustrated Contracts) Act 1943, in so far as the contract was performed up to the date of frustration and thereafter there is a claim for a *quantum meruit* with regard to the other work. The third claim which is said to be outside the submission to arbitration and, therefore, outside the scope of the arbitration is in relation to some further services which were alleged to have been performed by the first defendant outside the provisions of the agreement but consequential thereon, in particular one relating to some work done in assessing the quantities on another building altogether.

With regard to the third item which I have mentioned, that was not pressed as being wholly outside the province of the arbitrator and if the arbitrator is rightly entitled to adjudicate on the *quantum meruit*, which is claimed in two different ways for different amounts and is entitled to adjudicate on the claim under the Law Reform (Frustrated Contracts) Act 1943, then it was not sought to say that that item of claim would not be appropriate in the arbitration. The question, therefore, arises whether the submission of the plaintiffs is right that these heads of claim fall outside the ambit of the arbitration clause.

That matter was discussed by both counsel, but counsel for the first defendant said that, whatever the appropriate decision ought to be on that matter, this court had no jurisdiction to determine it, and he relied on *North London Ry Co v Great Northern Ry Co* (1883) which decided that:

> 'the High Court has no jurisdiction to issue an injunction to restrain a party from proceeding in a matter beyond the agreement to refer, although such arbitration proceeding may be futile and vexatious'.

That is the headnote, and I think that it is the effect of what was said by Brett LJ and Cotton LJ in that case. It was also supported by the decision in *Den of Airlie SS Co Ltd v Mitsui & Co Ltd and British Oil and Cake Mills, Ltd* (1912), where *North London Ry Co v Great Northern Ry Co (supra)* was followed.

Counsel for the plaintiffs sought to distinguish *North London Ry Co v Great Northern Ry Co* on the ground that the whole of the matter in dispute and under discussion was beyond the jurisdiction of the arbitrators and he pointed out that that was not the circumstance here, that this was only going to part of the arbitrator's jurisdiction and that, in the result, great injustice might be visualised because of the form in which the award might be framed, so that there could not be a clear differentiation between the decision on the matters which were appropriate for the arbitrator's consideration and those which the plaintiffs claimed to be outside his jurisdiction. I think that is clearly a distinction between those cases and the present one, but this is not a case where an injunction is sought against the first defendant, it is a claim for a declaration. Although a declaration was asked for in conjunction with an injunction in *Den of Airlie SS Co Ltd v Mitsui & Co Ltd (supra)*, it seems to me that there may be circumstances where the court could appropriately make a declaration where it might not, on those authorities, be able to grant an injunction. That position with regard to an injunction was modified in some way in the view of Kekewich J in a case which was cited, but however bad an application for an injunction may be, I would not have felt myself restricted in granting the declaration if I had come to the conclusion on the merits that it was one which I ought to grant in favour of the plaintiffs.

I must now deal with the merits of the claim as it is framed before me. The question has to be judged by an interpretation of the arbitration clause and the claims which are sought to be made in the arbitration.

In my view, this arbitration clause is very wide. It covers: 'any dispute or difference (which) shall arise or occur between the parties hereto in relation to any thing or matter arising out of or under this agreement'.

The distinction between matters 'arising out of' and 'under' the agreement is referred to in most of the speeches in *Heyman v Darwins Ltd* (1942) and it is quite clear that 'arising out of' is very much wider than 'under' the agreement. This clause incorporates a difference or dispute in relation to any thing or matter 'arising out of' as well as 'under' the agreement and, in my view, everything which is claimed here in this arbitration can be said to be a dispute or difference in relation to something 'arising out of' the agreement.

It is true that *quantum meruit* is a quasi-contract and arises, in a sense, on an implied contract and not on any express agreement but, in my view, in the circumstances of this case (although it may not be in all cases) the *quantum meruit* is an incident which arises out of the contract. It is not a remedy for breach or arising on frustration, but it is an incident, in my view, which does arise as a consequence of the contract or 'arising out of' it. One has only to look at the pleadings, at the points of claim, and to visualise what is involved in the arbitration to see the close association between the written contract and the claim advanced in this way on a *quantum meruit*.

The issue whether there has been a frustration giving rise to a *quantum meruit* or giving rise to a claim under the Law Reform (Frustrated Contracts) Act 1943 is one wrapped up with all the terms of the contract and its purported performance. Until the arbitrator has decided that issue on the contract and what took place in purported performance and all the circumstances, no question of the *quantum meruit* arises. Indeed, it would give rise to a difficult and highly unsatisfactory position if the arbitrator were to be left to decide whether the facts and circumstances amounted to a frustration or to a repudiation of the contract, or, putting it in another way, whether they were such that the contract had ceased to exist, and then, having arrived at that conclusion, it should be said that the matter as to *quantum* had to be referred to the court. Notwithstanding the effort counsel for the plaintiffs made to satisfy me that there were good reasons for this procedure (ie, this attempt to have the court invoked for part of the claim), I am afraid I have not been convinced. I can well understand that the more complicated matters, not of quantity, but of law and fact to decide the issues of frustration or repudiation, might be appropriate to the court. It seems to me most inappropriate that the court should be asked to assess the sum on the basis of the findings of the arbitrator in relation to other matters.

If, as I think, the claim for *quantum meruit* is incidental to this claim and, therefore, within the arbitration clause, so, I think, is the alternative claim under the Law Reform (Frustrated Contracts) Act 1943. It requires the same investigation of the contract and its terms and the performance under it and is so closely linked up with the contract which existed until it was frustrated that I think it properly falls within the submission.

Very little authority has been referred to with relation to this particular aspect of the case. The matter did not arise in the case which has been most referred to, *Heyman v Darwins Ltd (supra)*, although there are indications of the view their Lordships might have taken if a claim for a *quantum meruit* had arisen there. Viscount Simon LC says:

'By the law of England (though not, as I understand, by the law of Scotland), such an arbitration clause would also confer authority to assess damages for breach, even though it does not confer upon the arbitral body express power to do do'

which goes to show that, in the view of Lord Simon LC, incidental relief, although not expressly stated in the submission, would be within the jurisdiction.

Lord Macmillan, dealing with the effect of repudiation, said:

'I am accordingly of opinion that what is commonly called repudiation or total breach of a contract, whether acquiesced in by the other party or not, does not abrogate a contract, though it may relieve the injured party of the duty of further fulfilling the obligations which he has by a contract undertaken to the repudiating party. The contract is not put out of existence, though all further performance of the obligations undertaken by each party in favour of the other may cease. It survives for the purpose of measuring the claims arising out of the breach, and the arbitration clause survives for determining the mode of their settlement. The purposes of the contract have failed, but the arbitration clause is not one of the purposes of the contract.'

I think that the important words there are that 'it survives for the purpose of measuring the claims arising out of the breach', and it does not seem to me that that observation would have any less force if the words were 'claims arising out of the frustration'.

For those reasons, I find and hold that the plaintiffs are not entitled to the declaration for which they ask. It is, perhaps, not for me to emphasise, but I have already indicated that it would greatly inconvenience any further pursuance of this dispute if the view which I took of the matter had been different, and I had to give effect to the claim which is made and make a declaration that this particular dispute had to be tried in two parts, partly before the arbitrator and partly before the court. There may be cases where there is a clear separation of the issues and one or more may be said to be wholly outside the submission, but I do not find that to be the case here.

If I had felt that the declaration asked for was one which might be given but that I had discretion in the matter, I should not have exercised my discretion in favour of the plaintiffs' claim. I think good sense and good reason, in the particular circumstances of this case, do not justify a separation of the issues of the claim which the first defendant is making against the plaintiffs. Therefore, I dismiss the claim.

Claim dismissed

Ad hoc submission (see LPA 2.3)

Even if there is no contract between the parties containing an arbitration clause, it is open to the court to find that they have made an *ad hoc* submission to an arbitrator on the issue of whether there is a binding contract or not.

Luanda Exportadora and others v Tamari & Sons and others (Queen's Bench Commercial Court, 1967)

ROSKILL J:... There is however a separate and independent point raised by [counsel]. In the ordinary way, if a question arises in an arbitration whether or not there was a contract containing an arbitration clause, the jurisdiction of the arbitrators must depend upon the proof of the existence of the contract. If there was no contract, there is no consensual jurisdiction arising from the contract for there cannot be, in the nature of things, an agreement to submit disputes under the contract to arbitration if there never was a contract. But [counsel] has argued that, on the facts of this case which I shall have to examine ....there was, what I will call, a narrow *ad hoc* submission to the umpire of the question whether or not Colprogeca on the one hand and Tamari and Jaffa on the other were parties to this alleged contract. He seeks to say that there was such a narrow *ad hoc* submission and that, be the award right or be it wrong, that issue was determined against the buyers by the umpire.... I shall have to consider in detail hereafter whether there was a narrow *ad hoc* submission of the kind which I have just described.... As I said at the beginning of this judgment, an umpire faced with a dispute whether or not there was a contract from which alone his jurisdiction, if any, can arise, can adopt one of a number of courses. He can refuse to deal with the matter at all and leave the parties to go to the court, or he can consider the matter and if he forms the view that the contract upon which the claimant is relying and from which, if established, alone his jurisdiction can arise is in truth the contract, he can proceed accordingly. This is made plain by Lord Goddard, then Lord Chief Justice, in *M. Golodetz v Schrier and another* (1946). The learned Lord Chief Justice made plain what the rights of an umpire or arbitrator are in these circumstances. He said:

> 'He (that is counsel) says that the plaintiffs knew all along that the defendants' real defence was that there never was a contract, and he says that the Association (that is the Refined Sugar Association of London) were so informed when they were invited to arbitrate in the matter. That was perfectly true and, of course, if there is not a contract, it follows that there is not a submission, because the submission is contained in the contract; and, says (counsel), the House of Lords decided in *Heyman and another*

v Darwins Ltd (1942) that, where the dispute which arises is whether there is a contract, that dispute cannot be referred to arbitration because the submission to arbitration is contained in the contract. If there is not a contract, then there is no submission to arbitration.'

Let us see how that works out. One has to remember that in *Scott v Avery* (1856) there came up the very familiar point as to what is to happen where an action is started, and one party to the action, who was the defendant, comes forward and says: 'I ask under the appropriate section of the Arbitration Act that the action should be stayed, because there is a submission to arbitration'. When the court finds that the real dispute between the parties is whether there was a contract at all, then they say: 'We will not stay the action, but the action must proceed because, if it turns out in the action that there is no contract, then there is no submission to arbitration'. I am saying nothing here as to what might have happened if the defendants had appeared before the arbitrators, or taken some other steps, and said: 'The real dispute in this case is whether there was a contract or not'. I am not going to give any decision upon what would have happened if the arbitrators had said: 'We are at any rate going to proceed'. They might have been restrained. I do not know. But if they had proceeded and made an award, whether it would have made any difference it is not necessary to decide, because when the action is brought to enforce the award then that question must be determined, and if the arbitrators had no power to proceed because there was no contract, then the action on the award will fail. It will fail for the very good reason that there was no submission.

If one refers to the old books on pleadings, you always find one of the first defences that can be set up to an action on an award is: 'No submission'. So really it is as broad as it is long, because if the arbitrators do proceed, and it turns out there is no submission, then their award would be a nullity. But what is to happen? It is said here that the arbitrators ought never to have proceeded at all, but the defendant never appeared before the arbitrators. The plaintiff appears, and says to the arbitrators: 'Here is my contract', and shows it to them. 'I say that is a contract.' There being nothing to contradict the plaintiff's evidence, the arbitrators are entitled, as it seems to me, to proceed and say: 'We will hear your case, as the defendant does not appear, and we will then give our decision upon the contract which is placed before us, and stated to be a contract'. That is what they did here. The plaintiff, of course, in that case proceeds, so to speak, *ex parte*, and runs the risk that, when he seeks to enforce his award, he may be met with the answer: 'This award is a nullity, because there was never a submission, because there was never a contract'. The learned Lord Chief Justice continues:

> 'In this case, the arbitrators having made an award, I find that there was a contract and that that contract did contain a submission; therefore it follows that the arbitrators did nothing wrong in proceeding with the matter.'

In other words, as I understand what Lord Goddard CJ said, where the question arises before an arbitrator or an umpire whether or not there is a contract and, therefore, whether or not there is jurisdiction, it is open to an arbitrator or umpire, if he so chooses, to go ahead and to make an award. If he is right in the view he takes and there is a contract, the award is binding, and the other party will or may absent himself at his peril. But if the arbitrator or umpire be wrong, there is the risk of the award being declared a nullity in subsequent proceedings, which is, of course, what the buyers seek to achieve in one part of the present proceedings. It is because of that that the sellers argue in the alternative that even if they are wrong on the points which I have decided in their favour, there was nonetheless on the evidence an *ad hoc* submission on the very question what the contract was.

In order to determine whether or not that submission is right, one has to have regard to what happened in the course of the arbitration proceedings ... in which he [the umpire] purported to make the award which is sought to be impugned. A very similar question arose some years ago in a case which was decided by Mr Justice Devlin (as he then was) in this court in *Westminster Chemicals & Produce Ltd v Eichholz & Loeser* (1954). Later a similar point arose in *Aktiebolaget Legis v Berg & Sons Ltd* (1964) to which I have already referred. In each of those cases the court held that there had been an *ad hoc* submission and that, therefore, by the time the matter reached the court on proceedings brought to have the award in question declared null and void, it was much too late because the parties had agreed to submit to the umpire or arbitrator that issue.....

In the event, his lordship found that there was a contract between the parties and it was upon that contract that the umpire purported to make his award.

PART III

The courts and arbitration

'I know that there has been a very great inclination in the courts for a good many years to throw obstacles in the way of arbitration. I wish to speak with great respect of my predecessors the judges; but I must just let your Lordships into the secret of that tendency. There is no disguising the fact that as formerly the emoluments of the judges depended mainly or almost entirely upon fees and they had no fixed salary, there was great competition to get as much as possible of litigation into Westminster Hall, and a great scramble in Westminster Hall for the division of the spoil, and hence the disputes between the different courts about the effect of a *latitat*, a *capias*, and a *quo minus* — the *latitat* bringing business into the Court of Queen's Bench, the *capias* into the Common Pleas, and the *quo minus* into the Exchequer. They had great jealousy of arbitrations, whereby Westminster Hall was robbed of those cases which came neither into the Queen's Bench, nor the Common Pleas, nor the Exchequer.'

Lord Campbell in *Scott v Avery* (1856)

Ousting the jurisdiction of the courts (see LPA 3.1)

An agreement by the parties that they will not seek access to the courts by way of case stated is void as ousting the jurisdiction of the courts, contrary to public policy.

Czarnikow & Co v Roth, Schmidt & Co (King's Bench Division, 1922)

BANKES LJ: The parties to this appeal entered into a contract for the sale and purchase of a quantity of sugar fob Antwerp. The contract contained a clause in the following terms:

> 'This contract is subject to the rules of the Refined Sugar Association, as fully as if the same had been expressly inserted therein, and even though one of the parties to it be not a member of the association'.

The contract is made on the contract form of the association. Rule 7 of the rules of the association relating to the constitution provides that:

> 'It shall be an express condition of these rules that all members making contracts subject to them or on contract forms of this association shall be bound to refer any dispute arising to the arbitration of the council'.

Rule 17 provides that:

> 'All disputes from time to time arising out of any such contract including any question of law arising in the course of the proceedings whether arising between the parties thereto, or between one of the parties thereto and the trustee in bankruptcy or personal representative of the other party shall be referred to arbitration in accordance with the rules'.

Rule 19 (*inter alia*) provides that:

> 'It is expressly agreed that the obtaining of an award from the tribunal shall be a condition precedent to the right of either party to sue the other in respect of any claim arising out of any such contract. Neither buyer, seller, trustee in bankruptcy, nor any other person as aforesaid, shall require, nor shall they apply to the court to require any arbitrators, to state in the form of a special case for the opinion of the court any question of law arising in the reference, but such question of law shall be determined in the arbitration in manner herein directed'.

A dispute arose between the parties in reference to the sugar and was referred in accordance with the rules to the council of the association. The buyers applied to the arbitration tribunal to state their award in the form of a special case, or to state a special case, or to postpone making their award until the respondents had had the opportunity of applying to the court for an order requiring them to state a special case. The arbitration tribunal refused the application and proceeded to make their award. The buyers thereupon applied to the Divisional Court to set the award aside upon the ground of misconduct. No suggestion was made, on the one side, that the buyers, the respondents, were seeking to raise a frivolous point of law or, on the other, that the arbitration tribunal was not acting in good faith and in accordance with what it believed to be the binding agreement of the parties. The Divisional Court set the award aside on a somewhat narrow ground. They declined to decide whether rule 19 was against public policy, and, therefore, not binding, but they held that, inasmuch as that question was obviously a serious and important one, the arbitration tribunal should have acceded to the buyers' application in order that the question might be decided. The effect of this decision would be to involve the parties in further litigation in order to obtain the decision of some other court upon the point. This does not appear to me to be a satisfactory way of disposing of the matter, and as all the materials are before this court it should, I think, give a decision as to the validity of the rule.

The ground of objection to the rule is that as an agreement it ousts the jurisdiction of courts of law and is consequently against public policy and void. The importance of maintaining in its integrity the rule of law in reference to public policy is, in my opinion, a matter of considerable importance at the present time. Powerful trade organisations are encouraging, if not compelling, their members and persons who enter into contracts with their members to agree, as far as they lawfully can do so, to abstain from submitting their disputes to the decision of a court of law. The present case is a case in point. There have been others before the courts. Among commercial men what are commonly called commercial arbitrations are undoubtedly and deservedly popular. That they will continue their present popularity I entertain no doubt, so long as the law retains sufficient hold over them to prevent and redress any injustice on the part of the arbitrator and to secure that the law that is administered by an arbitrator is in substance the law of the land, and not some home-made law of the particular arbitrator or the particular association. To release real and effective control over commercial arbitration is to allow the arbitrator or the arbitration tribunal to be a law unto himself or themselves, to give him or them a free hand to decide according to law, or not according to law as he or they think fit; in other words, to be outside the law. At present no individual or association is, as far as I am aware, outside the law except a trade union. To put such associations as the Refined Sugar Association in a similar position would, in my opinion, be against public policy. Unlimited power does not conduce to reasonableness of view or conduct.

It is, however, with the purely legal question that we have to deal. No one has ever attempted a definition of what constitutes an ouster of jurisdiction. Each case must depend upon its own circumstances. Each agreement needs to be separately considered. To what an extent opinion may differ in respect of a particular agreement is well indicated by the difference of opinion which existed among the judges who advised the House of Lords in *Scott v Avery* (1856). ... The recent case of *Atlantic Shipping and Trading Co v Louis Dreyfus & Co* (1922) is another illustration of the same kind of difference of opinion, the House of Lords putting an entirely different construction upon the agreement between the parties from that which was put upon it in this court. In the present case the agreement is expressed in perfectly plain terms. By rule 19 it is provided as a first step that the obtaining of an award is a condition precedent to the existence of any liability. The effect of this is that either party can obtain an order staying an action if any action is brought in lieu of proceedings for arbitration. To a substantial extent, this is an ouster of the jurisdiction of the courts, but it has been said in *Scott v Avery (supra)*, to be legitimate and not contrary to public policy. In the present case the parties have expressly agreed by rule 17 that questions of law as well as questions of fact must be submitted to arbitration. If, therefore, the agreement that neither party shall apply to the court to state a special case is to stand, the only hold which the court can have over the proceedings is (i) if the arbitration tribunal itself states a case for the opinion of the court, or states its award in the form of a special case; or (ii) if either party applies to set aside the award for misconduct on the part of the arbitration tribunal or upon the ground of error on the face of the award. To hold that in these circumstances the agreement not to apply for a special case is not to oust the jurisdiction of the court within the meaning of the rule of law as I interpret it is in effect to decide that the appeal tribunal is entitled to be a law unto itself and free to administer any law, or no law, as it pleases. I cannot but think that this is against public policy. I therefore hold that so much of rule 19 as provides that neither party shall apply for a special case when incorporated into an agreement is unenforceable and void. The arbitration tribunal should, therefore, in my opinion, have acceded to the buyers' application and, having refused to do so, they have brought themselves within the decision in *Re Palmer & Co and Hosken & Co* (1898). I agree, therefore, in the result with the decision of the Divisional Court, though not on the same grounds. The appeal must be dismissed with costs here and below, and the award will be set aside.

SCRUTTON LJ: ... Arbitrators, unless expressly otherwise authorised, have to apply the laws of England. When they are persons untrained in law, and especially when, as in this case, they decline to allow persons trained in law to address them on legal points, there is every probability of their going wrong, and for that reason Parliament has provided in the Arbitration Act that not only may they ask the courts for guidance and the solution of their legal problems in special cases stated at their own instance, but that the courts may require them, even if unwilling, to state cases for the opinion of the court on the application of a party to the arbitration if the courts think it proper. This is done that the courts may ensure the proper administration of the law by inferior tribunals. In my view, to allow English citizens to agree to exclude this safeguard for the administration of the law is contrary to public policy. There must be no Alsatia* in England where the King's writ does not run. It seems quite clear that no British court would recognise or enforce an agreement of British citizens not to raise a defence of illegality by British law ... The

*Alsatia: at one time the name for the precinct of White Friars in London, a sanctuary for debtors and criminals — Ed.

courts always decline to recognise an agreement to refer all disputes to arbitration as compelling them to stay an action, and do so because such an agreement would oust the jurisdiction of the King's courts. I prefer the language of Lord Sumner, concurred in by Lord Buckmaster and Lord Atkinson, to the effect that so long as a clause does not exclude the claimant from such recourse to the courts as is always open by virtue of the provisions of the Arbitration Act 1889, but only requires certain conditions as precedent to a valid claim, it does not oust the jurisdiction. I think Lord Sumner would have regarded a clause depriving the claimant of the protection of the Arbitration Acts as an ousting of the jurisdiction and unenforceable. And I can conceive some conditions precedent to enforcing a claim which English courts would decline to enforce. I am of opinion that the view of the Divisional Court was correct in regarding the action of the tribunal as wrong in refusing an opportunity to apply for a special case. Arbitrators must understand that parties before them have a right to take the opinion of the court on whether the arbitrators should be given the guidance of the court in matters of law, and that they must not attempt to stop the action of the courts by interfering with or hindering such a right of parties. For that reason I think the decision must be affirmed, setting aside the award. I am also of opinion that the latter part of rule 19 is unenforceable and that parties are entitled in spite of it to apply to the court, and in a proper case obtain from it a special case on matters of law. I do not decide that the present case is a proper case; the matter has not been argued before us. The parties, however, should consider their position; they must obtain an award as a condition precedent to recovering anything, and therefore, must go to some arbitrators. I see no reason to assume that the present tribunal will not, if ordered to do so, state a proper special case, and it may be that the best course to take is to remit the matters to the arbitrators in the existing arbitration, when an application to order them to state a special case can be made in the usual way. This appeal, however, must be dismissed with costs.

ATKIN LJ: I agree with the judgments that have been delivered. ...The jurisdiction that is ousted in this case is not the common law jurisdiction of the courts to give a remedy for breaches of contract, but the special statutory jurisdiction of the court to intervene to compel arbitrators to submit a point of law for determination by the courts. This appears to me to be a provision of paramount importance in the interests of the public. If it did not exist, arbitration clauses making an award a condition precedent would leave lay arbitrators at liberty to adopt any principles of law they pleased. In the case of powerful associations such as the present, able to impose their own arbitration clauses upon their members, and, by their uniform contract, conditions upon all non-members contracting with members, the result might be that in time codes of law would come to be administered in various trades differing substantially from the English mercantile law. The policy of the law has given to the High Court large powers over inferior courts for the very purpose of maintaining a uniform standard of justice and one uniform system of law. Analogous powers have been possessed by the court over arbitrators and have been extended by the provisions of section 19 of the Arbitration Act 1889. If an agreement to oust the common law jurisdiction of the courts is invalid every reason for such a principle appears to me to exist for holding

be stated in this way: he says that under the terms of the contract, he (the plaintiff) is to be the judge of the question whether there are material defects or not, and if his surveyor says he found material defects, then the question of whether they objectively exist or not does not matter: that he, the plaintiff, is entitled to reject the yacht on the *ipse dixit* of his surveyor, and that, he says, is a matter of the construction of the contract, and that if he is right in saying that that is so then it would be a waste of time and money to proceed with the arbitration on the question of fact which the defendant regards as vital, because if the question of construction is decided in favour of the plaintiff, then it is wholly immaterial whether any defects, such as Mr Freeman [the surveyor] said, or has been said to have said, that he found, existed or not, or whether they were defects of the magnitude which I have mentioned.

In reply to that, [counsel] on behalf of the defendant, says: 'Well, that may be a point of construction, a point of law, but it is such a bad one that the court should not really pay any attention to it'.

I am not prepared to dismiss it as summarily as that. At the same time, the fact that an arbitration would involve the decision of questions of law is not of itself a reason why an arbitration clause should not be invoked.

But it is the fact here that, as I have already stated, the arbitrator who has been appointed by the president of the relevant federation is unwilling to arbitrate on the construction of the contract, and it seemed to me that there was a good deal to be said for regarding this as one of the cases of the order to which Lord Parker of Waddington referred in *Bristol Corporation v John Aird & Co* (1913), where he says this:

'It is, I know, a common thing to stay an action as to one matter in dispute and at the same time to allow it to proceed as to another, notwithstanding that both matters are within the reference; and I think it is obviously a desirable course in many cases, for this reason, that very often the matters subject to the reference include both the question of the true construction of the instrument containing the submission, and also various matters of detail, and it may be of account. Everybody knows that with regard to the construction of an agreement it is absolutely useless to stay the action, because it will only come back to the court on a case stated; therefore it is more convenient on a question of construction to allow the action to proceed; and at the same time with regard to accounts and matters of detail to allow the arbitration to proceed.'

It is fair to say that Lord Parker's opinion, that it is useless to stay an action on a question of construction because it will only come back to the court on a case stated, has been the subject of further observations in the House of Lords in the later case of *Heyman and another v Darwins Ltd* (1942); but the point for which I referred to that passage still holds good, namely, that the appropriate course in certain cases may be to refer part of the action to arbitration, but to retain it in the High Court in another. Therefore, subject to a matter to which I must refer in a moment, I think there is a great deal to be said for leaving what I would call Part I of the statement of claim in this division, because generally speaking what it is dealing with is purely a question of construction, but at the same time to stay the action in respect of what I would call Part II of the statement of claim — paragraph 7 of the statement of claim and the prayer which is referred to in that paragraph. I am convinced that that is the right course with regard to Part II of the statement of claim, and in so far as that is concerned I am going to grant a stay and let the question of fact go to arbitration.

But I now come back to Part I of the statement of claim. It seems to me that it has not been formulated in the way in which a pure question of construction, such as [counsel for the plaintiff] contends exists here, would have been formulated if it had been intended to be a pure question of construction and nothing else. There are certain ambiguities, to which reference was made in the course of argument, which could only be regarded as raising a pure question of construction and nothing else if that part of the statement of claim were amended.

As [counsel for the defendant] points out, I have got no amendments formulated before me. [Counsel for the plaintiff] answers that his submission would be that it is unnecessary to amend that part of the statement of claim, because as it stands it raises a question of construction as a matter of law, and raises no questions of fact.

I do not think that Part I of the statement of claim is satisfactorily formulated for the purpose of raising the point of construction on which [counsel] so strongly relies. Therefore, what I propose to do in regard to Part I of the statement of claim is to grant a stay there as well, on an undertaking by the defendant forthwith to issue an originating summons in this division, raising the question of construction. At the moment I say it in a deliberately vague form, 'raising the question of construction'.

But I will now discuss with counsel how best effect can be given to the course which I think is the right course to take in this case, and I hope that now the contest before me has been resolved by my judgment, both sides will be able to co-operate in giving some sensible effect to it, as I am sure they will.

Restraining arbitration by injunction (see LPA 3.6)

The English courts will not normally restrain parties from going to arbitration in London in accordance with their contract on the ground that legal proceedings are on foot in another jurisdiction.

Frota Nacional de Petroleiros v Skibsaktieselskapet Thorsolm (Court of Appeal, 1957)

> In this case neither of the parties nor the proper law of contract was English, but the contract provided for arbitration in London. The facts of this case are fully set out in the judgment of Denning LJ.

DENNING LJ: The plaintiffs in this matter are a Brazilian concern who took a long-term charter of a Norwegian vessel, the *Thorsoy*. The defendants are the Norwegian company who owned that vessel. The charter-party was for five years from August 1954, so that if it went its full term it would not expire until August 1959. In that charter-party there was a clause which said that in the event of a war involving Norway or Brazil, or involving any two or more of the following powers — Great Britain, the United States, Russia, France — both the owners and the charterers have the right to cancel the charter, either party to give in writing three weeks' notice of their intention to cancel the charter. There was in the charter-party an arbitration clause which provided for arbitration in London. I will read it a little later.

On 5 November 1956, when things were happening in the Suez Canal area, the owners of the ship gave notice of cancellation of the charter-party — their contention presumably being that there was a war involving Great Britain and France. That was denied by the charterers; but none the less, in pursuance of their notice of cancellation, the owners withdrew the vessel from the services of the charterers on 3 December 1956. I need hardly say, in view of the increase in freight rates, that they have utilised this vessel (it was an oil tanker) at a rate of freight greatly in excess of that provided in the charter.

In these circumstances, on 15 December 1956, the charterers brought proceedings in the District Court for the Eastern District of Pennsylvania, claiming damages. The ship was then at Philadelphia. The charterers brought those proceedings *in rem* against the ship, which was only released by the authorities on $500,000 being put up as security. When the charterers took those proceedings the owners promptly took exception to them. They objected to the jurisdiction of the Court of the United States because they said that there was an arbitration clause in the charter-party under which the matter had to go to arbitration. No ruling has yet been given by the United States Court on that matter. Meanwhile, the owners have taken steps to go to arbitration in London under the arbitration clause. The object of the present application is this: the charterers want to restrain the owners from taking those arbitration proceedings: and that is the question we have to determine.

This is the arbitration clause, agreed upon by both parties, the Brazilian charterers and the Norwegian owners:

> '49.   Any and all differences and disputes of whatsoever nature arising out of this charter shall be put to arbitration in the City of London pursuant to the laws relating to arbitration there in force, before a board of three persons, consisting of one arbitrator to be appointed by the owners, one by the charterer, and one by the two so chosen. The decision of any two of the three on any point or points shall be final. Either party hereto may call for such arbitration by service upon any officer of the other, wherever he may be found, of a written notice specifying the name and address of the arbitrator chosen by the first moving party and a brief description of the disputes or differences which such party desires to put to arbitration. If the other party shall not, by notice served upon an officer of the first moving party within twenty days of the service of such first notice, appoint its arbitrator to arbitrate the dispute or differences specified, then the first moving party shall have the right without further notice to appoint a second arbitrator, who shall be a disinterested person, with precisely the same force and effect as if the said second arbitrator has been appointed by the other party. In the event that the two arbitrators fail to appoint a third arbitrator within twenty days of the appointment of the second arbitrator, either arbitrator may apply to a judge of any court of maritime jurisdiction in the city above mentioned for the appointment of a third arbitrator, and the appointment of such arbitrator by such judge on such application shall have precisely the same force and effect as if such arbitrator had been appointed by the two arbitrators....'

I need not read more of that clause, because what has happened in this case is that the owners have called for arbitration in the City of London, in accordance with that clause, and they have stated that they have appointed Mr Chesterman in London as their arbitrator. They have asked the charterers to appoint their arbitrator; and that the charterers have not yet done. The charterers have got, under the clause which I have read, twenty days in which to do it, and the time is going to be up tomorrow.

The parties have been very co-operative in this matter and have brought these proceedings speedily before the court so as to have this matter determined, and we are in a position to determine it here and now. The question is whether this court should restrain the owners from proceeding to arbitration in the City of London, and also whether it should revoke the appointment of Mr Chesterman as arbitrator. The argument put forward in support of that application is mainly this: proceedings are now pending in the courts of the United States; security is lodged in that court. Is there not a danger of there being a conflict of jurisdiction in the two courts in the two countries if, while proceedings are pending in the United States, the arbitration proceedings are to go on in the City of London? It is said that there may be different decisions by the courts of the United States and by the arbitrators in the City of London. I am not oppressed by the difficulties which are set before us, because the courts of the United States view arbitration proceedings with the same respect as do these courts, and view a contract to go to arbitration in the same light.

The courts of the United States have not pronounced upon this document at all at the moment. It seems to me that here is a contract between the parties — a contract whereby they have provided that all their differences and disputes are to be put to arbitration in the City of London. That is a contract which binds them still; and I have heard of no reason in the course of this case why there should not be arbitration in the City of London according to their contract. I do not pause to consider whether the question of war or no war is a question of fact or a question of law. Suffice it to say that the parties have agreed that all their differences are to be put to arbitration in the City of London. I can see no reason why this court should intervene to hamper that contract or to say that the owners are not at liberty to proceed to the arbitration in the City of London when both parties have agreed that they should be. I can see no equity or any reason whatever for this court to intervene to prevent this arbitration going forward in accordance with the terms of the contract. I do not fear that there will be any conflict of jurisdiction. The courts of both these countries, the United States of America and the United Kingdom, can be trusted to see that in the end there is no conflict.

The other question was whether we should revoke the appointment of the arbitrator under section 1 of the Arbitration Act 1950. Suffice it to say that this arbitrator Mr Chesterman, has been appointed by one party, and I see nothing in section 1 of this Act which enables the court to revoke his appointment. It could in a proper case give leave for the party to revoke it; but I see no ground for saying that the court has power to revoke it against the will of the party who appointed the arbitrator. I am dealing, of course, only with the case where the provision is for an arbitrator to be appointed by each of the two parties who in their turn appoint an umpire.

For these reasons, it seems to me that the Judge below was quite right in the decision to which he came, and I would dismiss the appeal.

ROMER LJ: I agree, and there is nothing that I wish to add.

PARKER LJ: I also agree.

Appeal dismissed

See also *James Miller & Partners Ltd v Whitworth Street Estates (Manchester Ltd (1970)* and *International Tank and Pipe SAK v Kuwait Aviation Fuelling Co KSC* (1974), both in Part II.

Removal of an arbitrator (see LPA 4.10)

Section 23(2) provides that, where an arbitrator or umpire has misconducted himself, the High Court may, *inter alia*, set the award aside.

Luanda Exportadora and others v Tamari & Sons and others (Queen's Bench Commercial Court, 1967)

It was alleged that the arbitrators had misconducted themselves and therefore an award by the umpire could be set aside under this section.

ROSKILL J: [Counsel] argues from that that an award of an umpire may be set aside for the misconduct of an arbitrator. I can only say that I do not so construe the section.

PART IV

Appointment of an arbitrator

'Touching his Ordinance, he is Ordained by these two things, viz., by
the Election of the Parties and by his own undertaking of the charge.'

Fitz. *Arbit.* (1584)

Essentials for a valid appointment (see LPA 4.1)

Three things are essential for a valid appointment of an arbitrator: to ask the appointee, to obtain his consent, and to notify the other side.

Tradax Export SA v Volkswagenwerk AG (Court of Appeal, 1970)

This was an arbitration between owners and charterers in the standard shipping Centrocon clause:

'Any claim must be made in writing and the claimant's arbitrator appointed within three months of final discharge and where this provision is not complied with the claim shall be deemed to be waived and absolutely barred'.

One party notified the other side on 27 January of the nomination of their arbitrator, but they failed to notify the arbitrator himself until 24 July, when they were out of time. Motion to hold that there was a valid appointment within the three months allowed by the Centrocon clause.

DENNING MR: So we have to decide: what is necessary to constitute the appointment of an arbitrator? I think the answer is this: first, it is necessary to tell the other side. That is plain from *Tew v Harris* (1847). Second, it is necessary to tell the appointee himself. That is obvious because he often has to start acting at once. Third, it is necessary that he should be willing to act and have intimated his willingness to accept the appointment. In *Russell on Arbitration* (17th edition, 1963 at page 160) it is said: 'Acceptance of the office by the arbitrator appears to be necessary to perfect his appointment'. There is a passage in *Ringland v Lowndes* (1864), which gives some support to that statement.

[Counsel] by great diligence has discovered the case of *Cox v Johnson* (1914) where it is said:

'In my view all that is required by the section' — a similar section — 'is nomination by each party to the other of the person whom he has selected to act on his behalf'.

I think that statement may have been right in relation to the facts and evidence in that case. But I do not think it is of general application. I think in general it is essential not only that the other side should be told, but also that the arbitrator himself should be told.

[Counsel] took a special point. He said that Mr Chesterman was, so to speak, the standing arbitrator for Tradax. As long ago as 1960 Tradax had decided that, in any case of a charter-party arbitration in which they were involved, Mr Chesterman would be acting as their arbitrator. They appointed him, not on a permanent retainer, but habitually and regularly as their arbitrator whenever he was free to accept the appointment. In consequence, I think it may be fairly assumed that Mr Chesterman would have been willing to accept the nomination. But I do not think that is enough. Mr Chesterman ought to have been told that he was nominated as arbitrator, otherwise his appointment was not complete. I see no difficulty in complying with this rule. Tradax could have told Mr Chesterman that he was appointed at the same time as they told the owners. A telephone call, or letter, a telex message, or anything would do, so long as he was told. The three months' provision could easily be satisfied.

I am sure that it was an oversight that Mr Chesterman was not told. So much so that if Tradax — as soon as they discovered the omission — had applied to the court to extend the three months, it would certainly have been granted under section 27 of the Arbitration Act 1950, as explained in *Liberian Shipping Corporation 'Pegasus' v A. King & Sons Ltd* (1967). But no such application was made. Instead, Tradax come to the court on the simple point: must the arbitrator be told of his appointment? I think he must. So here the appointment was not made within the three months. And the claim is barred. I have less reluctance than I might have in holding the time bar effective, seeing that Tradax allowed so long a time to elapse before taking out this summons. I would, therefore, dismiss the appeal.

SALMON LJ: I agree. Indeed if it were not for the extremely attractive way in which [counsel] put his case and a passage in the judgment of one of the judges in New South Wales who decided *Cox v Johnson* (1914), I should have thought that the proposition for which he contends was unarguable. It is suggested that an arbitrator can be effectively appointed without knowing anything about it — without any communication being made to him. No doubt the word 'appointed' has different meanings in different contexts. We, however, are only concerned to construe it as used in the Centrocon arbitration clause, which my Lord has read and which I need not read again. Perhaps it is permissible, in considering the true meaning of the word in that clause, to see how businessmen appear to have understood it. We know from all the evidence in this case that, as a general rule, anyone who desires to appoint an arbitrator under this clause gets in touch with the proposed arbitrator to ascertain whether he is willing to act in the dispute in question. If he is willing to act, then the party authorises him to act and communicates with the other party, notifying him of the name of the arbitrator. It is argued, in effect, that everything except the notification of the name of the arbitrator to the other party is a ceremonial ritual performed only out of courtesy. I am afraid I cannot agree. In my opinion the ordinary businessman takes the view — no doubt what may be considered the prosaic view, which I share — that in order to appoint an arbitrator you must first get his consent to act as arbitrator.

How an agreement for arbitration can be enforced (see LPA 2.4)

Once a party has appointed an arbitrator, he has no power under section 7(a) of the Arbitration Act 1950 to appoint a new one in his place unless the one originally appointed conclusively refuses to act at all, not merely refuses to act in a particular way.

Section 7 states: 'Where an arbitration agreement provides that the reference shall be to two arbitrators, one to be appointed by each party, then, unless a contrary intention is expressed therein ...

(a)   If either of the appointed arbitrators refuses to act or is incapable of acting, or dies, the party who appointed him may appoint a new arbitrator in his place.'

Burkett Sharp & Co v Eastcheap Dried Fruit Co and Perera (Queen's Bench Division, 1962)

PEARSON LJ: .....The refusal required by section 7(a) is a refusal to act — that is to say, a refusal to act as arbitrator and not merely a refusal to act in a particular manner. Secondly, the refusal is in the section associated with the arbitrator becoming incapable of acting or his death — two events which would put the arbitrator completely out of action, if I may use that expression. A refusal should be something equally conclusive. It should be a definite and final refusal. Thirdly, as in any case of doubt or difficulty, application can be made under section 1 to revoke the authority of the arbitrator, there is no need to extend the meaning of the word 'refuse' beyond its natural meaning in its context....

The court has a discretion, under section 10 of the Arbitration Act 1950 (formerly section 5 of the Arbitration Act 1889), whether or not it may appoint an arbitrator under this subsection and it may do so subject to conditions. In the case of an applicant without residence or assets within the English jurisdiction, it may be proper to make the appointment subject to the condition that he provides security for costs.

Re Bjornstad and Ouse Shipping Co Ltd (Court of Appeal, 1924)

On an application by a foreign firm under section 5 of the 1889 Act (the same as section 10 of the 1950 Act) for the appointment of an arbitrator, a master made an order appointing a named arbitrator. Talbot J. affirmed that order unconditionally.

BANKES LJ: This appeal raises an important point under these circumstances. The parties are Norwegians on one side, and shipbuilders in this country on the other side, and an agreement was entered into in 1919 for the building of a number of ships by the shipbuilding company for the Norwegians. The agreement contained an arbitration clause. Disputes having arisen between the parties whether the ships were or were not of the contract carrying capacity, the Norwegian firm, who are parties, have claimed arbitration under the contract. The shipbuilding company have refused to concur in the appointment of an arbitrator, and the Norwegians have made an application under section 5 of the Arbitration Act 1889 to the court by an originating summons, asking the court to appoint an arbitrator, all conditions precedent under the section having been complied with. The section provides as follows:

> 'In any of the following cases: (a)   Where a submission provides that the reference shall be to a single arbitrator, and all the parties do not after differences have arisen concur in the appointment of an arbitrator ... any party may serve the other parties ... with a written notice to appoint an arbitrator....'

That has been done. The section goes on:

> 'If the appointment is not made within seven clear days after the service of the notice, the court or a judge may, on application by the party who gave the notice, appoint an arbitrator....'

The language of the section itself, apart from any judicial decision upon it, would appear to indicate that the court has a discretion with reference to the appointment of an arbitrator, because the words used 'the court may appoint an arbitrator', which are the same words as are used in section 4 of the same statute, which there is ample judicial authority for saying give the court a jurisdiction with reference to the matter.

Our attention, however, has been called to a decision of this court — *Re Eyre and Leicester Corpn* (1892) — as to the proper construction to be placed upon the language of section 5, and it is said that that is a decision to the effect that the word 'may' in section 5 must always be read as 'must', with the consequence that the court, when called upon to exercise its powers under section 5 has no discretion at all, but must appoint an arbitrator if the conditions precedent have been complied with. If that was the effect of *Re Eyre and Leicester Corpn* we must follow that decision, whether we agree with it or whether we do not; but in my opinion that decision does not cover this case, and for this reason. The parties in *Re Eyre and Leicester Corpn* were both resident in this country, and, therefore, the question which arises in this case was not before the court in that case. It may be that without that explanation the language used by Lopes LJ in particular would seem to be language wide enough to cover every case; but when one considers the facts of that case and the language used by Lord Esher MR and Kay LJ, I think it is plain that the intention of the court there was to confine its decision to the facts of that case or, at any rate, not to deal with a case which contains the exceptional features of the present case, namely, that it is a foreigner residing outside the jurisdiction who is seeking to invoke the assistance of the court....

I begin, therefore, by saying that in my opinion in this particular case this court has a discretion to refuse to appoint an arbitrator at all under the circumstances of this case, and to refuse because the applicant is a foreigner resident outside the jurisdiction. If the court has that discretion, it seems to me that it can attach any reasonable condition to the exercise of its discretion in granting the application. One knows that very often in applications under section 4 the fact that an arbitrator has no power to make an order for a commission to examine witnesses abroad is a ground for refusing to stay proceedings. Equally, I think, it would be a ground, or might in this case be a ground, for refusing to exercise one's discretion, that the applicant is a foreigner outside the jurisdiction and, I think, that it is perfectly competent to this court to make an order in this form, that if the applicant within a certain time gives security for the costs of the arbitration, and of this appeal, then the order of Talbot J may stand; but if the security is not given within the time limited then the order is discharged, and in either event that the respondents should have the costs here and below. One will consider that time should be allowed, or whether counsel for the applicants is prepared to consider the question of time; but I think myself that, not being bound by the decision referred to, and having a discretion, it is perfectly competent to this court to make an order in that form, and to attach that condition to the exercise of its discretion.

WARRINGTON LJ: I am of the same opinion. The application is one under section 5 of the Arbitration Act 1889, which provides that in certain circumstances enumerated in the section the court may appoint an arbitrator. Now, as far as the language of the section is concerned, it does appear to give to the court some discretion; but it is said that *Re Eyre and Leicester Corpn (supra)* has decided that there is no discretion in the court under that section. With all respect, I do not think that that point has been decided in the case referred to.... In the present case there arises a most material fact outside those which appear in *Re Eyre and Leicester Corpn*, namely, that the person who invokes the assistance of the court is a foreigner out of the jurisdiction. It seems to me that this is just one of those cases which were contemplated as likely to arise by the judgment of Kay LJ and I feel quite satisfied, reading Lord Esher's judgment, and with rather more hesitation Lopes LJ's judgment, that if any such fact had been in their minds or had been established in the case before them, the decision they gave would not have been what it was. At any rate, I do not consider that we are bound by that decision to hold that the court has in the present case no discretion at all. With regard to the form of the order, I have nothing to add. It seems to me that it is an order which is quite competent for us to make, an order which should be fair to both parties.

SCRUTTON LJ: Two Norwegian gentlemen trading in partnership made a contract with an English firm for the construction of a certain number of ships. The contract contained an arbitration clause as to disputes and differences and a clause providing that the Norwegian gentlemen should provide an English gentleman on whom writs should be served. The ships were built. By a supplementary agreement, the effect of which may have to be considered in the proceedings, the two Norwegian gentlemen dissolved partnership. One of them is alleged now to be in an impecunious position, the other to be in the employ of another firm. But the two gentlemen, describing themselves as formerly trading in partnership, desire to make a claim with respect to the construction of the ships, of the merits of which, of course, I know nothing. The English firm, for various reasons, does not want the proceedings under the arbitration clause, and, therefore, does not appoint an arbitrator. Thereupon the two Norwegian gentlemen come to the court and ask the court to exercise its powers by appointing an arbitrator in the case. It is said of them: 'But you are foreigners and as foreigners you ought to give security'. They reply through their counsel: 'It is quite immaterial that we are foreigners. It is quite immaterial even if we were both bankrupt; you, the court, must appoint an arbitrator, and start this arbitration, though we are foreigners, and even if we are bankrupt.' I do not think there is any justification for that haughty attitude.

It is a well-recognised principle of these courts that the courts do not as a matter of right give redress to foreigners. The courts do not allow a foreigner to claim protection as of right. The courts have always in their inherent jurisdiction refused to act at the instance of foreigners, unless the foreigners afford sufficient protection to the other party whom they desire to involve in litigation. I do not know any more striking instance of that than the attitude which the courts adopt towards foreign sovereigns. A foreign sovereign is not subject to the laws of this country, and his property is free from seizure under the laws of this country, but the courts, when a foreign sovereign has come and asked to institute an action in this country, have declined to allow him to proceed unless he gives security for a counter-claim brought by the defendant in respect of a collision with regard to which the foreign sovereign is claiming, see the decision of this court in *The Newbattle* (1885).

In that case the foreign sovereign was refused leave to proceed till he gave security for the counter-claim which the defendant he desired to proceed against wished to bring against him. That principle appears to me to cover this case. The applicants are coming here asking the court to do something. Their counsel agree that the court may refuse to do that something unless they secure the costs of this particular proceeding, but he says: 'Though I am asking you to institute an expensive arbitration in which I shall make the other side liable for costs, or make them incur costs, you have no power to say to me; "We, the court, will not accede to your application unless you secure the person against whom you are wishing to proceed against costs"'. I think that is entirely contrary to the principle on which the court acts with regard to foreigners.

It is further said that that may be so as a general principle but that in the case of arbitrations the Court of Appeal has decided that the court must act, and has no discretion. Of course, if the Court of Appeal has so decided, this court is bound by its decision, and I should loyally follow it, and leave the House of Lords to deal with the matter, if so requested. But I cannot find in *Re Eyre and Leicester Corpn (supra)* any trace that there was ever present to the mind of the court, or that they ever thought that they were deciding to act on the instance of a foreigner, not giving to the British subject against whom the foreigner was proceeding the protection that they would give in any other case. While I think that I am bound by the decision of *Re Eyre and Leicester Corpn*, however I should decide it myself, in cases which come within the facts on which that case was decided, I do not think I am bound in the case of an application by a foreigner on a question the merits of which were never before the court. It appears to me to follow that, if we say to their counsel in this case,'You shall not make this application at all till you have secured the other side against the costs', we may also say, 'You shall not make this application to us unless you are prepared to provide for the costs of the proceedings which you are asking to set on foot'. For that reason I think the appeal succeeds.

Order affirmed on terms

Disqualification as an arbitrator (see LPA 4.2)

It is not proper for one party to appoint himself as one of two arbitrators, notwithstanding that, under the procedure in force, if the two arbitrators disagree, they are entitled to act as advocates for the party appointing them before the umpire.

Veritas Shipping Corporation v Anglo-Canadian Cement Ltd (Queen's Bench Division, 1966)

> The claimants moved the court under the terms of section 23 of the Arbitration Act 1950 to remove the arbitrator appointed by the respondents and to appoint a fresh arbitrator under section 25(1). The respondents did not appear and the facts are laid out in the judgment.

MCNAIR J: In this matter counsel moves on behalf of Veritas Shipping Corporation for an order that Dr W. K. Wallersteiner, the arbitrator appointed by Anglo-Canadian Cement Ltd, in the reference to arbitration between Veritas Shipping Corporation and Anglo-Canadian Cement Ltd, under the arbitration clause contained in a charter-party dated 11 May 1964, be removed and that an arbitrator be appointed on behalf of Anglo-Canadian Cement Ltd in the said reference.

The matter arises in this way. Veritas Shipping Corporation were the owners and Anglo-Canadian Cement Ltd the charterers in a charter-party in the Gencon form [a standard shipping charter form: Ed] dated 11 May 1964, which charter-party contained by clause 30 an arbitration clause to the following effect:

> 'any dispute arising under this charter-party shall be referred to arbitration in London. One arbitrator to be nominated by the owners and the other by the charterers. In case such arbitrators cannot agree, then the dispute to be referred to the decision of an umpire who shall be appointed by the said arbitrators....'

Disputes arose between the parties, the shipowners advancing a claim amounting to a sum of just under £10,000 in respect of freight and demurrage. The shipowners, Veritas Shipping Corporation, are a Panamanian company and Anglo-Canadian Cement Ltd are a company incorporated in Nigeria.

These disputes having arisen, correspondence took place, and the correspondence on behalf of Anglo-Canadian Cement Ltd, part of which is exhibited to the affidavits in this case, was conducted by Dr W. K. Wallersteiner as their managing director. Correspondence proceeded for a long time. Finally the shipowners appointed Mr R. A. Clyde as their arbitrator and called upon Anglo-Canadian Cement Ltd to appoint their arbitrator. In response to that request, they received a letter from Anglo-Canadian Cement Ltd, signed by Dr W. K. Wallersteiner as their managing director appointing the same Dr Wallersteiner as the arbitrator to act on their behalf in this arbitration. The shipowners, through their representatives, objected to this appointment on the grounds of the close connection that Dr Wallersteiner had with Anglo-Canadian Cement Ltd and, indeed, with this particular dispute, or series of disputes, which they said disqualified him from acting as an arbitrator under this clause. In the course of further correspondence between the representatives and Anglo-Canadian Cement Ltd, and Dr. Wallersteiner personally, Dr Wallersteiner refused to withdraw and Anglo-Canadian Cement Ltd refused to appoint anybody in his stead.

In these circumstances, this motion, having been served both upon Anglo-Canadian Cement Ltd and Dr Wallersteiner out of the jurisdiction, comes before me, and by this motion the shipowners seek the assistance of the court to get the arbitration properly constituted. The order they ask for is that the court should remove Dr W. K. Wallersteiner under section 23 of the Arbitration Act on the ground that Dr Wallersteiner has misconducted himself in the arbitration in not only allowing himself to be appointed as arbitrator but having appointed himself, having as managing director of Anglo-Canadian Cement Ltd, signed the letter appointing him to act. Without making any reflections upon the propriety and skill of Dr Wallersteiner, I am quite satisfied that it would be quite wrong for him to be allowed to continue to act as arbitrator in a dispute of this nature. It is quite true that under the clause, if the two arbitrators disagree and the matter is referred to the umpire for his decision, the arbitrators, according to the customary way in which these matters are dealt with in the City of London, may if they so wish act as advocates. They need not do so but there is nothing wrong in them doing so. Until that moment arrives, the arbitrators must not only act judicially and show no bias at all but must also appear to be in a position to act judicially and without any bias.

In somewhat similar circumstances in the case of *Burkett Sharp & Co v Eastcheap Dried Fruit Company and Perera* (1962), Lord Justice Pearson, as he then was, expressed the view, with which the other members of the court concurred, that in view of the close association of Mr Perera with the Eastcheap Dried Fruit Company he was manifestly not a suitable arbitrator and their nomination of him as arbitrator was quite unsuitable and, indeed, astonishing. The same considerations seem to me to apply in this case. Accordingly, in the exercise of my discretion, I remove Dr W. K. Wallersteiner from his position as arbitrator in this matter.

The motion also asks that, if he is removed, an arbitrator should be appointed in his place on behalf of Anglo-Canadian Cement Ltd in this arbitration. That power so to do is contained in section 25(1) of the Arbitration Act 1950. Having had submitted to me a list of three gentlemen who are well qualified and experienced to act as arbitrators in charter-party disputes of this nature, each of whom has expressed his willingness to act, I appoint Mr J. Chesterman....

An arbitration agreement that provides for arbitrators to be 'commercial men' is complied with if the person appointed has had practical commercial experience

Pando Compania Naviera SA v Filmo SAS (Queen's Bench Division, 1975)

DONALDSON J: The arbitration clause in the charter-party provides:

> 'Should any dispute arise between owners and charterers, the matter in dispute shall be referred to three persons in London, one to be appointed by each of the parties...and the third by the two so chosen... The arbitrators shall be commercial men'.

Mr Clyde was originally appointed by the owners as one of the three arbitrators, but when the charterers failed to make a nomination the owners exercised their power under sections 7 and 9 of the Arbitration Act 1950 to appoint him sole arbitrator. It was in that capacity that Mr Clyde made his award.

No objection would have been taken to the procedure or to the award if Mr Clyde had been a 'commercial man' and so qualified initially to be appointed one of the arbitrators. The charterers, however, contend that at the time of his appointment he was not a 'commercial man' and have moved the court to set the award aside as being made without jurisdiction. Again it is conceded that if the premise is right, that result follows....

Is Mr. Clyde a 'commercial man'? [Counsel for the charterers] has emphasised that he does not attack his fairness and expertise or his personal or professional qualifications to act as umpire or arbitrator in maritime arbitrations. The sole issue is whether he falls, through neither fault nor virtue on his part, within the species of 'commercial man'.

In a letter Mr Clyde asserted that if he was not a commercial man, he was neither 'fish, fowl, nor good red herring'. He did himself an injustice. He is a great maritime arbitrator who, to the deep regret of his many friends and admirers on the Bench, in both branches of the legal profession and in shipping throughout the world, has retired because of ill-health. He has done so with a reputation for fairness, sound judgment and a knowledge of maritime law which is second to none, and the clarity and inimitable style of his awards will long be remembered. All this points to the fact that Mr. Clyde is an unusual man, but is he a commercial man?

Mr Clyde has practised for many years as a solicitor and was the senior partner in the firm bearing his name. In the late 1950s he became a full-time maritime arbitrator and surrendered his practising certificate. He subsequently became a director of a number of Channel Island companies, most of which were involved with the carriage of goods by sea. He was not an executive director in the sense of being fully employed in executing their respective policies. He could not be, for he was a full-time arbitrator. But he was far more than a 'name' and took part in the board discussions which formulated the policies of those companies. In doing so he was not acting as a legal adviser, but a man of business.

[Counsel for the charterers] submits, rightly, that 'commercial', is a word which takes its meaning from its context. Thus 'commercial action' in the Rules of the Supreme Court include a wide range of causes. In the phrase 'commercial area of the port', however, it has a different meaning, and yet another in 'commercial artist'. Counsel also submits, again rightly in my judgment, that Mr Clyde's qualification as a 'commercial man' has to be assessed as at the date of his appointment in the present arbitration.

The words have to be construed in the context of an arbitration clause in a charter-party. In that context, [counsel for the charterers] submits that 'commercial man' means (a) a business man who is employed wholly or mainly in the conclusion or performance of trading transactions, or (b) a person who is engaged wholly or partly in the conclusion or performance of trading transactions at the time of his appointment or is so employed for a substantial time previously.

The point has never been decided by the courts, although Mr Justice Mocatta in *The Captain George K* (1970) noted that 'it was not suggested that Mr Clyde, with his great experience in maritime arbitrations since he retired a good many years ago from commercial practice as a solicitor, was other than a "commercial man"'.

In *Rahcassi Shipping Co SA v Blue Star Line Ltd* (1969) Mr Justice Roskill considered at length the history of arbitration clauses which required the appointment of commercial men and concluded that it was not necessary to define 'commercial men' with precision. I respectfully agree and would only add that in my judgment any such attempt will fail. Like the elephant, commercial men are more easily recognised than defined. But Mr Justice Roskill also said that it was a general phrase which enabled the parties to choose the arbitrators or umpires from a wide field of persons with commercial experience.

That observation points to the real test. It does not matter whether or not the arbitrator has retired from commerce or is still engaged in it. What matters is his practical commercial experience.

The shipping industry has two sides: the marine and the commercial. The present parties wished the arbitrators to be chosen from the commercial rather than from the marine side. In some other cases it might be necessary to decide whether commercial experience which was unrelated to the carriage of goods by sea — the retail distributive trade for example — was sufficient under such a clause, but that does not arise in the present case.

The use of the words 'commercial men' also excludes those whose experience is as practising members of the legal profession. Some of them could rightly be described as 'commercial lawyers', but while they serve the commercial world, they are not of it. Mr Clyde was a commercial lawyer before he ceased to practise, but that fact could not disqualify him from becoming a 'commercial man' thereafter, if he would otherwise be qualified.

The crux of the matter is whether a whole-time professional maritime arbitrator is within the class of person to whom the parties to a charter-party must be deemed to be referring when they speak of 'commercial men'.

The shipping and commodity trades of the world are unusual in that they do not regard litigation or arbitration with abhorrence. On the contrary, they regard it as a normal incident of commercial life — a civilised way of resolving the many differences of opinion which are bound to arise.

As a result, a domestic arbitration service has grown up in London; 'domestic' because an important characteristic is that the arbitrators are not regarded as outsiders.

As I said in *The Myron* (1969): 'A person who is actively engaged throughout all available working hours in maritime arbitrations is regarded in practice as being engaged in the shipping trade'. And I could well have added 'and in the commercial side of that trade'.

There is no doubt that a member of the London Maritime Arbitrators Association practising as a full-time arbitrator would be regarded by most shipowners and charterers throughout the world as a 'commercial man'. Accordingly Mr Clyde was qualified to be appointed. The fact that he has also had practical experience of another aspect of the commercial side of the shipping trade by having been a director of shipping companies merely reinforces that view.

Motion dismissed

There is no reason why a professional man who is a servant of one of the parties should not be an arbitrator if the parties have so agreed: and even (apparently) if one issue is his own professional competence or still.

Eckersley and others v Mersey Docks and Harbour Board (Court of Appeal, 1894)

> The contract between the plaintiffs and defendants contained a clause that all disputes should be referred to the defendants' engineer as sole arbitrator.
>
> The plaintiffs began proceedings claiming damages for negligence of the engineer's son. An application by the defendants to stay the proceedings to allow the matter to go to arbitration was opposed on the grounds that the named arbitrator was likely to be biased.

LORD ESHER MR: In this case the plaintiffs are contractors, and they entered into a contract with the defendants, the Mersey Docks and Harbour Board, to do certain works within the ambit of the Liverpool Docks. The works were to excavate a certain piece of ground within the ambit of the docks for the purpose of making a new dock, or a new basin, to give some assistance to the Liverpool Docks.

They entered into a contract, and in that contract was a stipulation that:

> 'All disputes and differences of every kind which may arise between the contractor and the Board during the progress, or after the completion, of the works contracted for, in relation to or arising out of any of the plans or drawings, or any of the provisions of the specification or contract, or in relation to any of the works, or the payment to be made for the same, or as to the accounts between the Board and the contractors, shall be and the same are hereby referred to the engineer of the Board, as sole arbitrator, with power to make awards from time to time as he may think proper, and with power to make such orders in any such award as to the costs and charges of and attending any such reference, and of the award, as the said engineer shall in his discretion think proper, and every award of the engineer shall be finally binding and conclusive upon the parties in relation to the disputes and differences as to which such award is made.'

It seems to me that words cannot be larger, and that they are a submission to arbitration in the cases spoken of.

The plaintiffs allege that certain things were done by the servants of the Mersey Docks and Harbour Board, not on or within the space which was the subject-matter of the contract, that is to say, the portion of the ground which was to be excavated, but outside it, which caused water to flow into the part which the plaintiffs were excavating. In my opinion all those things are within the submission.

The plaintiffs say that the court ought not to stay the action, because there is sufficient reason why the matter should not be referred to the engineer. What is their ground for saying that? They say that he might be biased in that which he had to do for reasons which they state. They argue that it is sufficient for them to say that he might be biased, although the court should be of opinion that there is no ground for supposing that he would in fact be biased. This, therefore, is an attempt to apply the doctrine which is applied to judges — I do not mean only to judges of the Superior Court, but to all judges — that not only must they not be biased, but, even although it be proved to demonstration that they would not be biased, yet if the circumstances are such that people — not reasonable people but many people — would suspect them of being biased they ought not to sit as judges. That is the rule that is applied to judges. Is that a rule which can be applied to such a contract as this, where, as between the contractor and a principal, the parties both agree that the chief servant of one of the parties shall be the arbitrator? If you applied the rule which is applied to judges in such a case as this, it is obvious that such a servant, under whose superintendence the work was to be done, never could act as the arbitrator. Therefore the allegations must be further, and must go, in my opinion, to the extent that it must be shown, I will not say that he would be biased, but that there is a probability that he would be biased. That seems to me to be distinctly the decision in *Jackson v Barry Rail Co* (1893).

The case relied upon by the plaintiffs is *Nuttall v Manchester Corpn* (1892). That case has been discussed since it was decided and, as I understand it, it has been explained upon the ground, first of all, that there had been a very unseemly dispute between the engineer in that case and the contractor — a personal dispute raising a vindictive feeling — and also that he had expressed an opinion so strongly as to amount to a pre-judgment. If that is the ground of the decision in *Nuttall v Manchester Corpn.* that case is to be supported entirely, but it is not in point in this case, because such facts do not exist in this case and are not suggested. If it is said that, according to a reading of the report — which I cannot help thinking is not a full report of what the judges decided — the mere fact of the conduct of the engineer himself being likely, or being sure, to come into question is sufficient of itself to satisfy the court that there is a reason why the matter should not be referred to him, all I can say is that it seems to be contrary to other cases, and is absolutely contrary to *Jackson v Barry Rail Co (supra)*. If that be the right view of the case we ought not to agree with it, and we ought to say that we overrule it.

Therefore it must be shown, at least, that it is probable that the engineer in this case would be biased. What is relied upon by the plaintiffs to show that? It seems to be admitted that, if he had to consider whether he himself had given a negligent order, or whether he himself had given an unskilful order, that would not justify the court in saying that he should not be the arbitrator; but we are asked to say so where the very same negligence was committed, or an ill-advised or incompetent order was given, by his son. That involves that we must think that a man, of whom nobody could say it was possible that he would act with bias in judging of his own acts, would be probably biased to give a decision which he knew to be wrong in favour of his son. All I can say is that that is a view of human nature which I do not adopt. When we have a man of high character, one whose character for impartiality cannot be impeached when his own conduct is called into question, and I am told that such a man would not have strength of mind and honesty enough to act impartially where his son's conduct is called into question, all I can say is, I do not accept the suggestion. I certainly do not accept it in this case. I am, therefore, of opinion that the decision of the Divisional Court, of the judge at chambers, and of the master, all of which coincided, cannot be set aside by this court, and that this appeal must be dismissed.

LOPES LJ: I am of the same opinion... It is of the essence of the submission that questions are to be submitted to this engineer, as arbitrator, which must involve matters connected with his own competency, with his own case, with his own caution and with the way in which he may have discharged the duties which belonged to him under his contract. The parties agree that the arbitrator is to adjudicate on matters in which he has an interest. Further than that, I understand it was admitted and was not disputed at the Bar that, if the matter in question here were a matter which involved the professional competency or the professional skill of the engineer himself, he would not be disqualified. What is the additional fact in this case? What is there to distinguish it from a case where his own professional competency is involved? Simply that he would have to decide upon the professional competency of his son, instead of upon his own. It appears to me that that can made no substantial difference upon which this court ought to act. I am unable to say that that raises in my mind any reasonable probability of any partiality on his part....

DAVEY LJ: I am of the same opinion. Upon the first point, I think that the dispute, when one thoroughly understands the facts and the contentions of the parties, is one which is thoroughly within the arbitration clause. Upon the other point I confess I have had more doubt; but, upon consideration, I must say I do not think there are sufficient circumstances to make it right in the present case to deprive the defendants of the benefit of the provision in the contract for arbitration. No doubt, in a certain sense, the engineer will be the judge of his own conduct, and no doubt that is a position which *prima facie* raises some surprise in a judicial mind; but that is the contract of the parties. The parties have contracted that the servant of one of them shall be the arbitrator, and it appears to me that they have contracted that he shall be the arbitrator in cases which necessarily involve the correctness of his own opinion, the competency of his advice and opinion as engineer, and the regularity of his own proceedings... it is perfectly obvious that the parties did contemplate and intend that the engineer, notwithstanding the interest he would have in the subject-matter in dispute, should be the tribunal by which the disputes between the parties should be settled. It is therefore not, in my opinion, any objection to the engineer acting in this dispute that his conduct, or the conduct of his son as assistant engineer in directing the other works done in the Canada Dock, would be or might be called in question. It must have been within the contemplation of the parties that the engineer might have to superintend other works undertaken by the defendants during the progress of the contract works, and it seems to me to be an objection which the contractors waived and deprived themselves of the right to insist on when they agreed that the engineer should be the sole arbitrator as regards themselves.

I have only to add that I think that the suggestion that, although he might be trusted on a question concerning his own professional skill, he cannot be trusted on a question concerning his son's professional skill, is one which the court ought not to entertain. I am therefore of opinion that, having regard to the nature of the contract, we cannot disturb the order of the court below.

Appeal dismissed

PART V

Arbitration procedure

'I part with this case merely with this observation. I think that great care has to be used in reading the decisions of a century or half a century ago as to the powers of arbitrators today. As it has been pointed out on many occasions, by Lord Justice Scrutton and Lord Goddard and others, the growth of commercial arbitration in the City has been so wide and, as a whole, so beneficial, that the courts show increasing reluctance to interfere with the manner in which these trade bodies carry out their important functions and only interfere in the very rare case where it has been shown that some real impropriety has been committed.'

McNair J in *Henry Bath & Sons Ltd v Birgby Products* (1962)

Is a hearing necessary? (see LPA 7.1)

It is open to parties to make any agreement they like as to procedure. The 'usual way' in the City of London in disputes about quality is for two arbitrators to be appointed, one by each party, for no formal hearing to be held, and if they disagree for them to become advocates for the party appointing them before an umpire.

Naumann v Nathan (Court of Appeal 1930)

> A contract for the sale of cassia oil provided for the settlement of disputes in 'the usual way'. The buyer claimed that the oil had been adulterated. Two arbitrators were appointed, one by each party, but failed to agree and nominated an umpire. The buyer's arbitrator called on the umpire, neither the seller nor the seller's arbitrator being present, and put before him an analysis purporting to show the presence of adulterants. The umpire obtained a sample himself and submitted it to an analyst who found no adulterant and made an award for the seller. The buyer moved to have the award set aside on the ground that the umpire had not acted judicially in that he had not held a hearing and received evidence.

SCRUTTON LJ: I daresay that if this matter had come before the courts 100 years ago the appellant would have received a very sympathetic hearing. I think that quite possibly 50 years ago he would have received a sympathetic hearing. But during the last 30 or 40 years the attitude of the courts towards commercial arbitrations has considerably altered. We lawyers think, and have some justification for thinking, that the procedure of the courts, and the way they investigate questions, is excellently calculated to arrive at a true result; but there is no doubt that it does arrive at that result in a somewhat lengthy and expensive manner. During the last 30 or 40 years business men have formed the view that it is possible to be too accurate in investigating disputes and that it is better on the whole for business to have a rough and ready way of getting at the truth than the more accurate, expensive and dilatory method of the courts.

This is particularly the case with the class of disputes which are known as quality disputes. If a buyer rejects goods on the ground that goods do not comply with the contract in many particulars, the question is one which requires someone to understand the trade to decide it properly; and if that quality dispute is to be decided in the courts, the judge, who has the merit of complete impartiality and ignorance of the subject-matter, listens to three or four gentlemen who say it is in accordance with the contract and three or four gentlemen on the other side who say with equal positiveness that it is not. He may, if he is an exceptionally intelligent judge, manage to see through the contradictions of the witnesses; but he may not. At the end of the proceedings there will be a fairly expensive bill of costs, and commercial men may not be satisfied that the right result has been arrived at.

So in commercial arbitrations many trades have arrived at a system that they think is much better and which probably is very much better than the system of the law courts. They each appoint an arbitrator. That arbitrator is not in the least like a judge. He acts in a way no judge would act. He hears statements from one side without requiring the presence of the other. He uses evidence submitted to him by his client, putting it forward as an advocate and not as an arbitrator. It is useless to call an arbitrator a judge. He is a negotiating advocate, endeavouring to do the best he can for his client; and the system commercial men have acted on in these quality arbitrations is this. First of all, they say: 'We will appoint our arbitrator who will try to get the best decision he can from the other side' — and no doubt a great many of these commercial arbitrations are settled by give and take between the two arbitrators. But they may not agree; and when that happens these commercial men appoint an umpire. It is quite a usual practice in London in simple quality arbitrations that, when the umpire is appointed, he is told where the goods are, and no further hearing takes place. He sees the goods in the warehouse or gets an agreed sample. He performs the mystic operations of smelling, tasting, touching and handling, which one sees witnesses do in court; and these tell him the quality of the goods. There is never any further meeting; and there is never any intention of a further meeting; and he makes his award on his own judgment of the stuff submitted to him.

There is one further step. It may be that the nature of the goods is such that you cannot tell by view, or smell, or by taste or by touch, whether the goods are in accordance with contract. You can on analysis, and it may be that in certain trades a practice has arisen that the umpire may make his own analysis; and in this case the evidence seems to me to be overwhelming that the usual way of settling a quality dispute in respect of this class of goods is that the umpire may make his own analysis and need not have any further meeting, or submit the evidence to either side, unless he has a special request from either party that he shall do so.

What is the position of the courts to this? The courts are quite clear that no agreement of the parties shall oust the jurisdiction of the King. There is a celebrated passage in a judgment of Lord Justice James which begins: "The Stock Exchange is not an Alsatia* where the King's writ does not run"; and the same thing applies to the General Produce Brokers' Association of London. In one case I remember the courts, faced with a term in the contract of a Liverpool association, decided that it was contrary to public policy and refused to enforce it. They are quite capable of doing the same thing even with the General Produce Brokers' Association of London when the question arises. But if the term is not contrary to public policy, and has the effect that business people have agreed that the best way to settle their disputes is a particular way which is not contrary to public policy, the court does not interfere.

In this case — which is a contract for the sale of cassia oil, London analysis,

---

*Alsatia: at one time the name for the precinct of White Friars in London, a sanctuary for debtors and criminals — Ed.

with 'any dispute arising from this contract to be settled by arbitration in London in the usual way' — it appears to me that the evidence is overwhelming that this arbitration has proceeded in the usual way in this trade — a way which, according to the views of lawyers and the law courts, is quite irregular. The seller appoints what he calls his arbitrator. The buyer appoints what he calls his arbitrator. These two gentlemen remain in contact with their clients, getting information from them without communicating it to the other side. That is quite irregular if it is treated as a judicial proceeding, but business people find it works very well; and one starts with this, that the arbitrator is not a judge but is a negotiating advocate.

Now, the dispute arises as to the quality of the cassia oil. Apparently that dispute may be settled in some cases by mere smell. Evidently in some cases chemical analysis will also be necessary. The arbitrator for the buyer, the negotiating advocate, goes to the umpire who has been appointed and discusses the matter with him without the other side being present. That, of course, would be hopelessly irregular so far as legal proceedings are concerned, but it is the way business people accept as to the suitable way of investigating disputes like this.

In this particular case, the arbitrator, the negotiating advocate for the buyer, saw the umpire without the other arbitrator being present and saw him before the other arbitrator had been seen, and put his views and two analyses before the umpire. He admits that the umpire told him that he (the umpire) wanted a sample for analysis and he raised no objection. How, after that, it is possible for the client who appointed the negotiating advocate to object to the umpire taking a sample, I find it impossible to understand. He has appointed the negotiating advocate. The negotiating advocate has been told that the umpire is going to get a sample for analysis, and a sample is handed to him. When the buyer tells me he did not know what was to be done with the sample, he must think me a very credulous person. What does the umpire want a sample for unless he is going to judge it by his own skill and knowledge, or do what is usual in the trade and get an independent analysis.

The umpire gets an analysis from an independent chemist and he acts on it, and he does not have any further sitting and he does not communicate with the parties asking them to attend before him. The evidence is overwhelming that that is the usual way in which these quality arbitrations — and I am limiting my remarks to them — are conducted in this particular trade; and so far as the question of analysis is concerned I have not the slightest doubt it is the practice all through London.

The result, therefore, is that there is a clause in the contract 'any dispute arising from this contract to be settled by arbitration in London in the usual way'. This dispute according to the overwhelming evidence has been settled by arbitration in London in the usual way; and in my view there is nothing that would lead one to say that this procedure in the case of a quality arbitration is contrary to public policy....

I have had several cases before me in which this 'usual way' clause has been in the contract. This is the first case in which I have found the 'usual way' proved. The usual position has been that I have had seven or ten gentlemen signing the same form of affidavit, but I have had seven or ten on the other side signing exactly the opposite. So far my experience has been that it was not possible to get a trade to say what was the usual way. This is the first case in which I have known the trade prove the usual way, because it appears to me that the evidence here is overwhelming that the umpire has carried out the usual procedure in a quality arbitration. But, that being my experience up to the time I gave judgment in *Scrimaglio v Thornett & Fehr* (1924), I said:

> 'I do not think this means that you have to find out what is the usual way in which arbitrations are conducted in the trade. I think that generally would be a hopeless attempt'.

So far that was the result of bitter experience in hearing members of the trade trying to prove what was the usual way:

> 'What it means is this: once you have got the arbitrators appointed, they deal with the matter according to the law of England and the conditions laid down in the Arbitration Act 1889'.

Now, the law of England enforces an agreement between parties as to procedure unless it is so contrary to fundamental principles that it is treated as contrary to public policy. In my view there is nothing in this case which is contrary to public policy, though I have in another case held a clause to be contrary to public policy and not to be enforced by the courts. Therefore, I am afraid that in relying on this passage counsel, who is complaining that I have misled him, has not taken a sufficiently wide view of what is the law of England. Whether that will be any help to him in future I do not know. But I see nothing in that case to prevent me saying here that the trade has proved what is the usual way of conducting arbitrations, and that in quality arbitrations there is nothing contrary to public policy in enforcing the usual way in which the trade conducts these arbitrations.....

LAWRENCE LJ: I agree and have nothing to add.
SLESSER LJ: I agree.

Appeal dismissed

See also *Scrimaglio v Thornett & Fehr* (1924) in Part II for a further discussion of the term 'in the usual way'.

A commercial man acting as arbitrator is entitled to decide issues without receiving evidence and relying solely on his own knowledge and experience.

Mediterranean and Eastern Export Co Ltd v Fortress (Manchester) Ltd
(King's Bench Division, 1948)

LORD GODDARD CJ: By a contract dated 16 October 1946, Fortress Fabrics (Manchester) Ltd agreed to sell to the Mediterranean and Eastern Export Co Ltd a quantity of textile goods which subsequently the buyers refused to accept, alleging that the goods were not up to sample, but were unmerchantable and unfit for the purpose for which they were supplied, namely, export to South Africa. It appears that the sellers had a quota entitling them to export goods to that country, part of which they allocated to the buyers, which would enable them to sell those goods in that market to the extent of the quota transferred to them. In consequence of the refusal to accept, the parties agreed to arbitration in accordance with the rules of the Manchester Chamber of Commerce, and by a submission dated 16 August 1947, it was agreed that the dispute should be referred to arbitration by that chamber whose decision should be final and binding on both parties and, in accordance with the rules of the chamber, Mr G. W. Armitage was appointed sole arbitrator under the rules. Rule 1 states:

> The object of the tribunal of arbitration shall be the determination and settlement by commercial men of experience and special knowledge of the subject-matter in dispute or difference relating to trade, manufacturers and commerce (including customs of trade) by whomsoever submitted.

It is obvious, therefore, that parties who submit to the chamber's tribunal intend and expect that they will have benefit of arbitration before a person well acquainted with the class of business in which they are engaged, because he is selected for his knowledge of the trade.

The parties submitted statements to the arbitrator in accordance with the rules. The sellers' document, which was prepared without professional assistance, set out the contract, such letters as were admitted to be material, and certain facts to which I need not refer, and asked for an award of £2,455 2s 6d, the price of the goods plus interest at 5 per cent per annum. The buyers' statement set out their case and contentions, alleging that they were justified in rejecting the goods. In claiming the price of the goods the sellers, no doubt, fell into an error, often made in such circumstances, of asking for the price on the footing that the property had passed whereas, in fact, as it was a sale of future goods, the property had not passed, and what they were entitled to was not the price, but damages for non-acceptance. The arbitrator held a meeting at which both parties attended without professional representation, nor did they or either of them seek to call expert evidence. The reason for this is obvious. They had the advantage of an arbitrator who himself was an expert and he would be in a position as good as or better than expert witnesses to come to a decision on his own knowledge, which was the reason why he had been appointed. The arbitrator decided the questions submitted to him in favour of the sellers and by his award, dated 26 February 1948, found (i) that the goods delivered by the sellers were of merchantable quality and in accordance with the contract, and (ii) that, in refusing to accept delivery of the same, the buyers had committed a breach of contract by reason of which the sellers had suffered damage to the extent of £796 13s 11d, which sum he awarded to the sellers together with the costs of the arbitration.

The buyers now seek to set aside the award, and the first point which was taken by their counsel was that, because the sellers had claimed the value, by which they obviously meant the price of the goods, the arbitrator had no jurisdiction to award damages. In my opinion, that contention clearly fails. The arbitrator was obviously right in forming the opinion that no property had passed and therefore the price, as such, was not recoverable but, as all disputes had been referred to him and, as he had awarded in favour of the sellers on the merits and found a breach of contract on the part of the buyers, it was, in my opinion, clearly within his jurisdiction, while not awarding the price, to award damages, otherwise the matter would be left undecided as to what his finding entitled the sellers to recover. Because the sellers put forward a claim on a wrong basis it seems to me impossible to say that the arbitrator is not entitled to award compensation on the true basis, ie, damages instead of price.

The more serious question that was argued was that neither side had tendered evidence with regard to damage and, therefore, the arbitrator had no material before him on which he could fix the amount which the sellers were entitled to receive. This would be a formidable and, indeed, fatal objection in some arbitrations. If, for instance, a lawyer was called on to act as arbitrator on a commercial contract he would not be entitled, unless the terms of the submission clearly gave him power so to do, to come to a conclusion as to the amount of damages that should be paid without having evidence before him as to the rise or fall of the market, as the case may be, or as to other facts enabling him to apply the correct measure of damage; but, in my opinion, the case is different where the parties select an arbitrator, or agree to arbitrate under the rules of a chamber of commerce under which the arbitrator is appointed for them, and the arbitrator is chosen or appointed because of his knowledge and experience of the trade. There can be no doubt that with regard to questions of quality and matters of that description an arbitrator of this character can always act on his own knowledge. As Lord Esher MR said in *Wright v Howson* (1888), where it was suggested that the umpire ought to have received evidence from experts:

'What would this experienced manufacturer care for the opinion of the weaver? He was selected and appointed on account of his own superior experience'.

Lopes LJ said:

'Such a man is selected for the very purpose of deciding according to his own experience and examination.'

It is well known in the experience of the courts that many trades have their own tribunals of arbitration (the Corn Trade, the Produce Brokers' Association, the Oil and Fat Trades Association are instances) and no one has doubted — certainly not in modern times — that it is open to an arbitrator skilled in the trade to use his own knowledge and experience on many matters, such as quality, without having witnesses called before him. One of the reasons why commercial men like to go to arbitration before arbitrators of this description is because it saves the expense of calling witnesses and having the conflicting views of experts thrashed out and decided on. The parties are content and intend to accept the judgment of a man in their own trade on whose judgment they know they can rely.

This, indeed, I think, has long been the law. An early illustration is *Eads v Williams* (1854). The arbitrators were there appointed to settle the amount to be paid as the rent of a coal mine and Lord Cranworth LC said:

'I do not agree with the suggestion that it was incumbent upon those parties to examine witnesses; I do not think that is the meaning when a matter is referred to a surveyor, and people of skill to value and settle what the value of the property to be bought or let is... they are entrusted, from their experience and from their observation, to form a judgment which the parties referring to them agree shall be satisfactory; therefore I do not think that there was anything of importance in their now examining witnesses, provided *bona fide* they meant to say, "We know sufficiently of the subject to decide properly without examining witnesses" '.

There are other decisions to a like effect and I would only mention *Jordeson & Co v Stora, etc Aktiebolag* (1931) to which counsel for the sellers called my attention. Branson J in giving judgment, said:

'Now, I think that the fact that this umpire was an expert in the timber trade and was appointed because he was such an expert must not be lost sight of. I think the parties must be taken to have assented to his using the knowledge which they chose him for possessing; I do not mean to say knowledge of special facts relating to a special or particular case, but that general knowledge of the timber trade which a man in his position would be bound to acquire.'

I can see no reason why this principle should not be applied to a question of damages just as much as to a question of quality ... In this case, according to the affidavit of the sellers, they did take the point before the arbitrator that the South African market has 'slumped'. Whether the buyers contested that statement does not appear, but an experienced arbitrator would know, or have the means of knowing, whether that was so or not and to what extent, and I see no reason why in principle he should be required to have evidence on this point any more than on any other question relating to a particular trade. It must be taken, I think, that, in fixing the amount that he has, he has acted on his own knowledge and experience. The day has long gone by when the courts looked with jealousy on the jurisdiction of arbitrators. The modern tendency is, in my opinion, more especially in commercial arbitrations, to endeavour to uphold awards of the skilled persons that the parties themselves have selected to decide the questions at issue between them. If an arbitrator has acted within the terms of his submission and has not violated any rules of which is so often called natural justice, the courts should be slow indeed to set aside his award.

In my opinion, the arbitrator did act in this case within the submission, and I think also he has acted as the parties intended he should act and I see no reason for interfering with his award. This motion fails and must be dismissed with costs.

Motion dismissed with costs

Arbitrators acting as advocates before umpire (see LPA 7.1)

The court will take judicial note that in commercial arbitrations it is the practice in many trades for arbitrators who have disagreed to appear before the umpire as advocates for the party appointing them, to dispense with any formal hearing or evidence, and to be empowered to waive irregularities.

Wessanen's Koninklijke Fabrieken v Isaac Modiano Brother & Sons Ltd
(Queen's Bench Division, 1960)

At the 'hearing' only the two arbitrators were present, not the parties. The relevant facts appear in the judgment.

DIPLOCK J: This is a motion to set aside an award made in a commercial arbitration because of the misconduct of the umpire. It was made plain at the outset by counsel on behalf of the applicants that the misconduct which he alleges is technical misconduct and involves no reflection on the policy of the umpire.

The applicants were the buyers of certain rapeseed expellers to be shipped from Pakistan to Rotterdam by the respondents, who were the sellers. The contract was in the ordinary form of the London Cattle Food Trade Association (Incorporated), and it included the arbitration clause, clause 26:

'Any dispute on this contract to be settled by arbitration in London, in accordance with the rules and regulations of the London Cattle Food Trade Association (Inc), which are indorsed hereon and are deemed to form part of this contract.'

The rules are the familiar rules relating to arbitration, and it is sufficient that I should read only a portion of rule 1:

'Any dispute arising out of a contract embodying these rules shall be referred to arbitration in London, each party appointing one arbitrator, who shall be a member of the association, and not interested in the transaction, and such arbitrators shall have the power, if and when they disagree, to appoint an umpire, who shall be a member of the association, whose decision is to be final.'

A dispute having arisen between the buyers and the sellers as to the right of the buyers to reject the goods for an admitted breach of condition, each of the parties appointed an arbitrator under the provisions of the arbitration clause:

the buyers appointed a Mr Williams and the sellers a Mr Owen, and the buyers and sellers respectively at some time provided their arbitrators with documents relating to the dispute. The two arbitrators did not in fact meet; they had a conversation over the telephone, and, as is not unusual in these arbitrations which are not purely quality arbitrations, they disagreed. They appointed as umpire a Mr Phillips, and arranged with Mr Phillips for a hearing at Mr Phillips' office at some date in June 1960. All three were, as the arbitration rule 1 required, members of the association, and Mr Owen, the sellers' arbitrator, and Mr Phillips, the umpire, were men of long-standing experience in London Cattle Food Trade Association arbitration. It may be that Mr Williams was also, but the extent of his experience does not appear from his affidavit.

At the hearing Mr Williams presented the arguments in favour of the buyers. For that purpose he outlined the facts (which were not really in dispute) and addressed to the umpire his arguments on the effect of the law on those facts. When he had finished, Mr Owen, the arbitrator of the sellers, put forward his conflicting arguments, in the course of which he referred to counsel's opinion which had been obtained by the sellers, a copy of which had been furnished to him. He read out to the umpire a number of paragraphs of the opinion and, indeed, all the paragraphs of the opinion which dealt with the particular point which he was advocating. It is apparent from his notes that he stressed the importance of the opinion (the author of which he incorrectly described as 'a Queen's Counsel'), and suggested to the umpire that the opinion strongly confirmed, and was indeed conclusive in favour of, the contentions which he was advancing. This was done without protest by the buyers' arbitrator and, at the end of it, the umpire asked the buyers' arbitrator whether he wished to reply — whether he had anything to say in reply or whether he desired to obtain and submit a legal opinion such as the sellers' arbitrator had done. Mr Williams said that he did not. Both parties then handed to the umpire, without any objection from one or the other, their files of documents, which one now knows contained the relevant correspondence in the case of both the arbitrators and, in the case of Mr Owen, contained the copy of counsel's opinion from which he had read and also his own notes from which he had advanced his argument.

In the notice of motion it was contended that the umpire had misconducted himself in three respects: first, that he had not held a proper judicial investigation of the matter in dispute in the presence of the parties; secondly, that he had received as evidence the files of correspondence held by each arbitrator without the other arbitrator seeing the contents of the file; and, thirdly, that he took away counsel's written opinion without seeing the case on which such opinion was obtained. The first two grounds have not been persisted in in the argument before me.

It is, I think, plain and fully time that the court should take judicial notice of the fact that, in commercial arbitrations of this kind, under the rules of the London Cattle Food Trade Association, where arbitrators are appointed who, on disagreeing, appoint an umpire whose decision is final, the arbitrators, once they have disagreed and have agreed on an umpire, are *functus officio* as arbitrators and act at the hearing before the umpire as advocates for their respective appointors. That is a practice which two of the witnesses in the affidavits say has been going on for twenty-five years. A glance at the cases decided in these courts thirty and forty years ago shows that the practice has been going on since the beginning of this century. And it is clear that the practice, when arbitrators have been appointed in this way, is that the parties themselves are represented at the hearing before the umpire by the arbitrators and by no one else unless they express a desire to be otherwise represented.

As regards the second ground, namely, the reception of the file of correspondence held by the respective arbitrators without the other arbitrator seeing the contents of the file, that again has not been proceeded with before me. It is plain that the two arbitrators trusted one another and that this was done by each with the consent of the other. Now that the files have been seen, since they are exhibited to the affidavits, it is obvious that the trust which each had in the other was justified. But even if it had not been, I apprehend that the consent of each of the arbitrators to that course being adopted would waive any irregularity in the procedure which was concerned.

Counsel for the applicants has really limited his argument here to the contention: first, that the reading of counsel's opinion, with or without the case, was an irregularity; that the handing of it in to the umpire was a further irregularity (but, I apprehend, of the same kind); and that it was an irregularity which the buyers' arbitrator had no authority to waive. Counsel for the applicants, I think, concedes (as he must) that if his arbitrator had authority to waive the irregularity, then he cannot succeed in setting the award aside, for it is clear law that a party to an arbitration can waive an irregularity.

It therefore becomes necessary for me to consider what is the extent of the authority of an arbitrator when appearing before the umpire in a commercial arbitration of this kind. There is no authority directly on the point, but it seems to me that the position is fairly clear. Once the arbitrators have disagreed and appointed an umpire they are *functus officio* as arbitrators. If they attend, as they do, the hearing before the umpire, it is plainly as advocates for the parties who appointed them for unless they attend in that capacity as representatives of the parties, they have no right to discuss the matter with the umpire at all. As advocates for the parties they present the evidence and conduct the argument, as in this case Mr Williams presented the evidence and conducted the argument for the buyers and Mr Owen presented the evidence and conducted the argument for the sellers. It seems to me a necessary implication that a person appointed, as the arbitrators are at this stage of the proceeding, to act as advocate for the parties must have all the necessary powers to agree to the form of the procedure; to admit, for instance, facts, and to agree to the method of proof of fact. It does not seem to me that it can possibly be said to be outside the implied authority of an arbitrator acting in those circumstances to waive or agree to any irregularity in procedure which occurs.

Therefore, whether or not it was improper, strictly speaking, of Mr Owen to read the opinion of counsel without making it plain that he was adopting it as part of his argument, such an act, if it were an impropriety or irregularity, was one that could be waived by the advocate of the other side, and was plainly waived by Mr Williams.

This decision makes it unnecessary for me to consider whether the course adopted by Mr Owen was an improper course or not. He says in his affidavit that he read the opinion as a convenient way of putting his argument in support of the sellers' contention that the rejection was invalid, and that no objection was taken by Mr Williams to his doing so. I doubt very much whether that course would have amounted to an irregularity, even if an irregularity had not been waived. It has, however, been waived and the question does not arise.

In my view, there was no misconduct, however technical, on the part of the umpire in following a procedure, even if irregular, in which the irregularity was waived by the representative on each side, who, in my view, plainly had implied authority from the parties so to waive those irregularities.

The motion accordingly fails.

Motion dismissed

Amendment of pleadings (see LPA 5.15)

An arbitrator has power to allow any amendment to the pleadings at any time and should do so to allow the parties to raise the points not included in the pleadings.

E. Lloyd Ltd v Sturgeon Falls (Queen's Bench Division, 1901)

BRUCE J: .... we are of opinion that all points in dispute between the parties in reference to the contract for sale and purchase of Sturgeon Falls are included in the submission to arbitration and that the points of claim and the defence and counterclaim are in the nature of pleadings or particulars which are capable of amendment by the arbitrator. If any points in dispute arise between the parties in reference to the said contract which are not disclosed by these pleadings and particulars, we are of opinion that it is in discretion of the arbitrator to allow amendments on such terms as he may think fit in order to allow the parties to raise such points, and that if the claimants claim rescission of the contract it will be open to the arbitrator to make any amendment he may think fit to enable the claimants to give evidence of facts which entitle them to rescind the contract. If such question is raised it will be competent to the arbitrator to decide whether the claimants are or are not entitled to a rescission of the contract.

Arbitrator relying on own knowledge (see LPA 7.5)

It is not misconduct for an arbitrator to make use of his own knowledge of a trade or of facts not tendered in evidence, provided that this is not in such a way that the parties are taken by surprise.

Thomas Borthwick (Glasgow) Ltd v Faure Fairclough Ltd (Queen's Bench Division Commercial Court, 1968)

DONALDSON J: The complaint in the present case is simple. Both parties attended before the Board of Appeal [of their trade association]. They put their rival contentions before these bodies and asked them to decide which was right. Neither party sought to contend that there was any custom or practice which had any bearing on the matter. Had they been told that the board took a different view, either or both might have wanted to seek to persuade the board that it was wrong or to have placed further evidence before the board: the board did not give them an opportunity of doing so and this was unfair.

A trade arbitral tribunal is fully entitled to use its own knowledge of the trade. Indeed the fact that it has this knowledge is one of the reasons why it exists and performs a most useful purpose. Experience, however, dictates that this knowledge shall never be used in such a way as to take a party by surprise. If therefore a trubunal considers that both parties have missed the point — this sometimes happens both in litigation and in arbitration — it should invite the parties to deal with this point and, if the point arises for the first time in the course of deliberations after the hearing, should offer the parties a further hearing if either wish to avail themselves of the opportunity. Equally, if the tribunal has knowledge of facts which do not appear to be known to either party, it is only fair to reveal this knowledge to the parties, giving them an opportunity of putting those facts into different perspective or of persuading the tribunal that they are irrelevant. Such a course is not only fairer to parties; it also enables the tribunal to have additional assistance from the parties in arriving at a just decision.

No action is required on the motion because in my judgment the buyers succeed whether or not account is taken of paragraph 26 of the award. I have expressed my views upon the matters complained of because I know that the board would wish to act fairly and to be seen to act fairly. I hope and believe that the observations I have made may assist them and other tribunals faced with like problems in achieving this result.

Reception of evidence (see LPA 8.1)

Arbitrators are not guilty of misconduct if they accept evidence not in accordance with the strict rules of the court or do not require a document to be proved with the strictness required by the law.

Henry Bath & Son Ltd v Birgby Products (Queen's Bench Division, 1962)

The particulars of claim were delivered only on the morning of the arbitration and then contained the allegation, as the most important point, that one Lane as agent for the respondents' buyers had inspected material as they left a warehouse and had found it was according to contract and had actually seen it loaded on to the lorries. The buyers therefore got in touch with Mr Lane and in the course of the arbitration produced a telegram which read: 'Strongly repudiate any suggestion that at any time I saw and supervised any loading of material at Birgby warehouse. (signed) R.W. Lane.' An application to set aside the award, *inter alia*, on the ground that the arbitrators should not have admitted the document in evidence.

MCNAIR J: The arbitrators, receiving that telegram, did not refuse to admit it as a piece of evidence. Mr Wolff [one of the two arbitrators: Ed.] in his affidavit deals with the matter as follows:

'We decided to admit it (this telegram) in view of the very late delivery by the applicants of their statement of case. Confirmation of the said telegram was subsequently submitted to us and to Birgby Products in the letter from the said Mr Lane dated 28 October 1961... (Mrs) Joan Thomas [the sellers' representative: Ed.] did not dispute the authenticity of the said telegram though she denied its truth; nor did she apply for an adjournment nor ask for any opportunity to question the said Mr Lane and the hearing continued for about a further two hours. Had she wished to submit any further evidence on this matter it would have been open to her to do so because we delayed the making of our award and its publication in order to enable her to submit further evidence, if she was so minded, in regard to the amount owed by Henry Bath & Son Ltd to Birgby Products... That refers to the retained money on earlier contracts which had not been paid....'

Turning to Mrs Thomas's affidavit, she does not say that she saw Mr Lane supervising the loading of the material on to the lorries; nor does she controvert in any way Mr Wolff's affidavit, that she never made the point that she wanted to cross-examine Mr Lane.

The point taken here may be put quite shortly. It is said that this document was a very material document. Arbitrators are bound by the ordinary rules of evidence. This document was not properly proved according to the ordinary rules of evidence, and therefore the arbitrators permitted an irregularity going to the root of their award. For my part, I think that argument is fallacious in the following respects, at least. First, it is clear that parties can, by express or implied agreement, give their arbitrators power to act on any evidence they like; just as parties in the Commercial Court can give the judge power to act upon inadmissible evidence even if it is documentary evidence not strictly proved and even if it has not that power. Here the rules (which I have read) show, to my mind, abundantly clearly that the parties, assuming they had accepted the arbitration rules — and that is the assumption upon which the whole of this hearing has taken place — have agreed quite clearly that the arbitrators shall be able to act upon documents or copy documents presented to them with the case and upon statements of fact made in the case without anybody being obliged to support those allegations of fact or oral evidence. The whole basis of these documentary arbitrations (which result in the disposal of countless cases in the City of London) is that a certain amount of informality both as to evidence and as to other matters will be indulged in without any right of protest by anybody.

Regarding the rules, as I see it, throughout all these matters, when a court is asked to interfere with commercial arbitrations it does so very reluctantly, as it will not interfere with arbitrations if it is satisfied that the arbitrators have acted fairly and honestly in the matter and within the express or implied agreement as to documents which is contained in the rules. Though, no doubt, this telegram was an important piece of evidence on a highly material matter, and although, no doubt, it was not proved strictly, neither were the allegations which it was designed to meet proved at all because Mrs Thomas did not give any evidence in support of the sellers' case. And having regard to the fact that the sellers' case was not presented until the day of the hearing, it seems to me that no objection at all can be taken to the course taken ... in obtaining this telegraphic evidence from Mr Lane and submitting it to the arbitrators, or in the arbitrators allowing it so to be put in.

In my judgment there is no substance at all in that ground. Had there been any substance in it, I think that the sellers would be in grave difficulties indeed inasmuch as Mrs Thomas apparently raised no objection to the form of the evidence although she disputed its truth. The arbitration continued for a full two hours afterwards, and she made no protest. Whether that protest would have been effective, one does not know. But she clearly was faced with the knowledge, if the sellers' point was a good one at all, that inadmissible evidence was being tendered, and she stood by and did nothing about it.

Motion dismissed

Further evidence should not be admitted after closing the hearing

Eastcheap Dried Fruit Co v N.V. Gebroeders Catz (Queen's Bench Division, 1962)

SACHS J: The applicants by their notice of motion seek to have the awards set aside on two quite separate grounds. The first is that, after the hearing of the arbitration, the arbitrators improperly received further evidence....

Dealing with the first of those two grounds, there has been placed before me an affidavit by Mr Perera, who represented the applicants at the hearings at the arbitrations. He has stated that he has been informed and believes that the arbitrators, after the hearing had closed, had obtained and consulted a sworn statement from Holland as to the price there of pepper at the relevant date. As upon this application the respondents, although duly served, have not chosen to appear, the court is left with the position that it has to deal with the matter solely upon the material adduced by the applicants and also without having the benefit of argument adduced on behalf of the respondents. Having regard, however, to the authorities, and in particular to that of *Royal Commission on Sugar Supply v Trading Society Swik Hoo Tong* (1922), it appears that, when fresh evidence comes before the arbitrators after the conclusion of a hearing, then that is in law misconduct, vitiating the award unless, perhaps, it is affirmatively shown that it could not have affected that award. It is not as a rule for the court to embark upon conjecture as to whether their minds were affected or not.

An arbitrator has no power to call witnesses (see LPA 5.5)
An arbitrator in a case where a formal hearing akin to the procedure of the courts is held should not call witnesses of his own accord and against the will of the parties.

In re Enoch and Zaretzky, Bock & Co's Arbitration (Court of Appeal, 1910)

COZENS-HARDY MR: ....Another point which impresses me very much is this, that the umpire thought fit formally to rule that one of the parties to the arbitration, Mr Zaretzky — a gentleman who was not personally acquainted with the matter, and who had not been concerned with it — must attend and give evidence. What possible authority an umpire has to do that, I do not know. Mr Zaretzky was then in London; but my remark is still not without weight. The umpire took upon himself to rule that one of the parties to the arbitration, who was not really concerned and had no personal intimate knowledge of the matter, must come and give evidence. The next thing was this. The umpire took upon himself to call a gentleman whose name is Mr Kolway, a gentleman living in London, representing a company carrying on business at Burmah. What right the umpire had to call a witness, I confess I do not understand. But that.was not all. When this gentleman was called, he then produced copies of certain documents which it is really ludicrous to call evidence at all. He produced copies of certain documents which were said to show that certain parcels of rice had been purchased at Rangoon from certain people at certain prices, and of certain qualities. That being so, the vendors said that this was entirely a new point resulting from the witness whom the umpire had thought fit to call, and that they must have permission to send out to Rangoon, where they could get something deserving the name of evidence as to the place from which and the terms on which the parcels of rice which were in the cargo in question were obtained. The umpire would not allow the adjournment, and he actually proposed to make his award and deal with the matter, preventing the vendors from adducing evidence most obviously relevant in order to deal with a matter which, to my mind, it was equally obvious was not evidence, and which the umpire had no right to admit.

Then I am impressed with this, that the umpire has thought fit in this dispute to make a very long affidavit which is, to my mind, coloured throughout by an obvious bias in favour of the buyers and against the sellers. I wish to make it clear that I am not suggesting fraud on the part of Mr Von Limburg. But I do say that his conduct as umpire was such, as manifested by the particulars which I have given, that it would not be satisfactory, it would not be fair, it would not be just, to leave the rights of the parties, as they necessarily would be, in his sole hands to make the award unless we interfered. I, therefore, think that this appeal must be allowed.

FLETCHER MOULTON LJ: I am of the same opinion and for the same reasons. So far as they deal with the facts of the case other than one particular point to which I will presently refer, the same have been so admirably stated by the Master of the Rolls that I do not intend to refer to them. The point to which I wish to allude is the question of the umpire procuring evidence in the arbitration himself. It is quite clear, both from his conduct and from the line that has been taken up by counsel for the buyers and their arbitrator on this appeal, that there is an idea that an umpire, a person in a judicial position, has the power, and, I suppose, the duty, to call witnesses in a civil dispute which the parties do not either of them choose to call. In my opinion there is no such power. A judge has nothing to do with the getting up of a case. The argument is based on the case in the Court of Appeal of *Coulson v Disborough* (1894) in which certainly there are dicta that require to be carefully examined. The case itself presents no difficulty; nor does the decision. That was a case where, after both the counsel had spoken, the jury intimated to the judge that there was a person there to whom frequent reference had been made and they would like him to be called as a witness. The learned judge (Bruce J) called him as a witness, but obviously without any objection being raised by either party. He asked him one or two questions, the answers to which are wholly immaterial to the question, and then counsel for one of the parties asked leave to cross-examine, and the learned judge would not give him leave. When that was brought before the Court of Appeal, all the learned judges held that the answers were quite immaterial, and they said that under those circumstances there was no right whatever to cross-examine. Only one of the learned judges, Lord Esher MR, does give a dictum to which I wish to refer particularly. But it is quite evident that nothing was said throughout the argument as to this witness being called *in invitos* so far as the parties were concerned. Lord Esher MR said:

> 'If there be a person whom neither party to an action chooses to call as a witness, and the judge thinks that that person is able to elucidate the truth, the judge, in my opinion, is himself entitled to call him.'

If that means to call him when either side objects, I am satisfied that there is no basis for that dictum. It certainly was not necessary for the decision; and the consequences to which it would lead if so interpreted are such that I am satisfied that the Court of Appeal would never have made a decision so wide-reaching and so destructive of the fundamental principles of our laws of procedure without either authority or reasoning. It is not based on any course of reasoning and no authority is cited for it. I say that it would be destructive of the fundamental principles of our law of procedure because of this. According to such dictum, if supposed to apply to witnesses called against the will of one of the parties, the civil rights of a man might be decided by evidence given by a person whose personal credibility and the accuracy of whose statements he would have no right to test by cross-examination, because the Court of Appeal laid down that if a judge does call a witness then neither party can cross-examine him as of right. That may be most reasonable if the calling has been with the assent of both parties, because he cannot be regarded as a witness of the other party. But it would lead to consequences which I do not even like to contemplate if it were supposed to apply to cases where a judge calls a witness to facts of the case and then refuses, or has the power to refuse, that there shall be any cross-examination. Therefore I think that that dictum refers only to cases where a judge has called a witness without protest; that is to say, with practically the acquiescence of both parties, and has done so in order to get over the difficulty that, if either party calls a witness, he is supposed to be responsible for his personal credibility, though not for the accuracy of his statements. It is well known that if a party calls a witness he may not then attack his general credibility. There may be a person whom it would be desirable to have before the court. Neither party wishes to take the responsibility of first vouching his personal credibility, or that he is a witness fit to be called, and the judge may relieve the parties in this way, by letting him go into the box as a witness of neither party, and of course, if the answers are immaterial, he may refuse to allow cross-examination. But the dictum certainly does not justify in my opinion, and it is certainly not the law, that a judge, or any person such as an arbitrator in a judicial position, has any power to call witnesses to fact himself against the will of either of the parties.

FARWELL LJ: I am of the same opinion, and, as I have taken the opportunity during the adjournment to look into one or two of the cases, I will state my views on one or two of the points that have been argued. Where a case is referred to two arbitrators and an umpire, I think it is well understood that the arbitrators act as counsel who try and settle the case without going to court. But the umpire or a single arbitrator occupies a judicial position and exercises judicial powers, and is bound, as far as practicable, to follow legal rules, although, as Lord Halsbury says in *Andrews v Mitchell* (1905):

> 'We must not insist upon a too minute observance of the regularity of forms among persons who naturally, by their education or by their opportunities, cannot be supposed to be very familiar with legal procedure, and may accordingly make slips in what is mere matter of form without any interference with the substance of their decisions. I should be anxious myself, as I have no doubt all your Lordships would be, to give every effect to their decisions; on the other hand, there are some principles of justice which it is impossible to disregard, and, giving every credit to the desire on the part of this arbitration court to do justice, I think it is manifest that they proceeded far too hastily in this case, and, apart from imputing to them any prejudice or any desire to do wrong, I think that the mode in which the whole thing arose and was disposed of was so slipshod and irregular that it might lead to injustice.'

There are several matters which have arisen in the present case the cumulative effect of which is very strong....

The next objection is this. The witness who produced the copy award was found to be called by the umpire. The statement in the affidavit is:

> 'When Mr Zaretzky had finished, the umpire said, "Now I have a witness to call", and then began to examine Mr Kolway, an assistant of the Burmah Rice and Trading Co Ltd, who had been present during the proceedings. Mr Kolway produced an award, of which a copy is included in the

bundle forming the exhibit to this affidavit. This award was read out, and it was evident that the umpire attributed the greatest importance to it. The umpire then proceeded to examine this witness with a view of showing [certain things].'

This is in my opinion highly objectionable. If an umpire knows of a witness who can give evidence, he should inform both of the parties and invite them to call him. It puts the parties against whom the witness gives evidence, in a very difficult position when the umpire has made him his own witness by calling him and by examining him. How can he effectually object to the umpire's questions? How can he ask him to reject a document which the witness produced, on which the umpire relies? It is said that a judge of the High Court has the power to do this on the authority of *Coulson v Disborough (supra)* I am far from suggesting that is not the power, qualified in the way my brother Fletcher Moulton LJ has stated. I think there is such a power, if [that is what] Lord Esher MR meant to say, which is in accord with the facts of the case then before the court, and therefore I think one may fairly presume he did mean to say, 'if there be a person whom neither party to an action chooses to call as a witness, and the judge thinks that that person is able to elucidate the truth and neither party objects the judge, in my opinion, is himself entitled to call him'. In that particular case there was a man in court who apparently was supposed by the jury to know certain material facts, and they desired to have him called. No one objected, and the judge called him. To that I see no objection whatever. I confess that I feel some difficulty in assenting to the proposition that a judge ought ever to refuse cross-examination, but the learned judge says [in *Coulson v Disborough, supra*]:

'If what the witness has said in answer to the questions put to him by the judge is adverse to either of the parties, the judge would no doubt allow, and he ought to allow, that party's counsel to cross-examine the witness upon his answers. A general fishing cross-examination ought not to be permitted.'

To that I have no objection to offer at all, but I think, taking the facts of that case, what was meant was this. The jury thought that the man could give relevant testimony. He gave evidence which was not relevant, and then the judge said, 'We will treat him as not called', and he would not allow any general fishing cross-examination. To that I see no objection whatever. I would venture with respect to criticise what Smith LJ says that a witness called in this way is a witness of the judge and not of the parties. I venture to think it is not accurate to say a judge ever has a witness of his own. He is there to determine on the evidence called and in the case put, the witness, although called, would be a witness to be dealt with as an ordinary witness, the learned judge's qualification being true to this extent that it is not open to the counsel on either side to comment on the evidence given and to say he is either the plaintiff's witness or the defendant's witness. If he meant no more than that then I agree, but whatever power a judge of the High Court has to call such a witness, an umpire has no such power. He has not got all the power of a judge, but only such power as the Arbitration Act 1889, and Order 30, rules 48 and 55, give him in any case to which those rules are applicable. In my opinion, the conduct of the umpire in calling this witness and examining him and admitting the copy award as evidence is legal misconduct; and I cannot see that the objection to the admission of the document is waived because it was produced by the umpire's witness, and it would have been useless to object. Then he actually refused to allow an adjournment in order to enable the sellers to give evidence to test the testimony of the witness whom he had himself called. These facts appear to me to be amply sufficient even without the other matters...

Appeal allowed

It is misconduct if the arbitrator refuses to allow one of the parties to examine a witness he wishes to call unless custom, the arbitration agreement or the submission so provides.

Faure, Fairclough Ltd v Premier Oil and Cake Mills Ltd (Queen's Bench Division 1968)

The applicants were sellers of groundnut oil to the respondents and an arbitration about an allowance went on appeal to the Board of Appeal of the London Oil and Tallow Trades Association in accordance with the rules of the association. At the appeal they had present a Dr Williams, one of the world's leading authorities on the constitution and analysis of fats, but he was not allowed to give evidence, the Appeal Board holding in effect that they were traders and entitled to settle the allowance on the basis of 'look and sniff' (or in the words of the learned judge 'by visual and olefactory methods without the use of chemical or mechanical appliances') since the measure of damages for deficiency in quality was the difference between the market price of the goods of the contract description and the market price of the goods delivered. The evidence of a technical expert might therefore be irrelevant but could be received *de bene esse*, that is to say, admitted provisionally.

DONALDSON J: This is a motion to remit or set aside four awards of the Board of Appeal of the London Oil and Tallow Trades Association... The oil tendered by the sellers was admittedly not of good merchantable quality and the extent of the allowance to be made by the sellers was referred to arbitration in accordance with the rules of the London Oil and Tallow Trades Association. There rules provide for an initial arbitration before two arbitrators and, if necessary, an umpire, with a right of appeal to the Board of Appeal of the Association, consisting of four members of the Committee of Appeal. The appeal is by way of re-hearing but the rules provide that the award appealed from must be confirmed unless three members of the board decide to vary it.

The sellers were dissatisfied with the allowances awarded by the arbitrators and appealed to the board...

The hearing was attended by Mr Trigge for the buyers and Mr Faure for the sellers. Also present were Dr Williams, an eminent analytical chemist, and Mr Brett, a well-known independent cargo superintendent, whose firm had in fact superintended the loading of the cargoes on behalf of the crushers. Mr Trigge objected to the presence of Dr Williams and Mr Brett otherwise than as observers upon the ground that the board was a board of traders and not chemists and that the sellers could only be represented by one person and that person was Mr Faure and not Dr Williams or Mr Brett.

I am bound to say that I regard both these objections as wholly misconceived. It was precisely because the members of the board were not chemists that they would be assisted by evidence from a chemist, if chemical analysis was a relevant consideration, and while it is true that the line between expert evidence and advocacy often becomes somewhat blurred, both gentlemen could have given evidence without providing the sellers with additional representation.

The board should, in my judgment, have thereupon considered and if necessary ruled upon whether either gentleman could give relevant evidence. If so, they should have been allowed to give evidence in the usual way and in particular both parties should have been allowed to question them. No doubt some of the formality of examination-in-chief, cross-examination and re-examination may be inappropriate to a trade arbitration, but without some questioning by both parties it is impossible to be sure that all the relevant evidence which the witnesses can give has been put before the tribunal.

Unfortunately the Board did not adopt this course.... The sellers now apply for the award to be remitted or set aside upon the ground of the alleged misconduct of the board in refusing to hear relevant evidence and, further or alternatively, in not affording the sellers an opportunity of questioning a witness.

The much publicized activities of the Divorce Division of the High Court have given the word 'misconduct' a special meaning which is not only inappropriate but tends to give offence when applied to the activities of arbitrators. As a result variations have been introduced and counsel now speak of 'legal misconduct' or 'technical misconduct', with or without apology for the choice of language. The settlement of disputes by arbitration is a consensual process, and what is usually meant by misconduct is a departure by the arbitrators from the procedure which has the express or implied agreement of the parties, although considerations of public policy can be involved (see the *London Export Corporation Ltd* case (1958) per Mr Justice Diplock, as he then was). In deciding whether or not there has been such a departure, the courts now recognise that the parties may well intend to confer upon the tribunal of their choice a wide discretion as to the procedure to be adopted and are properly reluctant to intervene. However, in the absence of express agreement to the contrary, the courts assume that the parties, as reasonable people, intended that the procedure should be such as would not only tend, but appear to tend, to the achievement of a just result. It was suggested in argument that the famous dictum that justice must not only be done but seen to be done was inapplicable to private proceedings. I disagree. The importance of actual justice is, of course, paramount but, subject to that, the appearance of justice is just as important in arbitration as in litigation, even if the audience is more restricted and the parties are to be presumed to have agreed to arbitration on the basis that the procedure adopted would actually and apparently tend to a just result.

In the present case there may have been no actual injustice, but the procedure adopted was such as Mr Faure and Dr Williams both felt, and had reason to feel, that the sellers' case had not been fully deployed before the board. This is misconduct and justifies the intervention of the court.

I accept Mr Diamond's submission that the sellers have not shown that the evidence of either Dr Williams or Mr Brett is relevant; but relevance is a matter to be determined by the board, at least in the first instance. In so far as the board questioned Dr Williams, it may be inferred that his evidence was or could be relevant, but it may well be that the members of the board never really applied their minds to the issue of relevance.

I also accept fully that a trade tribunal is entitled to make use of its own knowledge and indeed in a quality dispute it is often wholly appropriate that the tribunal should itself 'look and sniff' if this is the best way of determining the issue between the parties. Indeed this is much better than evidence of others as to what they saw and smelt, i e, 'hearsniff' evidence. I have much more doubt about the proposition that trade arbitrators can refuse to hear relevant evidence upon the ground that such evidence would not assist them, because I find it difficult to conceive of circumstances in which arbitrators could *bona fide* conclude that relevant evidence would not assist without having first heard it. I completely reject the submission that arbitrators can refuse a party the right to examine his own witnesses unless there is express agreement to this effect, since such a procedure tends to result either in the tribunal entering the arena to the detriment of detached judgment or to the evidence being incompletely deployed, and in either event gives or may give the appearance of unfairness. . . .

I am confident that the members of the board will give full and fair reconsideration to the matter upon remission just as they would have done if there had been a consultative case. This confidence, which I am sure will not be misplaced, also decides me in favour of remitting rather than setting aside, and I need not therefore consider what is the effect upon the initial award in a two-tier arbitration where the appeal award affirming it is set aside.

The four awards will be remitted to the Board of Appeal of the London Oil and Tallow Trades Association to enable them to make fresh awards in the light of the evidence which they have already heard and further relevant and admissible evidence which either party may wish to tender. It is not always easy to determine whether evidence will be relevant without actually receiving it, but I can see no reason why arbitrators should not in a proper case receive evidence without prejudice to a later decision on its relevance. The admissibility of the evidence will, of course, fall to be judged by the rules appropriate to a London Oil and Tallow Trades Association arbitration and not by those which are appropriate to hostile litigation in the courts. If the board considers that evidence based upon analyses could be relevant, they will no doubt consider carefully whether it may not be advisable to allow experts on both sides to analyse the official samples which I understand are in the board's possession. . . .

Misconduct by an arbitrator (see LPA 7.5)

'Misconduct' does not mean delinquency.

There are learned discussions by Ulpian and Julian of the legal position in Roman law if an *arbiter* should select a brothel as the venue for an arbitration. They are not likely to have much relevance to modern conditions, even though they might well have done so in the last century (see Serjeant Ballantine: *Some Experiences of a Barrister*) or when a Lord Chancellor, Lord Campbell, was seen in the then notorious Cremorne Gardens 'to observe human nature', as he put it.

Nor has the word 'misconduct' any of its usual implications, as Donaldson J explained.

Thomas Borthwick (Glasgow) Ltd v Faure Fairclough Ltd (Queen's Bench Commercial Court, 1968)

DONALDSON J: The motion invites me to set the award aside or to remit it to the Board [of Appeal] for a further hearing upon the ground that the board misconducted itself in making the finding set out....

Lawyers are well aware that arbitrators take it ill if they are accused of misconduct, perhaps because the word has acquired a technical meaning in a quite different realm which occupies so much of the time of the Probate, Divorce and Admiralty Division of the High Court. It is therefore customary to add, in an apologetic parenthesis, that what is meant is technical misconduct. Whether or not 'misconduct' is an appropriate term, 'technical' is certainly inappropriate. What is complained of here — I venture to think that the same can be said of all allegations of misconduct by arbitrators — is that the board was in breach of its duty to act fairly and to be seen to act fairly. This is not to say that the board intended to be unfair or was aware that it might appear to have acted unfairly. Such cases are happily very rare, because the commercial community is fortunate in the skill and conscientiousness of those who devote time to the resolution of commercial disputes by arbitration.

An arbitrator who indicates to the parties that he intends to have a view of the property in dispute is guilty of misconduct if he does not do so.

Micklewright v Mulluck (Queen's Bench Division, 1974)

An arbitration between a house owner and the builder who carried out alterations for him included two points:
(1)   what was the reasonable price for work carried out and
(2)   what allowance ought to be made for work alleged to be badly done by the builder.
On a motion to set aside the award made in the builder's favour by the arbitrator, a fellow of the Royal Institution of Chartered Surveyors:

PARK J:......It was submitted on behalf of Mr Mullock [the house owner] that from the outset the arbitrator had expressed a clear intention to view the property, that Mr Mulluck and his advisers had relied upon that statement of intention and at no time had the arbitrator notified the parties that he had changed that intention, so that the parties had thereby been deprived of the opportunity of calling such further evidence as might be necessary in the light of the change of circumstances.

It is accordingly submitted that the arbitrator mis-conducted himself and reliance is placed on the case of *Pepper v Gorham* (1820). For Mr Micklewright [the builder] it is argued that an arbitrator has a discretion whether or not he should inspect the property in dispute and that there is no imperative duty on him to inspect.

Reliance is placed upon *Munday v Black* (1861) but in my view that case is distinguishable from the present case, where the arbitrator had stated at the outset that he intended to view the premises .....

In my judgment, an arbitrator who states that he intends to inspect the property in dispute and thereby induces a party to the arbitration to conduct his case on the basis that the arbitrator would do so, should not depart from his intention, or, if he did, should not do so without giving both parties notice of his intention to do so and an opportunity to call such further evidence as might be necessary in the changed circumstances ......

In the circumstances, I think that within the meaning of section 23(2) of the Arbitration Act 1950 [the arbitrator] misconducted himself ...... The award will be set aside.

Motion allowed

Proceeding ex parte (see LPA 2.4.4)

It may be misconduct for an arbitrator to proceed *ex parte* in default of defence, unless a clear warning has been given to the respondent.

The Myron (Queen's Bench Commercial Division, 1969)

DONALDSON J: . . . Tradax's second complaint is, as I have said, that they never intended to allow the arbitration to proceed in default of defence and should have received clear warning of the fact that this would occur if they did not take prompt action. [Counsel] also contends that Tradax were entitled to be informed of and to consider the owners' evidence and arguments. I doubt whether this submission would have been made, but for a dictum of Mr Justice Megaw (as he then was) in *Government of Ceylon v Chandris* (1963) that:

> 'It is, I apprehend, a basic principle, in arbitrations as much as in litigation in the courts (other, of course, than *ex parte* proceedings), that no one with judicial responsibility may receive evidence, documentary or otherwise, from one party without the other party knowing that the evidence is being tendered and being offered an opportunity to consider it, object to it, or make submissions on it. No custom or practice may override that basic principle.'

I say that I doubt whether this submission would otherwise have been made because there is no suggestion that Tradax were in the least taken by surprise by or wished or needed to be expressly informed of the owners' evidence and contentions. I respectfully agree with this dictum of Mr Justice Megaw in the context of the case with which he was concerned — it was a formal arbitration and evidence was submitted *ex parte* after the conclusion of an oral hearing attended by solicitors and counsel. I do not, however, think that he would have regarded it as applicable to this case in which, as I have said, Tradax knew full well that the owners were submitting evidence, knew broadly what that evidence was and had no wish to be further informed about it.

Tradax also rely on a dictum of Mr Justice Megaw in *Montrose Canned Foods Ltd v Eric Wells (Merchants) Ltd* (1965) where he said:

> 'In my judgment, it is incumbent upon arbitrators to take steps to ensure, so far as is reasonably possible, before they make an award, that each of the parties to the dispute before them know the case which has been put against them, and has had the opportunity to put forward that party's own case. Here that did not happen . . . . .
>
> There was no clear or specific statement by the buyers and no reason to suppose that it was their intention to allow this arbitration to go by

default without putting their case before the arbitrators and stand upon some submission that the arbitrators had no jurisdiction. Unless that had been made abundantly clear, it was the duty of the arbitrators as a matter of natural justice, before they proceeded to make an award on the basis of the arguments and submissions of one side only, to make sure that the buyers did not wish to put their case before the arbitrators.'

The learned judge is here dealing with two distinct, if related, matters, namely, first the duty of the arbitrators to ensure that each party knows the case which is being put against him and has an opportunity of dealing with it, and, second, their duty to make sure that a party does not wish to put his case before them if they are to proceed in default of defence.

As to the first point, the practice of allowing each party to submit their evidence and arguments to the arbitrators separately only works on the assumption that neither party will be taken by surprise by either the evidence or the arguments advanced by the other party. Normally both parties are fully aware of the issues, the arguments and the evidence available for consideration, and no problem arises. If, however, the arbitrators have the slightest grounds for wondering whether one of the parties has fully appreciated what is being put against him, or whether he might reasonably wish to supplement his evidence or argument in the light of what has been submitted by the other party, it is their duty to take appropriate steps to resolve these doubts. This would normally be done by one of the arbitrators writing to the party concerned summarising the case made against him and inquiring whether in the light of the summary he wished to add anything by way of evidence or argument.

Let me make two matters quite clear. First, it is not sufficient that the arbitrator appointed by party A shall know the case being made by party B. This must always be the case and an arbitrator is in no sense a representative of the party appointing him, unless and until there is a final disagreement. Second, I am not for one moment suggesting, and I do not think that Mr Justice Megaw has ever suggested, that the evidence and argument submitted by one party must be copied and submitted by the other with a right to reply thereto. That would lead to an indefinite exchange of correspondence. If either party wishes to see the whole of the other party's evidence and to be informed in detail of his arguments, he should require a formal hearing. Any such request must be granted and at the hearing the usual court procedure will be followed. The usual court procedure includes the granting of an adjournment on appropriate terms if the justice of the case so requires. What I am saying is that each party to an arbitration conducted on informal lines is entitled to rely upon both the arbitrators to safeguard his interests by ensuring that he is fully informed of any issue of fact or law which is raised by the other party and which he may not have anticipated.

There is no suggestion in the present case that Tradax were in any way taken by surprise. The owners' case was perfectly straighforward, although I naturally express no view as to whether it was right. The only unusual features were those which Tradax would have injected, and had Tradax submitted evidence and argument, it would almost certainly have been necessary to give the owners express notice of what was being alleged so that they could deal with it by supplementary evidence and argument.

I now turn to the second point, namely, the duty of the arbitrators to make sure that a party does not wish to put his case before them and is content that they shall proceed in default of defence. Taking full account of the initial inertia of the owners, Tradex nevertheless behaved in a most unbusinesslike and, indeed, discourteous manner. It is tempting to say that they deserve to suffer the consequences in the shape of the award which has been made against them, but the issue of principle is somewhat more important than the education of Tradax. In successive paragraphs of his affidavit, Mr Chesterman [as arbitrator] says that normally, if a party does not produce any papers, 'warning (is given) that an award will be made without them unless they are produced quickly' and notice is given 'that if none are produced the arbitration will proceed anyway'. If that had been done in clear terms in the present case, there would have been no ground whatsoever for interfering. However, the intimation in the letter of 13 May 1968 that Mr Chesterman could not resist fixing a date for hearing in June and that he 'hoped' to have the papers — not 'must' have them — before then is not sufficiently clear and definite to convey unequivocally to Tradex that if they did not produce the papers by June, their case would go by default. In the circumstances, the award cannot stand.

It has been submitted on behalf of Tradex that the arbitration should be begun again before different arbitrators, in the light of the fact that Mr Chesterman has expressed the view that (a) the court would not interfere with the award and (b) it is unlikely that a further award would be different in the light of the owners' evidence. I should not hesitate to adopt this course if I thought that Mr Chesterman or Mr Clark [the other arbitrator] was either incapable of applying or unwilling to apply his mind to the dispute afresh in the light of any evidence or arguments which Tradax may submit, but I do not think that this is the case.

The award will therefore be remitted to Mr Clark and Mr Chesterman to enable them to give further consideration to the dispute in the light of any or any further evidence or arguments which either party may wish to submit. If eventually they are agreed, they will make a fresh award. If they are not agreed, they will appoint an umpire.

Award remitted

Consulting lawyers (see LPA 7.3)

There is no reason why an arbitrator should not, if he finds himself in difficulties about the law, consult a qualified lawyer.

Giacomo Costa Fu Andrea v British Italian Trading Company Ltd (Queen's Bench Commercial Court, 1962)

> The motion was to set aside an award on the ground, *inter alia*, that the arbitrator has misconducted himself in that he had, in terms unknown to the parties, requested the advice of solicitors on the interpretation of a clause in the contract.
>
> McNAIR J discussed *Dreyfus and Co v Arunschala Ayya* (1931) and decided that it was no authority that an arbitrator, if he is in difficulty, cannot consult a lawyer, a qualified person on the subject.

McNAIR J: The other case cited in support of this branch of the argument is the case of *Ellison and others v Bray* (1864) which is not an easy case to follow owing to the abbreviated nature of the report. It appears that it was a rule to set aside an award, on the ground that the umpire had acted upon the opinion of his attorney, and one of the paragraphs of the statement of facts says:

> 'The affidavits showed that the umpire decided to make his award in favour of the plaintiffs, subject to the opinion of his attorney as to the legal effect of the agreement and resolution.'

Mr Justice Shee, who delivered the judgment, which made the rule absolute said this:

> 'It is clear that an arbitrator or umpire is allowed to consult others if he wishes to inform his own mind, but he must not substitute the opinion of another for his own. From the affidavits it appears that the award is that of the umpire's attorney, not the umpire's. The latter acted on his attorney's advice without a moment's consideration or discussion, and has substituted the judgment of another for his own.'

That again seems to me to be another illustration of the principle stated in the Privy Council case to which I have just referred, that an umpire cannot delegate to another the decision of the question where there is referred to him a dispute involving both questions of fact and of law.

I was also referred to the case *In re Hare, Milne and Haswell* (1839), where there are some interesting *obiter* observations by Chief Justice Tindal as to the right of an umpire to take opinion of counsel and he emphasises, obviously rightly, that if counsel's opinion is taken, the correct statement of facts should be laid before him otherwise the opinion could not be relied upon; and the case of *Rolland v Cassidy*, (1888), another decision of the Privy Council which is considered in *Russell on Arbitration*, 16th edition at pages 124 and 125. That case, however, was a case that came from Quebec and it seemed to involve questions under the French Code of Civil Procedure and I do not find in that case any statement of principle which is helpful to the decision of the matter before me.

I would, however, observe that it must surely be well-known common practice in these trade arbitrations for these commodity associations for the original umpire, or more particularly, the Board of Appeal, to have sitting with them at the hearing professional advisers, possibly a solicitor to the association, and it has never occurred to me for a moment, nor I have ever seen it suggested, that there is anything irregular in that or anything irregular in doing that without getting the express consent of the parties; and there is certainly nothing irregular in the Board of Appeal receiving advice from their legal advisers after the parties have completed their arguments. The umpire here has said in terms (and there is no reason for me to disbelieve his evidence on this point) that he had made up his mind, irrespective of the advice, before he had approached his solicitors. He had already formed the conclusion that the claimants' claim failed and that he intended to award against them, but he was merely asking for his lawyers' advice in case his view was erroneous. I see no reason at all why I should dispute that and it seems to me, subject to one point which I shall mention in a moment, that the course which he took was entirely right and unobjectionable.

The point which I have reserved in the last sentence is this, of course. As was pointed out by Chief Justice Tindal in *In re Hare (supra)*, it was essential that the correct facts should be put before whoever is called upon to give advice, otherwise the advice will be misleading and inaccurate. It is said here that the correct facts were not put before the solicitors. I do not know: there is no information at all before me as to whether the correct facts were so put before Messrs Waltons & Co. The suggestion is that they should have been told, as was well within the knowledge of the umpire and the two arbitrators, that the export of groundnuts from Gambia was wholly in the hands of a Gambia export monopoly board of some kind and, accordingly, the sellers could never themselves ship these groundnuts from Gambia, but would have to get them from the monopoly board. It is said that it does not appear that those facts were ever put before the solicitors. I do not know whether they were or not and I certainly am not prepared to express the view that they would be material facts in determining this question of construction. Accordingly, on the matters which I have dealt with so far, my judgment goes against the buyers.

An alternative argument was put forward on this same head of misconduct and that was this. In a passage which I have already read from the umpire's affidavit he said this:

'As the letter which I received from my lawyers was in my view additional evidence I considered it my duty as umpire to make it available to both arbitrators and this I did'.

On that it is submitted that it is plain law that, if an umpire obtains additional evidence and acts upon it in the absence of the parties, that itself would be a ground for setting aside on the ground of technical misconduct.

The answer to that, as it seems to me, is simply this that, although the arbitrator uses the words 'additional evidence' in relation to the letter from his solicitors, it is quite clear that it is not evidence at all; it is not evidence of fact, nor is it such evidence of opinion as sometimes is evidence of fact, namely, opinion as to foreign law or opinion as to any technical science. This is in no sense evidence and when the arbitrator said that this was additional evidence it seems to me to be reasonably plain that he merely meant: 'Well, this was an additional matter which I took after I had made up my mind and which I thought, as a matter of fairness, ought to be shown to the arbitrators', and that he did ...

Motion dismissed

Stating a case (see LPA 7.6)

Whether an arbitrator states a case or not is a matter for his discretion but he should state one if there is an issue which is real and substantial, capable of being expressed as a point of law, and if the resolution of it is necessary for a proper determination of the case.

Halfdan Grieg v Sterling Corporation (Court of Appeal, 1973)

Arbitrators were asked to state their award in the form of a special case. They refused in the following letter:

'With reference to the (owners') request that we should state our award in the form of a special case we have to advise you that we have decided not to do so for the following reasons:-
We do not feel that this is a proper case to be so stated. Whilst it may well be that there is a question of law it is our feeling that, whilst we do not presume to usurp the functions of the court, it is more suitable for decision by a commercial arbitration tribunal than by the courts since its interpretation is so closely allied to commercial practice and the interpretation that commercial men would give it. Counsel agreed that the court's decision would add nothing to the wealth of law which is already available to us and as there is no further principle of law involved we feel it unnecessary from the point of view of both time and expense to trouble their Lordships further. We have also decided to delay the issue of our award for fourteen days so that the parties may, if they wish, apply to the court.'

The owners applied for an order under section 21 of the Arbitration Act, that the arbitrators be directed to state their award in the form of a special case. Keer J refused and the owners applied to the Court of Appeal, who allowed the appeal.

DENNING MR: When one party asks an arbitrator or umpire to state his award in the form of a special case, it is a matter for his discretion. If the issues are on matters of fact and not of law, he should refuse to state a case. If they raise a point of law, it depends on what the point of law is. He should agree to state a case whenever the facts, as proved or admitted before him, give rise to a point of law which fulfils these requisites. The point of law should be real and substantial and such as to be open to serious argument and appropriate for decision by a court of law (see *Re Nuttall and Lynton and Barnstaple Railway Co* (1899)) as distinct from a point which is dependent on the special expertise of the arbitrator or umpire (see *Orion Compagnia Espanola de Seguros v Belfort Maatschappij voor Algemene Verzerkgringeen* (1962)). The point of law should be clear-cut and capable of being accurately stated as a point of law — as distinct from the dressing-up of a matter of fact as if it were a point of law. The point of law should be of such importance that the resolution of it is necessary for the proper determination of the case — as distinct from a side-issue of little importance.

If those three requisites are satisfied, the arbitrator or umpire should state a case. He should not be deterred from doing so by such suggestions as these: it may be suggested that a special case should be reserved for cases which are of general application (such as the construction of a standard form) or which would elucidate or add to the general principles of law (such as the doctrine of frustration or repudiation). I would not so limit the stating of a special case. In most cases the parties themselves are concerned, not with general principles, but with their particular dispute. If the case does involve a point of law which satisfied the requisites which I have mentioned, either of the parties should be enabled to have it decided by a judge of the High Court. When the parties agree to arbitrate, it is, by our law, on the assumption that a point of law can, in a proper case, be referred to the courts.

It may be suggested that if the point of law is only as to the construction of a particular document or of the words in it — as applied to the proved facts — then it should be left to the arbitrator or umpire. I do not agree. Most of the special cases are stated on points of construction. No one hitherto has thought that they should be refused on that ground.

It may be suggested that, if the point of law is only as to the proper inference, or the appropriate implication — to be drawn from the proved facts — then it should be left to the arbitrator or umpire. Again, I do not agree. Some of the most important awards have been of that kind: see, for instance, *Re Comptoir Commercial Anversois and Power Son & Co* (1920).

It may be suggested that if only a small sum is in dispute, a special case should be refused. Sometimes a small sum can involve big issues of much importance for the parties. In those cases a special case should be stated. But when the sum is so small as not to justify further time or money being spent on it, it should be refused.

Whilst setting out those guidelines, I would give a word of warning. The arbitrator or umpire should be watchful to see that the procedure by special case is not abused. The conference of Commercial Court Users, over which Pearson J presided in 1962, drew attention to abuses such as a special case on 'whether upon the facts found by the umpire his ultimate decision is correct'. That is why I have said that the point of law should be clear-cut. Other abuses spring readily to mind. A party may seek to raise a point of law which is too plain for serious argument. Or he may seek to use it as a means of delaying the day when a final award is made against him. In all cases where *the arbitrator or umpire is of opinion* that the application is not raised *bona fide but for some ulterior motive*, he should, of course, refuse it.

In the present case there is no suggestion that the application is not made *bona fide* or that it is an abuse of the process of a special case. But the judge has refused to order the arbitrators or umpire to state a special case for two main reasons: (1) that the question of law is one which is well within the experience and capacity of arbitrators; and (2) a delay of three years between 1969 and 1972 appeared to him 'to have been due to inaction on the side of the owners'. As to (1), whilst the experience and capacity of the arbitrators and umpire is undoubted, I do not think that the point of law is one which is specially within their expertise. It seems to me that the point at issue depends on the true construction of the agreement which the court is well qualified to decide, and which a party is entitled to ask the court itself to rule on. The court would, of course, give great weight to the views of the arbitrators and umpire on it, but should come to its own decision...

Counsel for the charterers referred to the words of Lord Wilberforce in *Compagnie Tunisienne de Navigation v Compagnie D'Armement Maritime SA* (1969) and suggested that when the decision of the arbitrators was followed by the decision of the commercial judge — refusing a special case — that should end the matter. In the ordinary way I would agree. But this case was treated by the judge as raising a question of principle. So it has been in this court. His decision would, I think, alter the practice hitherto adopted. The judge said that he did not wish to do this. He emphasised that his decision:

'should not be taken as any indication... that special cases should be stated less frequently in the future than in the past'.

But I think that it would inevitably tend to do so. This is a typical case where the court in the past would order a special case. If the residual discretion (to which the judge referred) is to be applied in this case, it would fall to be applied in many others like it. I would keep to the existing practice and order the arbitrators to state their award in the form of a special case. I would allow the appeal, accordingly.

MEGAW LJ delivered a concurring judgment.

Appeal allowed

In asking an arbitrator for a case stated, the party should make clear to him all the points on which findings of fact are necessary.

Aruna Mills Ltd v Dhanrajmal Gobindram (Queen's Bench Commercial Court, 1968)

DONALDSON J: It is the duty of parties to an arbitration who desire to raise questions of law for the decision of the court to make plain to the arbitrators all the points on which they wish the facts to be found for the purpose of arguing the questions of law. (See *Sinason-Teicher Inter American Grain Corporation v Oilcakes & Oilseeds Trading Company Ltd* (1954).) The Court is reluctant to remit an award for further findings of fact where there has been a failure by the parties in this respect, because remission adds considerably to the cost of the proceedings and creates delay. However, this reluctance is much reduced if the parties are prevented by the rules of the arbitration from being represented by lawyers, as it is unreasonable to expect the parties themselves to appreciate all the points which are or may be relevant. I can well understand the Liverpool Cotton Association Ltd considering that the assistance of lawyers is irrelevant to the decision of a dispute which turns solely upon matters of quality or description, there being no dispute as to the legal rights and duties of the parties. However, once any question of law creeps into the dispute, the position is quite different. The assistance of lawyers may then save both time and expense. Members of trade associations are fully entitled to agree that their rules shall forbid all legal representation at arbitrations conducted in accordance with those rules, but I venture to think that they are most unwise to do so. Contrary to popular belief, lawyers do not regard it as any part of their duty either to their client or to the tribunal to make confusion worse confounded. On the contrary, they can and do bring their professional expertise to bear upon the problem of crystallising the issues, thus saving time and money to all concerned, while at the same time ensuring a just result in accordance with law.

As there is no finding on this essential point and as the buyers were denied legal representation, the award will be remitted for such a finding if the buyers' contention is otherwise correct.

A case stated should include the recital of facts, the question and little else.

Universal Cargo Carriers Corporation v Pedro Citati (Queen's Bench Division, 1957)

DEVLIN J: Strictly speaking, a case stated should contain nothing but findings, positive or negative, of fact. In practice, it is always necessary to include some explanatory matter, but it should, I think, be kept to a minimum, its purpose being simply to make the findings easily intelligible. The award in this case would be admirable if the court had full appellate jurisdiction or even had power to draw an inference of fact, but it has not. Unless the question is whether there is any evidence to sustain a finding, the court is not concerned with the evidence, nor with the processes by which the arbitrator arrived at his inference or conclusions of fact. The effect of setting out the evidence may conceivably be to cause the judge to entertain doubts, which he ought not to entertain, about the value of the findings, and almost certainly will be to allow the argument at the hearing to range much more freely than it ought to.

No doubt the reason that lies behind this type of award is that the arbitrator wants to give the parties as good a run as he can at the hearing of the argument. But that is not, in my opinion, the proper object of arbitral proceedings, which is to cut out all further argument on questions of fact; and that object should be achieved as firmly and concisely as possible.

Another disadvantage about this type of case stated — and the one that is material to the point I have to decide — is that it is very difficult to make sure how much of it is meant to be a firm finding of fact and how much merely narrative or disputable evidence.....

A case can be stated in general terms, as the example given in the following case.

Universal Cargo Carriers Corporation v Pedro Citati (Queen's Bench Division, 1957)

'Whether upon the facts found and upon the true construction of the charter-party the claimants were entitled on 18 July 1951 to treat the charter-party as discharged by the respondent's breach and to claim damages accordingly'.

DEVLIN J: When the question of law is left in this general form, a party is entitled to argue any point of law that arises on the facts found. The purpose of arguing the law before the arbitrator — and the only useful purpose, as far as I can see, once it becomes clear that a case is to be stated — is to enable him to know what facts to find as relevant to the points of law which the parties are taking. It is the duty of each party, when he gets the case stated, to consider it and satisfy himself that the relevant facts are found. If they are not, he should apply to the court within the six weeks allowed by Rules of the Supreme Court, Order 64, rule 14, to have the case remitted for the findings he wants. If the relevant facts have not been stated, it must, strictly speaking, be the fault either of the party for failing to make his point properly or of the arbitrator for failing to apprehend it. I say 'strictly speaking' because there may be cases of complexity where it is difficult to put the blame on anybody. If, however, it is the fault of the arbitrator, the applicant is, I think, entitled to remission almost as of right; if it is his own fault, he must ask for indulgence. The court must then exercise its discretion, which is a wide one.

The importance of making an application in time is two-fold. It may be a case which it is best to remit at once before the argument of law begins. If it is not, and if the court thinks that time and money may be saved by first hearing the argument, the result of which may make the remission unnecessary, the application will nevertheless make it clear beyond doubt that the applicant's grievance was one which occurred to him at once on reading the case, and that the point of law is not an afterthought which arose for the first time during the hearing of the argument. If the application is not made in time and the applicant has to ask for an extension, he must, I think, not only explain the delay, but also show 'a strong case on the merits indicating a really definite issue for consideration': per Lord Justice Scott in *Temple Steamship Company Ltd v V/O Sovfracht* (1943).

An arbitrator can be called upon to state as a question of law whether there is any evidence to support his findings. If he does so, he should only set out the relevant facts which support his findings and not append a transcript of the evidence or a full summary of the whole of it.

Tersons Ltd v Stevenage Development Corporation (Court of Appeal, 1963)

UPJOHN LJ: ...When an arbitrator is preparing to state a case raising the question whether there was evidence upon which he reached a certain conclusion of fact, he must in principle proceed in exactly the same way as when he is preparing a case stated to raise some other question of law. He must set out the relevant facts, but the facts, when his conclusion of fact is so questioned, must consist of the evidence on which he relies to support his conclusion. When he is setting out this evidence, he must remember that he is bound only to set out the evidence on which he relies to support his conclusion. He is not bound to set out the whole of the evidence for and against the conclusion of fact which he has reached. Indeed, strictly it is wrong for him to set out the evidence tending to show that his conclusion was wrong, for it is irrelevant. The court is not concerned with his finding of fact; the court is concerned only to see that there is evidence to support his finding. If there is, then the arbitrator's decision is final. Thus, an arbitrator could perfectly properly state: 'The evidence of Mr Smith was to the following effect' (setting it out) 'and I accepted it'. It is then quite immaterial that there were twenty witnesses who gave evidence in a contrary sense. With all respect to argument to the contrary, it is, in my judgment, the arbitrator's duty to state the effect of the evidence which he accepted, and not to set out question and answer in a transcript or even his own note. That this must be so is, I think, clear when one considers that very few witnesses, however honest, give evidence-in-chief which is not to some extent affected by cross-examination; and if all that the arbitrator does is to set out some questions and answers, the court is left with the task of evaluating that evidence, and deciding what is its effect. That is the very task that the parties have committed exclusively to the arbitrator. Consequently it is his duty to evaluate the evidence himself, and therefore to set out in summary form the effect of the evidence on his mind. It is wrong to leave that task to the court which, furthermore, has not seen or heard the witnesses, and therefore is denied the right of assessing it properly.

The arbitrator can in a few simple cases, where it is easy and practicable, set out the evidence in the form of a transcript or his own note, but normally that will not be so.

At this state, one word of warning, however, must be introduced. It is the duty of the arbitrator, as I have said, to set out the effect of the evidence which supports his conclusion. It is for him to select what evidence he regards as relevant to support his conclusion. It is for him to decide how fully or how summarily it shall be stated. But having selected the evidence upon which he does rely, that must be set out fairly in the sense of setting it out truly and accurately and the evidence must be credible, that is, such that a reasonable man could accept that evidence as the truth. If a party can successfully challenge those matters, then he establishes misconduct on the part of the arbitrator and the award can be attacked on that ground....

We have been referred to a number of cases, but none of them really decide this point. It is, of course, clear that in the ordinary case the arbitrator must not set out evidence; he must merely state his conclusion of fact; see *East Yorkshire Motor Services Ltd v Clayton (Valuation Officer)* (1961). And even where the question arises whether there is evidence in support of the arbitrator's finding, the court has very recently protested in *Festiniog Railway Company v Central Electricity Generating Board* (1962) against the appendage of lengthy transcripts, but it was not there necessary to decide this point of principle....

DENNING LJ and PEARSON LJ delivered concurring judgments.

PART VI

The award

The publishing or notifying of an Award is either provided for and ordered by the submission itself. Or else it is left and permitted to the discretion of the Arbitrator.

In the form of every Arbitrement six things are specially to be regarded:

1. That it be made according to the very submission touching the things submitted or necessarily depending thereupon, and every other circumstance, as aforesaid.
2. That it ought to be certain.
3. That it ought to be equal and appoint either Party to give or do unto the other something beneficial in the appearance at the least.
4. That the performance therefore be possible and lawful, and with the power of the Parties.
5. That there be a means how either Party may by Law attain unto that which is thereby awarded unto him.
6. That it be a final end of the Controversies submitted.

And if it fail in any of these points, then it is said that the whole Arbitrement shall be void.

Arbitrium Redivivam (1694)

[NB: This is still good law save for point No 3, which was part of the then emerging doctrine of consideration: Ed]

Essentials of a valid award (see LPA 9.1)

The award should name both parties to the arbitration correctly.

S.G. Embiricos Ltd v Tradax Internacional SA (Queen's Bench Division, 1967)

ROSKILL J: . . . There is one other small matter to which I wish to allude, not by way of criticism but in order to help those who are daily making awards. The charter-party in this case is expressed to be:

> '... between S. G. EMBIRICOS LIMITED (the well-known agents in the City of London), as Agents for disponent Owners G. Andronicos, Athens ... and Messrs TRADAX INTERNACIONAL SA Panama City (as the charterers)...'

When the umpire prepared his special case, he described the parties as 'MESSRS S. G. EMBIRICOS LTD (Agents for disponent owners) Claimants' and 'MESSRS TRADAX INTERNACIONAL SA (Charterers) Respondents'. The description in the body of the special case of the claimants as being Messrs S. G. Embiricos Ltd (albeit as agents) is in fact, with respect to the umpire, quite wrong. One has seen over the years awards made in this form but where a contract is made between X as agent for Y on the one hand and Z on the other, the contract is between Y and Z and not between X and Z. To make an award in the present form is to make an award under a contract which in truth was never made. Of course, in the majority of arbitrations the point is not important because everyone knows that the award will be honoured whatever technical defect it may contain. But if an award is made in this form and questions of summary enforcement under the relevant provisions of the Arbitration Acts arise, I apprehend that no court would summarily enforce an award in this form. I draw attention to this point, not by way of criticism but to avoid any possibility of misfortune arising through a practice which, while I know it has been followed for a good many years, is, with all respect to those who pursue it, wrong and can lead to trouble.

An award for the payment of money which is not a mere declaratory one must be in a form which is capable of being enforced as a judgment of the court.

Margulies Brothers Ltd v Dafnis Thomaides & Co (UK) Ltd (Court of Appeal, 1958)

There were six contracts of sale between the parties, three for the purchase of cocoa by one party and three for the purchase of cocoa by the other. The contracts were not for specified quantities but were for 'about' figures, ie '3 per cent more or less'. Disputes having arisen, the Board of Appeal of the Cocoa Association of London Ltd made an arbitration award:

'that contracts nos 2101, 2168, 2174 shall be applied against contracts nos 2184, 2207, 2265 respectively and the resultant differences plus interest at eight per cent per annum from 14 December 1957 to date of payment shall be paid by (the applicants) to (the respondents) within seven days and we further award that the fees and expenses of the original arbitration shall be paid by (the respondents)'.

A Queen's Bench master ordered that the above award should be enforced as a judgment of the court in accordance with section 26 of the Arbitration Act 1950. Havers J dismissed an appeal against that order; the Court of Appeal, in a judgment which does not appear to have been reported, allowed an appeal, holding that the award was too uncertain to be enforced as a judgment.

A motion was then made to remit it to the appeal board for calculation of the sum due to be paid.

DIPLOCK J:... This award does not purport to be a mere declaratory award; but although it is one for the payment of money, it does not specify the actual sum to be paid but sets out the manner in which the sum ordered to be paid is to be calculated.

It was determined by the Court of Appeal that an award in this form cannot be enforced in the same manner as a judgment under section 26 of the Arbitration Act 1950; and the purpose of the present application is to get the award amended to a form in which it can be so enforced. The application is resisted on two grounds: first, that the award is complete and valid on its face and the circumstances disclosed give me no jurisdiction to remit it, or, perhaps more accurately, the authorities show that it would be an unjudicial exercise of my discretion if I were to do so; secondly, that in the particular circumstances of this case I ought not to exercise my jurisdiction to remit the award, since the applicants' proper remedy, even if the award were amended, would be to bring an action on the award, and this they can do with the award in its present form....

The contracts are not for fixed quantities of cocoa but for 'about' the specified quantities — 'three per cent more or less' — and could have been performed with least loss to the respondents so far as their sales were concerned by delivery of three per cent less than the specified quantities. The award (and the documents referred to in it) does not, I think, in the absence of extraneous evidence, define what quantity of cocoa within three per cent each way is to be taken into account for the purposes of the calculation. On its face, therefore, I think that there is a good deal to be said for the view that it is uncertain.

Counsel for the respondents argues that, even if there were uncertainty on the face of the award and the documents referred to in it, the parties are agreed as to the method of calculation. The applicants have stated their views as to the method of calculation in an affidavit, and counsel for the respondents agrees with it. This is a matter (he says) like the shares in the ship in *Wohlenberg v Lageman* (1815) which is not in dispute between the parties. It is quite true that the point that the award was uncertain was first raised by me and not by counsel for the applicants. Indeed, the whole basis of his unsuccessful application to enforce the award in the same manner as a judgment which went to the Court of Appeal must, I think, have been that it was certain. But counsel for the applicants is naturally not unwilling to avail himself of the point, even at the eleventh hour, if he can; and I see nothing to stop him from doing so if he wants to. I think that this award on its face is uncertain and comes within the first category approved in *Montgomery, Jones & Co v Liebenthal & Co* (1898) in which awards can be remitted to the arbitrator.

Even if I am wrong in thinking that the award is uncertain on its face, I still think that I have jurisdiction to set it aside. It is, in my view, an implied term of an arbitration agreement made since 1889 (when the provision for enforcing an award in the same manner as a judgment was first introduced) that an award for the payment of money — as contrasted with a mere declaratory award — shall be in a form which is capable of being enforced in the same manner as a judgment. That this remedy should be available is one of the main purposes of an arbitration agreement, and I have no hesitation in holding that I have jurisdiction to remit an award for the payment of money so that it may be amended to put it in a form in which it will be so enforceable...

Order made remitting the award to the appeal board

The form of the award (see LPA 9.2)

If there are two arbitrators, it is preferable that they both sign the award in the same place at the same time.

Eads v Williams (Court of Appeal in Chancery, 1854)

LORD CRANWORTH LC:...I am inclined to think, contrary to my first impression when the matter was stated, that it was also an objection that they did not sign together. On that I give no opinion, for reasons which will appear, inasmuch as it is not necessary to decide it. One objection to the validity of an award, if taken in a proper way, and the parties are not now precluded, is as good as a hundred. I think that there is a great deal of good sense in saying, when a matter is referred to two persons to decide a thing by a statement in writing, that that writing must be made by the two together a contemporaneous act; because if one person signs at York on one day, and another signs at Exeter another day, how are we to know that something may not have occurred in the meantime to induce one party to change his mind if he could. It is the duty of two persons to keep the matter open to the last moment, and it is not competent for the one to sign at one time and the other to sign at another. That is not a question necessary to decide here, but I wish to guard myself against the notion that I do not accede to that as being a correct statement of the law.

An award should not contain more than the arbitrator's decision on the points at issue.

Universal Cargo Carriers Corporation v Pedro Citati (Queen's Bench Division, 1957)

DEVLIN J: In this connection it is not, I hope, out of place for me to comment upon a form of award that appears to me to be in a new style. The award in this case consists of 46 pages of foolscap; and another that I have had before me this term, also by a legal arbitrator, was of the same length. Both these documents are cast as judgments rather than awards; they set out the evidence *in extenso* with the views and comments of the arbitrator on it and on the matters of law discussed. The Court of Appeal has several times said that arbitrators ought not to annex bundles of correspondence to their awards, and I think the same principle applies to extended narratives of evidence.

An award should not have documents annexed to it:

Thomas Borthwick (Glasgow) Ltd v Faure Fairclough Ltd (Queen's Bench Commercial Court 1968)

DONALDSON J: The question comes before the court in an award in the form of a special case stated pursuant to section 21(1) of the Arbitration Act 1950.

The buyers have also moved the court, pursuant to section 22(1) and section 23(2) of the Act, to remit the award or to set it aside.

The contract of 25 January 1966 was on the printed form No 6 issued by the Cattle Food Trade Association (Inc) and is headed:

CONTRACT FOR IMPORTED FEEDING CAKES AND MEALS: CIF TERMS

The contract provides for the settlement of disputes by a two-tier system of arbitration, the award of the arbitrator or umpire being subject to appeal to the Board of Appeal of the association. In the present case the umpire found in favour of the sellers, and the Board of Appeal affirmed that finding subject to the court's decision on the question of law.

In *Oricon Waren-Handelsgesellschaft GmbH v Intergraan NV* (1967) Mr Justice Roskill drew attention to the difficulties which can arise if arbitrators annex to an award in the form of a special case documents which formed the raw material on which they have formulated their findings of fact, as contrasted with documents which are themselves directly relevant to the decision of the question of law, for example, the contract documents. The award in the present case has a bundle of correspondence annexed to it in addition to the copy of the contract and this bundle should not have been before the court. No doubt the decision in the *Oricon* case (*supra*) was not present to the minds of those who drew the award and in the event no difficulty has arisen.

The parties seek to resolve their dispute by arbitration rather than litigation for a number of reasons, and one of those reasons must be assumed to be a desire to ensure that questions of fact are determined by the arbitrators of their choice and not by the court. If the arbitrators submit to the court all or a part of the material upon which they have based their findings of fact, they complicate the task of the court and run the risk of the court inadvertently taking upon itself the fact-finding function with which they have been entrusted by the parties. In drawing attention to the matter again I am not seeking to criticise but only to assist arbitrators in the by no means easy task of stating an award in the form of a special case.

A common practice in maritime arbitrations in London is for arbitrators to make their award and at the same time to explain their decisions to the parties in a separate document. There is apparently no English judgment which considers this practice but the following Australian case would no doubt represent the views of an English court if such an issue were raised.

Madafferi Construction Co v Morling (Supreme Court of Western Australia, 1973)

> In a building dispute, the arbitrator had made his award and at the same time, separately, to both parties delivered a document headed 'Arbitrator's Notes on Award: without prejudice: these notes do not form part of the award and may not be used in any action without my permission'.

FOSTER LCJ: It was contended for the builder that the notes should be read as forming part of the award, notwithstanding the express declaration to the contrary because, it was said, the document itself coupled with its contemporaneous delivery indicated an intent to make it, in truth, part of the award. I am unable to agree. It seems to me the arbitrator has made his meaning clear, not only by his express statement that the notes do not form part of the award, but also by the somewhat inept phrase 'without prejudice' and by directing that the notes may not be used in any action. To add the words 'without my permission' does not depart from the intention thus expressed.

Contents of an award (see LPA 9.2)
Neither the pleadings in a case, nor the contract, form a part of an award unless specifically incorporated.

Belsfield Court Construction Co Ltd v Pywell (Queen's Bench Division, 1969)

The arbitrator's award provided (*inter alia*) as follows:

'NOW I . . . Herbert Anthony Clark . . . having heard and considered all the allegations, witnesses and evidence of both parties find:
A. In respect of the CLAIMANT'S CLAIM as set out in the Schedule of Claimant's Points of Claim and Supplementary Claim for the CLAIMANT as follows:

Item	£	s	d
1. Extra coats emulsion paint	Nil		

[The arbitrator then set out a further 21 items in respect of which he awarded a total of £105 9s 6d]
B. In respect of the RESPONDENT'S COUNTER CLAIM as set out in the Respondent's Claim for Defects and Omissions and Claim for Damages for Delay in Completing Work for the RESPONDENT as follows:

Item	£	s	d
1. Clearing away rubbish etc	20	0	0

[The arbitrator then set out 20 further items, awarding a total of £407 9s 6d, including £156 10s, in respect of damages for delay in completion]

and I:
1. DO HEREBY AWARD AND DETERMINE that the CLAIMANT do pay to the Respondent the sum of THREE HUNDRED AND TWO POUNDS (£302 0s 0d).
2. DO HEREBY DIRECT that the CLAIMANT shall pay the costs of the RESPONDENT and the costs of this Arbitration upon a party and party basis and that
3. The CLAIMANT shall also pay and bear the costs of this my award . . . .'

WILLIS J: This is a motion to set aside an award of an arbitrator, Mr Herbert Anthony Clark, dated 29 January 1969, on the ground that the award, when compared with the issues raised in the applicants' points of claim and the respondent's points of defence, is bad on the face of it, in that it contains statements of mathematical error. It is agreed that there is no error on the face of this award unless the pleadings can be looked at and compared with the award, and if that is permissible [counsel for the plaintiffs] submits that it will be made clear that the arbitrator has gone wrong. So by agreement of both counsel, the first matter which has been argued is whether the pleadings are documents which are so incorporated in this award that I am entitled to look at them.

I am greatly indebted to both counsel for the citation of authorities which bear upon what seems to me to be a very difficult point. The way [counsel] puts his case, as I understand it, primarily at all events, is that pleadings are in a special category and whether they are in fact referred to in any way whatever in the award or not, they must always be available for a court to look at if there is alleged to be an error on the face of the award when compared with the pleadings. If he is wrong about that, he submits that in this case, in accordance with the line of cases in which documents have been held to be so incorporated in the award, they may be looked at, the reference in the award to the pleadings entitles me to look at them. What [counsel] says is that the way in which the arbitrator has referred to the pleadings in the award really invites the reader to look at the pleadings with the award, and, in effect, I think he said that the award cannot really be understood without reference to the pleadings.

I deal with the second submission first. It seems to me in this case that, unless [counsel] can succeed on his first submission, I have to approach the question of the incorporation of the pleadings in this award in the same way in which the courts have approached contracts and particular clauses in contracts. If this is right, it seems to me difficult to bring the so-called 'incorporation' of the pleadings in this case within the category of contracts. The sort of category I have in mind, without referring specifically to the cases, is that which the court was considering in *D.S. Blaiber & Co Ltd v Leopole Newborne (London) Ltd* (1953). It is perhaps useful to refer to that case because the court was there referring to the very early case which is really the *fons et origo* of this particular matter, that is to say, *Hodgkinson v Fernie and another* (1857). The judgments of Mr Justice Williams and the other members of the court all laid down the clear position that the courts are only entitled to interfere with an award of an arbitrator if there is an error of law upon the face of the award. Although the particular exception was referred to by all the learned judges with regret in that case, it has now been accepted by the courts as one in which, even though there is not an error upon the face of the award itself, the document can be looked at if it is incorporated in the award. It is clear, as it seems to me, in the later cases, particularly *F.R. Absalom Ltd v Great Western (London) Garden Village Society Ltd* (1933), and *Champsey Bhara & Co v Jivray Balloo Spinning and Weaving Company Ltd* (1923), that the courts are determined to maintain the position that only within the very limited sphere which I have indicated will they interfere with an arbitrator's award and have set their faces against any extension of that position. I simply refer for the purposes of this part of [counsel's] submission to what Lord Justice Denning (as he then was) said in the *Blaiber* case (*supra*):

'I have a strong suspicion that the arbitrators went wrong in law, but we are not able to say so without looking at the contract, because the terms of the contract may vary the ordinary legal rights and implications. The difficulty is that we are not at liberty to see this contract. It is not expressly incorporated into the award, nor can I see that it is impliedly incorporated. The question whether a contract, or a clause in a contract, is incorporated into an award is a very difficult one. As I read the cases, if the arbitrator says: "On the wording of this clause I hold" so-and-so, then that clause is impliedly incorporated into the award because he invites the reading of it; but if an arbitrator simply says: "I hold that there was a breach of contract", then there is no incorporation.

In this case there is simply a recital of a contract which is not incorporated into the award and therefore we cannot look at it. I have no regrets on this score. . . .'

Now in this case, as it seems to me, the reference to the claimants' claim and the respondent's counterclaim and the itemisation of the 22 items under the claim and the counterclaim is simply a convenient method adopted by the arbitrator of making clear the items in respect of which he was making or not making an award. It is simply an indication that in respect of the matters which were referred to him in detail he has in fact taken them into account in considering the evidence and in considering his final award. That seems to me, with respect to [counsel], to be a long way from the strict approach to the incorporation of the document in the sense that the award can really only be understood by reference to that document: it would have been quite unnecessary for the arbitrator to have made any reference to the pleadings in this case apart from setting out his findings in a convenient form. However, [counsel] has referred me to page 318 of *Russell on Arbitration* (17th edition 1963), in which this passage appears:

'Thus if there are pleadings, and the arbitrator so refers to them as to incorporate them into the award, they may be looked at.'

Reference for that statement is given as *F. R. Absalom Ltd v Great Western (London) Garden Village Society Ltd (supra)* in which Lord Russell of Killowen (and this is really the basis for [counsel's] submission in relation to pleadings) says this:

'There still remains the question whether this error of law is apparent on the face of the award. I think it is. The award recites the contract and refers in terms to the provisions of condition 30.'

Pausing there, there is, as it seems to me, a clear warning in Lord Russell of Killowen's observations up to that point to the specificity of the reference to the document before it can be said to be incorporated. He goes on:

'Condition 30 accordingly is incorporated into and forms part of the award just as if the arbitrator had set it out verbatim and had then proceeded to state the construction which he placed upon it. The court can look at it just as it looked at the answers of the Divisional Court in the *British Westinghouse Co's* case (1912), at the contract in *Landauer v Asser* (1905), and at the pleadings in the *Kelantan* case (1923).'

Not surprisingly, [counsel] relies strongly upon those words and upon the reference to pleadings in *Government of Kelantan v Duff Development Company Ltd* (1923) to which I should refer. The reference in the latter case appears only in one short passage in the speech of the Lord Chancellor. There is nothing in the argument. There is nothing in the headnote which refers to pleadings, but Viscount Cave LC said this:

'The appointment of the arbitrator showed that differences had arisen as to construction, and the arbitrator was appointed to determine those differences. In the pleadings delivered in pursuance of the arbitrator's direction, the questions of construction were again clearly raised.'

It is really from that passage, as I understand it, [that pleadings can] be looked at in the same way as clauses in a contract or a contract. That is really the basis for the submission that, whether pleadings are a special case or not, they are documents which can be looked at, provided they have been so referred to by the arbitrator as to incorporate them into the award.

Looking at this award, I am not prepared to say that the pleadings have been referred to by the arbitrator so as to incorporate them into the award. I am very conscious of the difficulty of construing in any particular case the phrase so 'as to incorporate them into the award', but doing the best I can with the terms of this award, it does not seem to me that they have been referred to in that sense at all.

I pass, therefore, to [counsel's] first submission, namely, that no authority really is required at all for the proposition that pleadings can be looked at in this case because they can be looked at in every case. Pleadings, he says, are documents of such a specialized nature in relation to an arbitration that they can always be looked at, indeed whether the arbitrator has referred to them in the award specifically or by implication or not. In my judgment, there is no basis for that submission to be found in the authorities. At this point in time I would have thought that with a line of cases which starts as far back as 1857, if pleadings are documents which can always be referred to, there would have been some indications of this in the cases to which I have been referred, and if that had been the case, I would not have thought that so authoritative a book as *Russell on Arbitration* would have referred to pleadings at page 318 in the way in which they are there referred to. It is possible, I suppose, that Mr Spafford may be right in this sense, that his first proposition is the explanation of the somewhat cursory manner in which pleadings were dealt with in both *Absalom's* case (*supra*) and the *Kelantan* case (*supra*) but I do not think he is, sympathetic though I am to his submission. I think I am bound to hold that pleadings are not in a special case and that they have got to be looked at in exactly the same narrow and critical way in which the courts have looked at contracts and clauses in contracts.

[It is for] these reasons ... I find that the submissions of [counsel] that the pleadings can be looked at cannot be acceded to. [In] those circumstances it is ... conceded by him that, if I am not entitled to look at the pleadings, there is no error in law on the face of the award, and therefore this motion must fail.

Motion dismissed

A contract is not incorporated into an award unless the arbitrator specifically refers to a clause of it.

D.S. Blaiber & Co Ltd v Leopole Newbourne (London) Ltd (Court of Appeal, 1953)

DENNING LJ: I have a strong suspicion that the arbitrators went wrong in law, but we are not able to say so without looking at the contract, because the terms of the contract may vary the ordinary legal rights and implications. The difficulty is that we are not at liberty to see this contract. It is not expressly incorporated into the award, nor can I see that it is impliedly incorporated. The question whether a contract, or a clause in a contract, is incorporated into an award is a very difficult one. As I read the cases, if the arbitrator says: 'on the wording of this clause I hold' so-and-so, then that clause is impliedly incorporated into the award because he invites the reading of it; but if an arbitrator simply says: 'I hold that there was a breach of contract', then there is no incorporation.

In this case, there is simply a recital of a contract which is not incorporated into the award and therefore we cannot look at it. I have no regrets on this score. It seems to me that, when traders go to lay arbitrators to decide a dispute between them, then the matter ought in the ordinary way to be left to those lay arbitrators without their decision being queried thereafter in point of law. The lay arbitrators have decided according to the justice of the case as they see it. If people want to raise points of law then they ought to ask at the time for a case to be stated on a point of law. If no such request is made, they should leave the law to the arbitrators. Applications should not be encouraged which seek to set aside the award on the ground of error on the face of it in point of law.

I agree, therefore, that the appeal should be dismissed.

SOMERVILL AND ROMER LJJ delivered similar judgments.

Appeal dismissed

If any document such as a contract is intended to be incorporated in an award, it should be appended or set out in full.

Giacomo Costa Fu Andrea v British Italian Trading Co Ltd (Court of Appeal, 1962)

> A motion to the High Court asked for an award to be set aside, *inter alia*, on the ground that there was an error of law on the face of it if the contract was read as part of the award. The motion was rejected on appeal.

DIPLOCK LJ: It seems to me, therefore, that on the cases there is none which compels us to hold that a mere reference to the contract in the award entitles us to look at the contract. It may be that in particular cases a specific reference to a particular clause of a contract may incorporate the contract, or that clause of it, in the award. I think that we are driven back to first principles in this matter namely, that an award can only be set aside for error which is on its face. It is true that an award can incorporate another document so as to entitle one to read that document as part of the award and, by reading them together, find an error on the fact of the award. But the question whether a contract, or a clause in a contract, is incorporated in the award is a question of construction of the award. It seems to me that the test is put as conveniently as it can be in the words of Denning LJ which I have already cited from *Blaiber & Co Ltd v Leopole Newborne (London) Ltd* (1953):

> 'As I read the cases, if the arbitrator says: "On the wording of this clause I hold" so and so, then that clause is impliedly incorporated into the award because he invites the reading of it'.

I, therefore, apply that principle to the award in the present case — that is to say the award of the Board of Appeal, incorporating that of the umpire, in which he says 'I hereby award that buyers have failed to declare the final port of destination by 1 February 1961'. This is a finding of fact, and there is nothing about any clause of the contract there. Then he goes on to state the consequences of that finding — 'and therefore the contract is void'. There is no reference to any specific provision of the contract from which that consequence flows. It seems to me that it is quite impossible to say, reading those words, that he has incorporated the contract in the award, in the sense that he has invited those reading the award to read the contract.

This case seems to me to be far away from either [*Absalom v Great Western Garden Village* (1933)] or [*Landauer v Asson* (1905)] or [*Hillas & Co Ltd v Arcos* (1932)]. The principle of reading contracts or other documents into the award is not, in my judgment, one to be encouraged or extended and in my view, we are not entitled in this court on any award where there is a purely general reference to 'the contract' — and a reference only in that part of the award which deals with the consequences of the finding of fact — to look at the contract and search it in order to see whether there is an error of law. . . . .

PEARSON LJ agreed.

SELLERS LJ: . . . With regard to error of law on the face of the award, it seems to me that the law with regard to which one has to look at is clear. The difficulty is in its application. In *Champsey Bhara & Co v Jivraj Balloo Spinning & Weaving Co Ltd* (1923), to which reference has been made Lord Dunedin said:

> 'An error of law on the face of the award means . . . that one can find in the award, or a document actually incorporated thereto, as, for instance, a note appended by the arbitrator stating the reasons for his judgment, some legal proposition which is the basis of the award and which one can then say is erroneous. It does not mean if in a narrative a reference is made to a contention of one party that opens the door to seeing, first, what that contention is, and then going to the contract on which the parties' rights depend to see if that contention is sound'.

Neither does it open the door to look at a contract because it happens to be mentioned in the recital, or mentioned in what is in effect the conclusion or the order which the award makes. The difficulty is in its application — not, I think, whether any particular document has been expressly incorporated in an award but whether it has, in the circumstances, to be regarded as the intention of the tribunal which made the award to include the document in question as part of its award and its reasoning. Of course if any document is intended to form part of an award, it should be, if things are properly conducted, appended or set out in full. It should be made clear that it is the intention of the award that the document should be actually incorporated into it. It is only infrequently, I hope, that an arbitrator or tribunal making an award fails to include in an award all the relevant matters which it intended so to do. In this case I find no difficulty in agreeing entirely with the learned judge that the contract was not incorporated, or intended to be incorporated, in this award, and I would uphold the learned judge's decision on that head without any qualification. . . .

Appeal dismissed

Interest on claims (see LPA 9.3)

An arbitrator has power to include in his award interest on damages or debt and at any rate he sees fit up to the date of his award.

There appears to have been no doubt about this earlier (see *Beahan Wolfe* (1832), *Sherry v Okes* (1835) and *Armitage v Walker* (1855)) or from the date of the Common Law Procedure Act 1850 until the Arbitration Act 1934. However in *Podar Trading Co v Tagher* (1949) the Queen's Bench Divisional Court, presided over by Lord Goddard LCJ, decided otherwise. Their error was corrected by the Court of Appeal in the following case.

Chandris v Isbrandtsen-Moller Co (Court of Appeal, 1950)

DENNING LJ: . . . . I cannot see why any distinction should be drawn between the duty of an arbitrator to give effect to such statutes as the Statute of Limitations and his jurisdiction in his discretion to award interest. An award of interest is only a part of the damages recoverable and, adapting to the facts of this case the language of Lord Salvesen in the case to which I have just referred — language which was approved by Lord Maugham — it would read as follows:

> 'Although the Law Reform (Miscellaneous Provisions) Act 1934 does not in terms apply to arbitrations, I think that in mercantile references of the kind in question it is an implied term of the contract that the arbitrator must decide the dispute according to the existing law of contract, and that every right and discretionary remedy given to a court of law can be exercised by him.

To that there are certain well-known exceptions, such as the right to grant an injunction, which stand on a different footing. One of the reasons why an arbitrator cannot give an injunction is that he has no power to enforce it, but such an objection does not apply to an award of interest.

This matter was dealt with fully by Lord Goddard CJ in delivering judgment of the court in the *Podar* case (*supra*). He dealt with the power to give interest at common law and under the Civil Procedure Act 1833, and he then proceeded to say:

> 'The case which would seem to be directly in point is *Edwards v Great Western Ry Co* (1851). In that case the court approved of the allowance of interest by an arbitrator because it was allowable in the circumstances of that case by the provisions of the Civil Procedure Act 1833. Accordingly, we think we must take it to be the law that before the Law Reform

(Miscellaneous Provisions) Act 1934 an arbitrator had the same powers as the court with regard to the award of interest, but no greater power.'

The Lord Chief Justice then goes on to deal with the Law Reform (Miscellaneous Provisions) Act 1934 and he said:

'Moreover, sections 28 and 29 of the Civil Procedure Act are repealed, we feel driven to hold that not only have arbitrators no power to give interest on damages, but they have been deprived of the powers which they had so long as the sections of the Civil Procedure Act were in force and can now only give it in circumstances in which it was recoverable at common law'.

Counsel for the charterers argued that that judgment was based on the assumption that it was the Civil Procedure Act 1833 which gave the arbitrator his power to award interest and that, once that Act was repealed, all such powers had gone, and unless the arbitrator had been given fresh powers, he had none. I think, however, that the real basis of *Edwards v Great Western Ry Co (supra)* was that the arbitrator derived his powers, not from the Act of 1833, but from the submission to him which necessarily gave him the 'implied powers' referred to in the language of Lord Salvesen which I have just quoted, and I see no reason why, since the Act of 1934, an arbitrator should not be deemed impliedly to have the same powers. Therefore, with diffidence, having regard to the view expressed by the Divisional Court on this matter, I have come to the conclusion that in such a case as the present the arbitrator has power to award interest and accordingly to that extent, I think this appeal should succeed and the *Podar* case (*supra*) be overruled.

COHEN LJ: I am of the same opinion. I agree with counsel for the claimant that this case is really decided for us by the decision of the Court of Common Pleas in 1851 in *Edwards v Great Western Ry Co (supra).* That case is not binding on us, but it had stood unchallenged for over eighty years when the Law Reform (Miscellaneous Provisions) Act 1934 was passed, and I agree with the words of Lord Goddard CJ when he stated in the *Podar* case (*supra*) that before the Act of 1934 an arbitrator had the same powers as a jury to give interest. I think the Court of Common Bench reached its conclusion, not because it thought that as a matter of construction of the Civil Procedure Act 1833, sections 28 and 29, the arbitrator fell within the description of a 'jury on the trial of any issue, or on any inquisition of damages', but because it considered that an arbitrator had all the powers in regard to awarding damages which a jury had. In this connection it is to be remembered that in 1833 all relevant cases would have been heard by a judge with a jury. In my view, the decision of the court was not based on any statute, but the court considered that, apart from any statute, an arbitrator had all the powers of the appropriate court including the power to award interest in the cases indicated.

By the Law Reform (Miscellaneous Provisions) Act 1934, sections 28 and 29 of the Civil Procedure Act 1833 were repealed, and in lieu there has been substituted section 3 of the Act of 1934 which provides:

'(1)   In any proceedings tried in any court of record for the recovery of any debt or damages, the court may, if it thinks fit, order that there shall be included in the sum for which judgment is given interest at such rate as it thinks fit on the whole or any part of the debt or damages for the whole or any part of the period between the date when the cause of action arose and the date of the judgment.'

The Divisional Court had decided in the passage which my Lord has read that the effect of that sub-section is to deprive the arbitrator of the power to award damages in accordance with the Civil Procedure Act 1833, sections 28 and 29, without conferring on him the increased powers conferred by the sections on a court of record. The Divisional Court arrived at that conclusion with reluctance, and I am glad not to feel myself compelled to agree with it. The section does not purport to deal in any way with the powers of arbitrators. It may, of course, have curtailed their powers, but I do not think that in the present case it has done so.

In my opinion, the right of arbitrators to award interest was not derived from the Civil Procedure Act 1833, sections 28 and 29, but from the rule that arbitrators had the powers of the appropriate court in the matter of awarding interest. In my opinion, therefore, the effect of the Act of 1934 is that, after it came into force, an arbitrator had no longer the powers of awarding interest damages conferred on juries by the Civil Procedure Act 1833, sections 28 and 29, but he had the power conferred on the appropriate court in the Act of 1934 described as a court of record. The change of description may be due to the fact that damages are now usually awarded by a judge sitting alone. I agree with my Lord that, for the reasons he has given, the conclusion we have reached is supported by the decision in the *Naamlooze* case [*Chandris v Isbrandtsen-Moller Co Inc,* 1951], and I cannot help thinking that if the attention of the Divisional Court had been directed to that case, they might have reached a different conclusion. For those reasons, and for the reasons given by my Lord, I think this appeal should succeed.

ASQUITH LJ: I agree. I should have found it very difficult to resist the argument presented by counsel for the respondents if *Edwards v Great Western Ry Co (supra)* had not been decided as it was and had not stood unchallenged for over three-quarters of a century before the Act of 1934. But for those circumstances it would have been difficult, it seems to me, to resist a construction of section 3(1) of the Act of 1934 which would limit the discretion conferred by that section. But by parity of reason the right given by the Act of 1833 should have been limited to proceedings before a jury yet, in the *Edwards* case, that contention was impliedly or expressly rejected, and it was held that an arbitrator could award interest in cases in which, by statute, a jury was given power to do so.

For those reasons, and for the reasons given by my Lords, I think this appeal should succeed.

Appeal allowed with costs

An arbitrator should include interest in an award at a reasonable commercial rate from the date when the money should have been paid until the date of the award.

The Myron (Queen's Bench Division, 1969)

DONALDSON J: All matters of costs in the arbitration and interest upon any money found due are for the arbitrators or umpire. However, it may assist if I express my views upon the principles which are applicable. It is of paramount importance to the speedy settlement of disputes that a respondent who is found to be under a liability to a claimant should gain no advantage and that the claimant should suffer no corresponding detriment as a results of delay in reaching a decision. Accordingly, awards should in general include an order that the respondent pay interest on the sum due from the date when the money should have been paid. The rate of interest is entirely in the discretion of the arbitrators, but I personally take the view that in an era of high and fluctuating interest rates the principle which I have expressed is best implemented by an award of interest 'at a rate one per cent in excess of the Bank of England discount rate for the time being in force'. When interest is awarded arbitrators commonly award it for a period ending with the date of the award.

'A sum directed to be paid by an award shall, unless the award otherwise directs, carry interest as from the date of the award and at the same rate as a judgment debt': section 20, Arbitration Act 1950.

The plain meaning of this section would appear to be that the arbitrator is at liberty to specify the rate of interest an award shall bear, but if his award is silent on this point it bears interest at the same rate as a judgment does.

That, at any rate, was the view of one experienced commercial judge.

The Myron (Queen's Bench Division, 1969)

DONALDSON J: The consequence is that, unless there is a direction to the contrary, the award carries interest at the rate of 4 per cent per annum from the date of the award until payment (see Judgments Act 1838, section 17). With bank rate at its present level, this is a positive disincentive to payment. . . .

It would seem from the terms of section 20 of the Arbitration Act 1950 that arbitrators, unlike a judge, can, in addition to awarding interest, direct that the award itself carry interest at a specified rate in excess of that prescribed for judgments and this is a power which, if it exists, might well be used generally.

However, a majority in the House of Lords decided otherwise.

Timber Shipping Co v London Freighters Ltd (House of Lords, 1971)

The arbitrator in exercise of his powers under section 20 had awarded interest at 8 per cent from the date of his award at a time when the court and counsel concerned believed (incorrectly) that the current rate on judgments was 4 per cent. Unknown to any of them, the rate had been raised by statutory instrument SI 1971/491 Judgment Debts (Rate of Interest) Order to 7½ per cent.

LORD WILBERFORCE: The decision on the second question depends on the proper interpretation of section 20 of the Arbitration Act 1950 which provides:

A sum directed to be paid by an award shall, unless the award otherwise directs, carry interest as from the date of the award and at the same rate as a judgment debt.

Are the words wide enough not merely to give a discretion to an arbitrator to decide whether the award will carry interest but to give him a general discretion to direct that his award should carry interest at whatever rate he chooses to fix? In my view they are not. My first impression to that effect remains as my second impression. The words seem to me to assume the making of an award as the completion of the arbitrator's function and to provide that so far as interest is concerned the award will be equated with a judgment unless the award otherwise directs. The result will be that in the absence of a direction to the contrary an award will carry interest from its date as though it were a judgment and at the rate as though it were a judgment. The arbitrator has a veto by the exercise of which he may direct that the award will not carry interest at all. Unless he so directs the award will automatically carry interest at the same rate as a judgment debt.

If a general discretion were being conferred there would have been no necessity to make any reference at all to a judgment debt. Furthermore, the use of the word 'otherwise' suggests to my mind not a range and diversity both as to rates and dates of possible orders as to the awarding of interest, but a choice between the two alternative courses of equating the award (in this respect) with a judgment debt, with an automatic date and rate of interest bearing, or of directing that this automatic rate is not to follow.

If this were your Lordships' view there would remain the question as to how to give effect to it. The result would be that the arbitrators had no power to award interest at the rate of 8 per cent in relation to the period after the date of their award though their award of interest at that rate down to the date of their award was within their power. Their award was:

'that the Charterers do pay interest on the said sum at the rate of 8 per
cent per annum from 1 June 1969 until the said capital sum shall in
fact be paid'

On the view which I have expressed, and that which I understand others of
your Lordships hold, the award of interest at the rate of 8 per cent should only
have been made for the period down to the date of the award (which was 6 January 1970) interest as on and at the rate applicable to a judgment debt would
then by reason of section 20 be payable in respect of the period subsequent to
6 January 1960. It would be unfortunate if some mere technicality involved
the necessity of further proceedings with a possible consequence of a result
which would differ from that which on your Lordships' view of the law would
have been correct and should have followed. Any more fruitless expenditure
of time and money should if possible be avoided. . . . .

Power to correct slips (see LPA 9.5)

The power contained in section 17 of the Arbitration Act 1950 (formerly section 7 of the 1889 Act) for an arbitrator to correct 'slips' in his award does not empower him to alter it so as to correct errors in expressing his intention.

Sutherland & Co v Hannevig Bros Ltd (King's Bench Division, 1920)

Motion to set aside an award.

ROWLATT J: In this case an extremely difficult and important question has arisen with regard to the extent of the powers conferred on arbitrators by clause (c) of section 7 of the Arbitration Act 1889. Section 7 of the Act of 1889 provides that:

> 'The arbitrators or umpire acting under a submission shall, unless the submission expresses a contrary intention, have power . . . to correct in an award any clerical mistake or error arising from any accidental slip or omission.'

On the construction of those words as a matter of grammar 'clerical' belongs to 'mistake' only, and "error arising from any accidental slip or omission" is a second and independent limb of the clause. The words of the clause are similar to those found in Rules of the Supreme Court Order 28, rule 11 and, in my opinion, the greater part of the difficulty has arisen owing to the extent of the meaning which has been given to the words of that order. I cannot help feeling that, as applied to arbitrators, the words ought to be construed rather strictly. Before the passing of the Arbitration Act 1889, it is clear that the courts regarded it as very dangerous to allow arbitrators to alter or amend their awards after they had made them. The well-known case on that point is *Mordue v Palmer* (1870). In that case the error corrected by the arbitrator arose from the mistake of a clerk in copying the draft award, and it was held that the arbitrator could not put the mistake right, being *functus officio*. Such a state of things as that has been clearly altered by section 7, clause (c) of the Arbitration Act 1889. The difficulty, however, which still remains is to see how far the alteration has gone.

In the present case, the arbitrator made an award and he included in his award certain costs incurred in a matter between one of the parties and a third party, and the question arose whether the words he had used included all those costs or only some of them. The award was sent back to the arbitrator and he told Mr Lewis, of the firm of solicitors representing the respondents, that he certainly had made an error in writing his award, and he amended it so that it read, as he said, as he had originally intended that it should read. That was not correcting a clerical mistake within the meaning of clause (c) of section 7 of the Act of 1889. What is meant there is something almost mechanical — a slip of the pen or something of that kind. Then the question is did the arbitrator correct an error arising from an accidental slip or omission? Here we get upon ground which is almost metaphysical. An accidental slip implies that something has been wrongly put in by accident, and an accidental omission implies that something has been left out by accident. That raises a further question, namely: what is an accident in this connection, an accident affecting the expression of a man's thought?

Such an accident is a very difficult thing to define, but I am of opinion that what took place in connection with the award in this case was not an accident within the meaning of the clause. I cannot pretend to give a formula which will cover every case, but in this case there was nothing omitted by accident. The arbitrator, in fact, wrote down exactly what he intended to write down, although it is doubtful what that really meant when considered from a legal point of view; and he has now really assumed a jurisdiction to expound what he had purposely written down. That is a thing which he has no jurisdiction to do. Counsel for the respondents has contended that it was by inadvertence that the arbitrator did not put down all that he meant to put down. I am of opinion that inadvertence is not the right word to use in this case. A man may inadvertently write down a word which, if he had thought more about the matter, he would have written differently, but that merely means that he has gone wrong. I am of opinion that, in substance, the arbitrator assumed a jurisdiction which he did not possess, namely, to insert in the award an exposition of his words, because he found the words that he had used were not so well chosen as they might and ought to have been if chosen after further deliberation. The motion succeeds, and the award must be set aside.

MCCARDIE J. concurred.

Award set aside

PART VII

Costs of arbitrations

'. . . there is a settled practice of the courts that in the absence of special circumstances a successful litigant should receive his costs, and that it is necessary to show some grounds for exercising the discretion of refusing an order which would give them to him, and the discretion must be judicially exercised. Those words "judicially exercised" are always somewhat difficult to apply, but they mean that the arbitrator must not act capriciously and must, if he is going to exercise his discretion, show a reason connected with the case and one which the court can see is a proper reason.'

Lord Goddard LCJ in *Lewis v Haverfordwest RDC* (1953)

How an arbitrator's discretion as to costs should be exercised (see LPA 10.2)

An arbitrator ought not without special reasons deprive a successful party of his costs, still less award costs to a completely unsuccessful one.

Pepys v London Transport Executive (Court of Appeal, 1975)

A claim for compensation for injurious affection caused by the construction of the Victoria Line extension of the underground was referred to the Lands Tribunal which has power to receive 'sealed offers' under its statutory rules (an arbitrator has no such power). A sealed offer was made but the claimant was awarded nothing; nevertheless the tribunal gave her costs up to the date of the sealed offer.

LORD DENNING MR: . . . . . London Transport had won, yet they were ordered to pay those costs. They wrote to ask the President of the Lands Tribunal whether that was a slip. The reply was that it was a matter in the tribunal's discretion and was not to be altered. So London Transport asked for a case to be stated on the question whether the tribunal 'properly ordered the acquiring authority to pay the claimant her costs up to the date of the sealed offer, having regard to the provisions of section 4 of the Land Compensation Act 1961'.

The Lands Tribunal Act 1949 and the Lands Tribunal Rules made under it give the tribunal quite a wide discretion as to costs.

The practice of the courts, as also of tribunals and arbitrators, is that if a plaintiff or claimant fails altogether, no order is made whereby the successful party is to pay the costs of the plaintiff or claimant, except for very special reasons. If that rule is departed from, the tribunal or arbitrator or whoever it might be ought to set out the reasons, particularly where there is an appeal on costs to a higher court or tribunal which will want to see whether they are proper reasons. . . . .

No sufficient reasons have been vouchsafed here, either in the case stated or in the letter from the Lands Tribunal registrar, as to why the tribunal should have ordered London Transport to pay Dr Pepys's costs up to the date of the sealed offer. That part of the order cannot stand, leaving only the order that, from the date when the sealed offer was communicated, Dr Pepys should pay the costs.

ROSKILL LJ concurred.

SIR JOHN PENNYCUICK: If the tribunal awards costs to an unsuccessful claimant, it should give reasons for so doing. In the present case the tribunal did give a reason — but it was a bad reason. The fact that an acquiring authority had seen fit to make an unconditional offer which was not accepted by the claimant was clearly not of itself a good reason for ordering the authority to pay the claimant's costs up to the date of the offer.

The appeal was allowed

Where there are 'string contracts' of sale and the arbitration relates to whether the goods are of contract quality, each party is entitled to receive the costs he has to pay out to the previous party and not merely his costs against his supplier.

L.E. Cattan Ltd v A. Michaelides & Co (a firm) (third party, Turkie; fourth party, George, trading as Yarns & Fibres Co) (Queen's Bench Division, 1958)

An action commenced by specially endorsed High Court Writ was remitted by consent of all parties to the tribunal of arbitration of the Manchester Chamber of Commerce.

The arbitrator made an award which contained the words:

'viii: that the defendants shall pay the plaintiffs costs of and incidental to this reference and to the said action but not including the amount paid by the plaintiffs to the third party under paragraph (vi) hereof. By that paragraph (vi) the plaintiffs were condemned to pay the costs of the third party'.

DIPLOCK J: Counsel for the plaintiffs submitted that the order in regard to the plaintiffs' costs (paragraph (vii) of the award) was a very odd order for costs. The oddity is that, whereas the third party has recovered his costs against the plaintiffs, and also the costs which he has been ordered to pay to the fourth party, the plaintiffs are not entitled to recover any of those costs against the defendants, who set the train of actions in motion. Counsel says that in a particular case an arbitrator or a judge may say that the plaintiffs should not pay the costs of the defendants' third-party proceedings on the ground that such proceedings were unjustified for a number of reasons; but, he says, it is wholly inconsistent with that principle that the plaintiffs in the present case should be compelled to pay the costs of the fourth party when they were not responsible for him being made a party to the proceedings.

The order in regard to the plaintiffs' costs strikes me as very remarkable, but it was contended by counsel for the defendants that my jurisdiction to remit the award back to the arbitrator was limited to cases where I came to the conclusion that there could be no possible reason for an award in the form in which the arbitrator had made it. . . .

This is a border-line case. This award is, I think, a speaking award. The arbitrator has not limited himself to awarding that the counterclaim be disallowed and that the consequences as to costs follow, but has put forward, I think, the findings on which his award is based and in particular the finding that, consequent on the finding that the counterclaim fails, the questions of indemnity by the third party to the plaintiffs, and by the fourth party to the third party, do not arise. On those findings — and they represent the only findings in the case — it seems to me that the award as to costs clearly cannot stand. It would be an injudicial exercise of discretion to award against the plaintiffs and third party's costs, including the costs of the fourth party, and not to award to the plaintiffs against the defendants the plaintiffs' costs including the costs of the third and fourth party proceedings, which the plaintiffs have been compelled to pay. On those findings it is impossible, in my view, to draw the distinction which the arbitrator has drawn between the position of the third party and that of the plaintiffs as regards the costs of the further proceedings. I think, therefore, that that part of the award which deals with costs should be remitted to the arbitrator for his reconsideration.

In remitting that part of the award, I think that I should make these observations about the way in which costs should be dealt with where third, fourth, fifth and sixth parties have been brought in in these string contract cases, which are very common. In doing so, I want to make it clear that I am not seeking to substitute my discretion for that of the arbitrator, or to suggest that there may not be reasons in some circumstances for making a different award. In the ordinary way, however, where damages are claimed for breach of contract on one contract in a string of contracts, and the seller brings in his immediate seller as a third party, and the third party brings in his immediate seller as a fourth party, then, provided that the contracts are the same or substantially the same so that the issue whether the goods comply with a description is the same, the defendant (in this case it was the plaintiffs because it was a counterclaim), if successful, should recover against the plaintiffs not only his costs but any costs of the third party which he has been ordered to pay; the third party in like manner should recover from the defendant his own costs and any costs of the fourth party which he has been compelled to pay, and so on down the string. That is the normal way in which costs should be dealt with in this kind of action where there is a string of contracts in substantially the same terms. In saying that, I am not excluding the possibility that there may be special reasons for departing from normal practice. Whether it was reasonable for the defendant to bring in a third party at all is always a question to be considered, and that is a matter on which a lot of facts may be relevant.

Why I think that it is plain that the arbitrator cannot have applied the right principles in this case is the fact that the award as to costs is inconsistent, in that it has adopted one method towards the plaintiffs — who were the defendants to the counterclaim — and another method towards the third party. I think, therefore, that this is a case where I should, in the exercise of my discretion under section 22(1) of the Arbitration Act 1950, remit to the arbitrator for further consideration part of his award, namely, paragraphs (vi), (vii) and

(viii) which deal with costs. I do not think that I should limit myself to remitting merely paragraph (vii) which relates to the defendants' costs, because there may be matters unknown to me which will affect the matter of costs or which he may think, in his discretion, should affect the matter of costs.

Part of the award remitted

It is no ground for depriving a successful claimant of his costs in a building dispute that the builder was given no opportunity of putting right the defects.

Dineen v Walpole (Court of Appeal, 1969)

The award of the arbitrator read:

> 'I award the Claimant D. M. Dineen against the Respondents the sum of Forty Pounds . . . to put right the items under clause 3 of the Points of Claim under (a), (b) and (c). I award that the costs of the arbitration be paid by the Claimant'.

DAVIES LJ: What apparently was argued before the arbitrator — the argument that succeeded — was that, despite the fact that the respondent had failed on liability by reason of the matters pleaded in the points of defence (what I might call the history and all the circumstances), the claimant not merely should not be awarded his costs but ought to be ordered to pay the whole of the costs.

Those are the facts that were before the arbitrator. In a couple of sentences, what the respondent was saying was: 'You did not give me notice in time (he is technically wrong about that) but when you did give me notice I was ready and willing to do the work if you had only given me an opportunity. I still am ready and willing, and you ought not to have brought these arbitration proceedings which are premature'. It is to be supposed that, although he found against the respondent on liability, it was considerations of that kind that led the arbitrator to make the award which he did.

[Counsel], who has said everything that could be said on behalf of the builder in this case, makes, I think, two submissions. First he says that, in order to displace the order made by the arbitrator in the exercise of his discretion, there is an onus upon the claimant to show that there were no materials on which the arbitrator could exercise that discretion. For myself, I doubt whether that is correct. It seems to me, from a consideration of the authorities to which we have been usefully referred by learned counsel, that before such a drastic order as this can be made it must be shown on behalf of the person seeking the order that there were materials on which the discretion could be exercised in the way it was. But I do not think that this case falls to be decided on any question of onus. We have had all the correspondence and all the factors put before us, and at the end of it all I have come to the conclusion that in fact there were no materials in the instant case on which the arbitrator could so order. . . .

Part of the award set aside

Failure to award costs (see LPA 10.1)

An arbitrator who does not deal with costs has not adjudicated upon all matters referred to him.

Re Becker Shillan & Co and Barry Bros (King's Bench Division, 1920)

ROWLATT J: This is a motion to remit an award to an umpire on the ground that he has not dealt with all the matters referred to him. He has awarded in favour of the buyers, and has made an award with regard to the costs of the award, including the expenses of the hire of the room for the arbitration and the shorthand notes. It is said that he has not made any award with reference generally to the costs of the parties to the reference. The case was an important one. It was attended by counsel on either side, and it involved the examination of a number of documents. It was not a trade arbitration depending upon the inspection of goods. It was a litigation extending over five days, and the costs of the parties to the reference must have been very considerable. That being so, I do not think that, upon the terms of the award, one can read it as having dealt with the costs by leaving them where they fell. I think the award must be read as not having dealt with these costs at all. In these circumstances it seems to me that we are bound by authority to say that the umpire has not adjudicated on all the matters referred to him. . . . One of the terms was that the costs of the reference and award should be in the discretion of the arbitrator. That does not mean that it is in his discretion whether he will deal with them or not, but that he must deal with them by exercising his discretion upon them, if he likes, by saying that he leaves them to be borne by the parties who incurred them, and making no order that either party should pay the other. But he must exercise his discretion . . . I think that this case must go back to the umpire.

MCCARDIE J: I agree. The buyers and the sellers agree to submit to the umpire all matters in dispute between them with reference to a contract for Australian honey. No express reference to costs was made in the submission. The arbitration proceeded and occupied five days. Heavy correspondence was put in, counsel were employed, and the costs were heavy. The umpire has delivered his award and by it he has dealt with certain costs which I may call his personal costs, together with the costs of the arbitrators, the cost of the shorthand writer, who no doubt had given him a copy of the notes, the hire of the arbitration room, and the expenses of the award; in other words, he dealt with the minor or personal costs of the reference, but with the serious matter of the costs of the parties he did not deal at all. The sellers were successful; the buyers recovered nothing against them. The sellers now seek to remit the award to the umpire in order that he may consider whether they ought not to receive the costs. The ground upon which the award must be remitted to the arbitrators is that an award, in order to be valid, must deal with all the matters referred. The point here taken by counsel for the buyers is that the umpire has failed to carry out that requirement. . . .

In my view, it would be most unsatisfactory to infer from his silence that he has dealt with them. Upon the face of the matter it is clear that the successful sellers should *prima facie* get their costs. They had had vast expense and had defeated a claim for over £8,000. Can it be supposed that the umpire is to deprive them of costs by mere silence? I cannot think so. In my view it is reasonably clear that the umpire has not dealt at all with the question of the successful seller's costs. . . . In my view it is reasonably clear that we are justified in remitting it under section 10(1) of the Act of 1889, and in so doing we incidentally approve of the view taken by Moulton LJ, in *Warburg & Co v McKerrow & Co* (1904). The award must be remitted to the umpire.

Award remitted

But now see section 18(4) of the Arbitration Act 1950:

'If no provision is made by an award in respect of costs of the reference, any party to the reference may, within fourteen days of the publication of the award, or such further time as the High Court or a judge thereof may direct, apply to the arbitrator for an order directing by and to whom these costs shall be paid, and thereupon the arbitrator shall, after hearing any party who may desire to be heard, amend his award by adding thereto such directions as he may think proper with respect to the payment of costs of the reference'.

Costs of the reference and costs of the award (see LPA 10.1)

There is no distinction in principle between the costs of the reference and the costs of award; it is only a matter of convenience that they are often dealt with separately.

Smeaton, Hanscomb & Co v Sassoon I. Setty, Son & Co (No 2) (Queen's Bench Division, 1953)

An arbitrator had given his award in the form of a case stated and, as to costs, had ordered:

'However the court answers the three questions or any of them I award and direct that each party shall bear their own costs of the arbitration and that the sellers shall pay the costs of this my award.'

DEVLIN J: . . . In *Lloyd del Pacifico v Board of Trade* (1953) Mr Justice Wright laid it down as a principle that an arbitrator's discretion as to costs must be exercised judicially, and he set aside the part of the award in that case which dealt with costs on the ground that the umpire had not exercised his discretion judicially; and that principle was followed by Mr Justice Atkinson in the case of *Stotesbury v Turner* (1943). In the latest edition of *Russell on Arbitration*, the 15th edition, the principle is stated at page 233 in the following terms:

'The discretion must be exercised judicially, and it will be reviewed by the court to the same extent as a judge's order as to costs will be reviewed upon an appeal.'

That principle [counsel] has not disputed, but he does dispute its application in this case and, I think, mainly upon two grounds. The first of them is that he distinguishes between the costs of the arbitration or the reference and the costs of the award. He concedes that if a successful defendant is made to pay a part of the unsuccessful plaintiff's costs it is not *prima facie* (unless there are, of course, some exceptional grounds) a judicial exercise of his discretion. But he says that that principle does not apply to the costs of the award, which stand upon a different footing.

I do not feel able to draw any distinction in principle between the costs of the award and the costs of the reference. It is a mere matter of convenience, I think, that the costs of the award are kept separate. They are usually kept separate because the parties have to pay the arbitrator directly, and the practice is now universal that the award is not handed over except to a party who takes it up and tenders the necessary payment of the arbitrator's costs. It is, therefore, convenient that the costs of the award shall be set out separately and mentioned in the award; but in principle I think they are just as much costs in the arbitration as court fees are costs in the action. I see, therefore, no grounds for drawing any distinction there. . . .

Reasons for award of costs (see LPA 10.3)

There are grounds on which a successful plaintiff can properly be deprived of all or part of his costs, but the court is not entitled to require an arbitrator to state his reasons where the award is silent.

Matheson & Co Ltd v A. Tabah & Sons (Queen's Bench Division, 1963)

MEGAW J: The position in law as I understand it on the authorities in relation to the awarding of costs is that in an arbitration the principles on which the arbitrator has got to act are identical with the principles on which a judge in a court has got to act in awarding costs. Where a party is successful, by which I understand to be meant that he obtains judgment for a sum of money, in the ordinary way, he is entitled to recover the costs which he has incurred in the proceedings which have been necessary for him to obtain an order for the payment of that sum to which he is entitled. But that is subject of course to exceptions and provisos in relation to particular cases. If, for example, the claim has been grossly exaggerated and the award is for a much smaller sum than the award claimed, that is a factor which the court is entitled to take into consideration in depriving a successful claimant of his costs or of part of them. There are all kinds of other matters which may also properly be considered in the exercise of the court's discretion. They would include the conduct of the parties in the course of the hearing, they would include questions whether one particular facet of the claim failed on which a large amount of time had been spent and so forth. The principles which an arbitrator is, by his legal duty, obliged to apply are the same but there is this difference in practice that whereas if a judge in court makes what I may call an unusual order for costs, such as depriving a successful claimant of his costs or a large part of them, the judge would normally be expected to indicate his reasons for following that course and his decision would of course be available to a higher court, and if that court took the view that he had applied the wrong principle having regard to the matters which he had stated as being his grounds for decision, or if it were apparent from the proceedings in the court that he had applied a wrong principle or had failed to act on a proper principle, then his award as to costs could and would be upset.

But it has been held by authority by which I am undoubtedly bound that, where there is an order as to costs in an arbitration and that order is challenged in the court, the court is not entitled to require the arbitrator to state the reasons why he made that order . . . .

I, therefore, have to decide this matter on the material before me, and as I understand it I have got to look at the award and what is said in the award in order to see whether anything there appears which makes it clear that the arbitrator was exercising his discretion without the material on which he could properly exercise it. . . .

In *Perry v Stopher* (1959) . . . the Court of Appeal, having heard that the arbitrator could not be required to state his reasons, went on to consider whether in that case it was shown that the arbitrator or umpire had exercised his discretion wrongly, and the court there came to the conclusion that he had not. But as I understand it the matter, and the only matter, which the Court of Appeal regarded itself entitled to look at in that case was what appeared in the award itself. The references in the judgment of Lord Justice Hodson and Lord Justice Morris are to matters which appear on the face of the awards. In that case, the award was a comparatively lengthy document which went into the details of the dispute and gave the different items and the decision of the arbitrator on those items one by one. There was, therefore, material on which the court could consider matters on the face of the award, and they held that considering those matters the decision of the umpire was not an incorrect exercise of his discretion.

So far as the award is concerned here there is nothing on the face of it which shows one way or the other whether the arbitrator exercised his discretion correctly. What I am being asked to do in this case is to look beyond the award and to look at affidavits which have been put in by one party and the other in order to consider whether on the matters there shown there was material on which the arbitrator could properly have exercised his discretion in this way. There may be cases in which it would be proper to look at affidavits in relation to matters connected with the proceedings before the arbitrator, as for example the point which [counsel] for the claimants made very strongly, if there had been some question of a payment having been offered by one party to the other it would, in my view, be a proper factor to be taken into consideration in relation to the award of costs. But what I am asked to look at here is not such a matter as that, but is really a review of the facts of the proceedings before the arbitrator, the pleadings, the payments that were made, the contentions of the parties and so forth. In my view, at any rate, in the normal case it is not proper in considering this question whether the arbitrator has rightly exercised his discretion as to costs for the court to have regard to those matters. If for no other reason it would be for this reason, that if one starts to look at all at the proceedings in order to see what has influenced the arbitrator's mind, one cannot stop short of a review of the whole of the proceedings in the arbitration, the speeches on behalf of the parties, the evidence and so forth, because it may be that in any of those matters there would be material on which the arbitrator could properly have relied in exercising his discretion as to costs. Once one is precluded from obtaining from the arbitrator himself in a case where the award as to costs seems somewhat unusual — if he does not choose to give it — his statement of his reasons, in my view, it would normally be wrong, and it would be wrong in this case, to look at affidavits as to what I may call the merits of the proceedings. To do so would be in effect for the court to review the whole of what took place in the arbitration. Unless one did that, one could not be confident that one had seen all the material on which the arbitrator might properly have exercised his discretion in the way in which he did. It follows that I am unable here to come to the conclusion that there was no material on which the arbitrator could exercise his discretion as he did.

I ought, I think, however in deference tó [counsel's] powerful argument to say this, that on the material that I have been asked to look at without objection by either side, that is the affidavits, I feel a great deal of difficulty in seeing how the arbitrator in accordance with the principles on which the courts act and therefore an arbitrator ought to act, could have exercised his discretion properly in the way in which he did, but I am not satisfied that I have or could have before me the material which would satisfy me affirmatively that there was nothing which gave ground for the exercise of a discretion in that way. All that I can really say about it is this, that the parties should realise that if they adopt the procedure of arbitration they will find that, if an arbitrator makes an award as to costs which they regard as being unjust or unfair, the possibility of their being able to procure a review and a remedy for that in the courts is very limited almost to the point of non-existence unless the arbitrator himself sees fit, when the exercise of his discretion is challenged, to state what were the reasons so that the court can see whether the reasons are sound in principle. It may be that parties with their eyes open to that matter prefer to adopt the arbitral procedure rather than the procedure in the courts where, if such an order had been made, it could have been fully investigated and challenged in a higher court, but that is a matter for the parties. I am driven therefore, as I say reluctantly, for reasons which will be apparent from what I have said, to the conclusion that this motion fails and must be dismissed.

Motion dismissed

An arbitrator is not obliged to give reasons why he departs from the normal rule that 'costs follow the event' and a court will not disturb his order if there are grounds on which he could have exercised his discretion in this way.

Perry v Stopher (Court of Appeal, 1959)

A builder's action for £54 in the county court was referred to arbitration. He did not succeed in most of his itemised claim being awarded only £11 and the arbitrator stated: 'I award the defendant costs on Scale 3'.

The courty court judge refused to set aside that award and the plaintiff now appealed to the Court of Appeal.

HODSON LJ: In all cases where the exercise of discretion as to costs is concerned, the relevant authority is *Donald Campbell & Co v Pollak* (1927) where one of the matters emphasised by the House was that the discretion:

'must be exercised judicially, and the judge ought not to exercise his discretion against a successful party on grounds wholly unconnected with the cause of action'.

But so far as matters connected with the cause of action are concerned, the tribunal has a discretion which is unfettered.

The submission in this case is to me the novel one that, the order for costs being an unusual one in the sense that, having partly succeeded, the plaintiff was ordered to pay the defendant's costs, the arbitrator should have stated a reason for so finding. I say at once that, in my judgment, there is no authority for such a submission at all.

I begin with *Donald Campbell & Co v Pollak* (1927) and the speech of Lord Atkinson, on which the plaintiff sought to rely, because I think the words of Lord Sterndale MR in *Ritter v Godfrey* (1920), quoted by Lord Atkinson must have been very much in the mind of Lord Goddard in the case principally relied on by the plaintiff. Lord Sterndale MR in *Ritter v Godfrey (supra)* said:

'But there is such a settled practice of the courts that in the absence of special circumstances a successful litigant should receive his costs, that it is necessary to show some ground for exercising a discretion by refusing an order which would give them to him. The discretion must be judicially exercised, and therefore there must be some grounds for its exercise, for a discretion exercised on no grounds cannot be judicial. If, however, there be any grounds, the question of whether they are sufficient is entirely for the judge at the trial, and this court cannot interfere with his discretion.'

Lord Atkinson said *Donald Campbell & Co v Pollak (supra)*:

'My Lords, I think this judgment of Lord Sterndale contains a clear, condensed and accurate statement of the law and of the prevailing practice on the points with which it deals'.

After *Donald Campbell & Co v Pollak* had overruled the actual conclusion in *Ritter v Godfrey* but affirmed his expression of view as to costs in it, Lord Sterndale MR used these words in *Pitkin v Sanders & Forster Ltd* (1923):

'In this case, therefore, we have to see if the judge had any grounds for the exercise which he made of his discretion; and if there were any grounds on which he could exercise his discretion in the way in which he did, we cannot interfere'.

So far I do not think any language found in the cases indicates that the tribunal is required to state its reasons before it exercises its discretion in a particular way, even when it makes an order as to costs which may be or appear to be unusual.

On its facts, this case is not such a clear case as one in which a plaintiff wholly succeeds or wholly fails. It is a case of an itemised claim where, in the event, the plaintiff has succeeded to a far less extent than the defendant. Even assuming, however, that an unexpected order was made in it, in my opinion there is no justification for the contention that, in departing from the rule, it is necessary for a judge or an arbitrator to say 'I am departing from the rule for' this, that or some other reason. . . .

MORRIS LJ delivered a concurring judgment as did WILMER LJ who also said:

It seems to me, if it is proper to refer to authority on a matter which is so eminently one of discretion, I could not do better than adopt what was said by Diplock J in *Heaven & Kesterton Ltd v Swen Widaens A/B* (1958) in a passage which was referred to by the learned judge in his judgment in the present case. Diplock J said:

'I have no doubt that the umpire in an arbitration of this kind has power to deprive a successful claimant of his costs and, indeed, to order a successful claimant to pay the costs of the other side in appropriate circumstances. The mere fact, therefore, that on the face of the award the buyers have succeeded as to the sum of £73 but have nevertheless been ordered to pay the costs of the sellers would, in my view, of itself be no ground for setting aside the award.'

Appeal dismissed

PART VIII

Impeaching an award

'And note, It has been held, That an Averment shall not be allowed to shew the intent of the Arbitrators, if it be not expressed in the Award, either directly or by Circumstance.'

Dyer's Reports 242

Awards bad on the face of them (see LPA 12.5)

When invited to say that there was an error of law on the face of the award, a court is not entitled to look at the facts or receive affidavit evidence of them.

R.S. Hartley Ltd v Provincial Insurance Company Ltd (Court of Appeal, 1957)

Arbitration was on a clause in a policy of insurance as to whether the assured had taken reasonable precautions to prevent accidents (sometimes known as the 'trap clause').

Mr Gerald Gardiner, acting as counsel for the respondents, said that the motion was on the grounds that the arbitrator was guilty of misconduct within the meaning of section 23(2) of the Arbitration Act 1950, and that there was an error in law on the face of the award.

Lord Goddard: 'Why on earth have not your clients applied for a special case? I cannot deal with this matter. Mr Fenton Atkinson has heard the arbitration and given his award. I am not going into the facts because I have no jurisdiction to do so.'

Counsel said that he had an affidavit as to the facts, but Lord Goddard said that he could not look at it.

Counsel (continuing) said that he was well aware that the motion presented considerable difficulties and he was under no illusion about it. On the question of misconduct, the word was of very general application and the precise meaning of it in the Act had never been clearly defined. His clients were a small concern — really a one-man business — which had never been in a position to meet a claim for serious injuries and had therefore been insured. A 17-year-old girl was scalped in the accident at their factory premises, and manifestly had a claim for breach of statutory duty. It might be of the order of £7,000 and if the company went into liquidation most of the assets might go to her. The dispute had gone to arbitration because of a clause in the insurance policy to that effect. The sole ground on which the insurers had repudiated was a clause sometimes known as 'the trap clause'. This provided that the assured must take reasonable precautions to prevent accidents. There was no question but that a party to an arbitration was entitled to apply for the award to be set aside because there was on its face an error of law.

Lord Goddard: 'There is nothing wrong on the face of the award. Your clients should have applied to the arbitrator to state a special case. I cannot go into the facts found by the arbitrator.'

Counsel said that the only point contended by the insurers was that the lathe concerned was not guarded.

Lord Goddard: 'If you had applied for a special case the matter could have been argued. I am not going to try the case on affidavit evidence. I think you know that this is a matter for a special case or nothing. Whether you can get the time extended and get the arbitrator to state a special case I do not know.'

Counsel said that it was not suggested that the factory was run improperly, and in counsel's submission it was a wrong construction to hold that the clause in the policy could apply in those circumstances. The onus of proof was upon respondents to show that the terms of their conditions applied and, he submitted, they failed to do so.

Lord Goddard: 'I dislike these clauses as much as anyone, but I am bound to say that I cannot go into this matter at all. I have no findings of fact, and this award is perfectly clean.'

LORD GODDARD CJ: In this matter [counsel] has moved to set aside an award on the ground that the arbitrator misconducted himself and/or the proceedings in that:

1. He failed properly to interpret the law as laid down by the Court of Appeal in the case of *Woolfall & Rimmer Ltd v Moyle and another* (1942) to the facts of the claim as given in evidence.

2. That there was no evidence on which having regard to the law as so laid down the arbitrator could find (as he did) that the claimants did not take reasonable precautions to prevent accidents.

3. That in interpreting and applying the law as laid down in the case of *Woolfall & Rimmer Ltd v Moyle and another*, the arbitrator misdirected himself and failed properly to interpret and apply the said law.

Of course, the first thing that strikes anybody reading that notice of motion is that the decision of the case in the first instance must depend upon the facts which are found by the arbitrator. Whether he has applied the law properly or not depends on the facts. Of course, what ought to have been done in this case, if the applicants wished to argue this point before the court, was to apply to the arbitrator to state a special case. They did not do so.

The arbitrator has issued an award in which the material portions are these:

'Having considered the evidence and arguments of the claimants and respondents respectively that were submitted and addressed to me and having directed myself in accordance with the law laid down by the Court of Appeal in the case of *Woolfall & Rimmer Ltd v Moyle and another (supra)* I now find and award as follows:

(a) I am satisfied that the claimants did not take reasonable precautions to prevent accidents.

(b) Accordingly I award in favour of the respondents and find that the claimants are not entitled to the indemnity claimed.

The question was whether the claimants in the arbitration were entitled to an indemnity, and the insurance company was relying upon a clause in the policy to the effect that the insured should take reasonable precautions to prevent accidents and disease.

I do not know what facts the arbitrator found or what the facts of the case are. I do not think I am entitled to look at the affidavits because it is for the arbitrator to find the facts and not for the court to do so. The court has no right to find the facts unless the arbitrator or the parties state a case. But the parties have gone to arbitration, and it is for the arbitrator to find the facts. If the applicants wanted to argue that the facts which the law laid down in the case of *Woolfall & Rimmer Ltd v Moyle and another (supra)* would oblige the arbitrator to find in favour of the insured, they should have applied for a special case. They have not done so, and in my view this motion is misconceived and should be dismissed, with costs.

Motion dismissed

No valid arbitration agreement as a ground for setting aside an award (see LPA 12.3)

On a motion to set aside an award on the ground that the arbitrators offended a fundamental rule of justice in that they failed to afford the respondent proper opportunity of presenting the whole of his case, the judge concluded that there was no agreement to submit the dispute to arbitration, in spite of both parties believing that there was, and set aside the award.

Altco Ltd v Sutherland (Queen's Bench Division, 1971)

> Motion to set aside an award on the ground: (1) that the arbitrators offended a fundamental rule of administration of justice in that they failed to afford the respondent *viva voce* hearing on about 50 per cent of his case to which he was entitled (by the rules of the London Cocoa Terminal Market Association); and (2) that the contracts which formed the basis of the award were non-enforceable because they were not signed, and also that conditions of the contracts were broken by Altco Ltd. The facts appear in the judgment.

DONALDSON J: This has been a somewhat unusual motion, to set aside an award made by the London Cocoa Terminal Market Association in an arbitration between Altco Ltd and Mr Thomas Cunningham Sutherland. Altco Ltd are London commodity brokers. Mr Sutherland is a gentleman who, as I understand the matter, invests in or deals in the market, but not being a member of any of the commodity associations he has to employ the services of a broker. He accordingly contracted with Altco in terms of a document known as the customer's agreement. The agreement was dated 10 September, 1969, and the clauses which are relevant to my decision are as follows:

> 'In consideration of your acting as broker for the undersigned ...I agree as follows:
>
> 1. All transactions shall be subject to the constitution, by-laws, rules, regulations, customs and usages of the Exchange or Market (and its clearing house, if any) where executed.'

And then it goes on to deal with liens, margins, communications, modifications of agreement, revocation, and termination of the agreement and the effect on current transactions. Then we get to the next relevant clause, which is clause 7, which reads:

> 'This agreement shall be governed by the laws of England and any con-

troversy arising out of it or its alleged breach will be settled by the competent courts of London'.

By way of explanation of the rather unusual form of clause 7, I should add that Altco are a parent company who have offices in Hamburg, Lausanne, London and New York. This particular agreement appears to have been with Altco Ltd of 10/11 Lime Street, London, EC3, and no doubt this is a form of agreement which is common to the various international aspects of their business

Altco acted as Mr Sutherland's brokers for a period and disputes then arose. It is a reasonable inference from some of the things which Mr Sutherland said to me that the difficulties first began to arise when there was a change in the level of prices on the commodity market in such a way as to show losses to Mr Sutherland. This is common experience in the Commercial Court and is not a reflection either on Altco or on Mr Sutherland. But Mr Sutherland was very dissatisfied and he took the view that these disputes not only should be decided but must be decided by one of the commodity market associations. Since the contracts which gave rise to the dispute, and showed on the face of it a debit balance owed by him to Altco, were in cocoa he formed the view that the proper way, indeed the only possible way, to determine these disputes was by arbitration under the rules of, and before arbitrators appointed by, the London Cocoa Terminal Market Association. That view was based upon the fact that he considered that on its true construction the customer's agreement so provided. Altco, be it said, certainly did not dissent from that view and, from what has been said in court today, think that Mr Sutherland is entirely right, and it may well be that that view is shared by other broker members of the London Cocoa Terminal Market Association who, for all I know, use agreements with their customers which are substantially in the same form as the Altco agreement. Those parties, recognising, as they would say, that they had signed an agreement to arbitrate, and, in view of the subject-matter of the dispute, an agreement to arbitrate in front of the London Cocoa Terminal Market Association, appointed arbitrators or applied to the association for the appointment of arbitrators. Subsequently, a statement of case was delivered by Altco as claimants and a statement of defence and counterclaim was delivered by Mr Sutherland. Mr Sutherland, at that stage, conceived the idea that the proper way to dispose of the matter was to deal by way of preliminary point with his contention that the contracts—and by that I think he meant the market contracts, not the contract between him and Altco—were unenforceable because they were not signed by Altco, and that those that were signed by him were signed in error. None of the contracts was signed by Altco and only some were signed by Mr Sutherland. None of the sale contracts was signed by anybody.

The contracts to which he was there referring are what I would describe as brokers' bought and sold notes reporting to their customer what they had been doing on the market, and are not, I think, contracts at all. They are just like an insurance broker's notification to his customer that an insurance has been placed. But that does not matter. I am not concerned at any stage of these proceedings with the merits of Mr Sutherland's defence, or indeed, the merits of Altco's claim. But that was his preliminary point. He put forward an alternative defence on the merits which potentially sounded as a counterclaim in that, as he said, Altco had failed in their general responsibilities to him as a client and had failed in their special responsibilities to him under the customer's agreement . . . .

Mr Sutherland suggested to the arbitrators that they should deal with this preliminary point, namely that the contracts were unenforceable because they were not all signed by him and none of them was signed by Altco, by way of preliminary hearing. The arbitrators, as they were fully entitled to do, decided that that was not the proper way to deal with the matter and that it should all be dealt with at the hearing proper. It was here that things started to go wrong, in the sense that misunderstandings started to arise, because I think it probable that the arbitrators meant 'We will deal with everything at the hearing'; Mr. Sutherland thought that they meant 'We will deal with the enforceability point first, and if we are in favour of Mr. Sutherland of course we need go no further, but if we are against him we will hear the rest.' If I am right in my suspicions, the arbitrators thought, as I say, that they were going to deal with everything. So Mr Sutherland turned up by himself, without counsel or representation of any sort, and Altco were represented by Mr Godfrey of counsel, instructed by solicitors....

The course that the arbitration appears to have taken on the basis of affidavits from Mr Sutherland and Mr Phillips, who was and is Mr Godfrey's instructing solicitor, was that Mr Godfrey outlined Altco's claim and also dealt in some measure with some of the matters which had been indicated in the written defence and counterclaim of Mr Sutherland. Mr Sutherland then dealt with the unenforceability of contract point and replied—as he told me—to what counsel had said. It may well be that the impression got about, as a result of Mr Sutherland replying to what Mr Godfrey had said, that Mr Sutherland was putting forward the whole of his defence and counterclaim. Mr Sutherland says he was not. He said that he was dealing purely with the preliminary point, the unenforceability of contract point, and that he fully expected them to go on and deal with the substance of his other complaints which were the basis of his alternative defence and counterclaim. But he says that at that point the parties were asked to retire and the arbitrators deliberated for over an hour. It is common ground that that is the course that was taken. Then the parties were asked to come back and the chairman of the arbitrators asked if Mr Sutherland's defence depended entirely upon the invalidity of the contract, and Mr Sutherland said 'No', it did not, that he had an alternative defence based on various matters (which I think in fairness to all concerned I will not elaborate upon in this judgment) and Mr Sutherland says that he was stopped from going into those matters by the chairman, and that the chairman then said:'We will adjourn the hearing and let the parties know if the arbitrators want to hear further evidence or argument.'

Either Mr Phillips in his affidavit, or Mr Godfrey agree that the chairman did say on this occasion, the second occasion, 'We will adjourn' but there is a substantial difference of opinion between the views of Mr Phillips as expressed in his affidavit and the views of Mr Sutherland as expressed in his affidavit and in addressing me in this court, as to whether Mr Sutherland had plainly at that stage said all that he wanted to say, or appeared to have said all he wanted to say. Mr Sutherland says it was perfectly clear to the tribunal that he had other matters that he wanted to say: Mr Phillips—not perhaps in very express terms—does suggest in his affidavit that Mr Sutherland had 'run down' (if that is the right term) and I have no doubt at all that that is what Mr Phillips means to say in his affidavit.

It is common ground between the parties that Mr Sutherland did, at an early stage, give notice under the rule 134 of the arbitration rules of the London Cocoa Terminal Market Association saying that he required a *viva voce* hearing. The relevant part of rule 134 is in these terms:

> 'Unless either party shall, not later than the submission of the statement of defence, request a *viva voce* hearing, with or without witnesses, the board of arbitration may in its discretion decide the case on the written statements and documents submitted to it without a *viva voce* hearing or it may call the parties before it and request the attendance of witnesses or the provision of further documents or information in written form. It may also consult the legal advisers of the Association.'

Mr Sutherland says—and in this I think he is right, and I am not even certain that the contrary is contended—that in circumstances in which there is such a request there is no room for the arbitrators, operating under the subsequent parts of that sentence, either to determine the matter on written submissions or evidence or partly on a *viva voce* hearing but limited to such extent that the arbitrators themselves may request the attendance of witnesses or the provision of further documents or information in written form. So what Mr Sutherland is saying is that, in accordance with the ordinary rules of natural justice, this being an arbitration which, by the rules, had to be conducted on the basis of a *viva voce* hearing (and this, of course, is the normal position unless the rules otherwise provide) he was entitled to be heard fully in support of his case. He says he was not heard fully.

I am left on the evidence in very grave doubt as to whether he was heard fully. The probability is that there was some sort of muddle. I would not suggest, and I have no reason to suggest, that there was anything consciously unfair about the arbitrators' conduct. They may have got themselves into a state of some confusion as to what is the proper course where a party has required a *viva voce* hearing as contrasted with the more normal type of arbitration in that market, which is no doubt on documents supplemented on certain aspects perhaps by witnesses. They may have got in a muddle over that, or they may have simply misunderstood Mr Sutherland, who, if he will forgive me for saying so has not the facility of the trained advocate for putting the position with great clarity. But I am satisfied that where a party has solid grounds for considering that he was not able to put his full case before the arbitrators, the court must intervene, and that it is no bar to the court's intervention that the arbitrators may have acted with the best of motives. It might mean that an award was set aside unnecessarily in the event; it might mean that arbitrators were required to further hear a case on an order for remission, where that order was unnecessary in the sense that the result ultimately would be the same. But the importance of parties not only being given justice but as reasonable men knowing that they have had justice, or, to use the time-hallowed phrase, of justice not only being done but being seen to be done, far exceeds the importance of any individual case, and I have no doubt that, apart from one matter to which I will return in a moment, this is a case where I ought either to remit the award to the same board of arbitrators to hear the matter further, and to give Mr Sutherland a full opportunity of putting his case forward, or to another board, in fact, to put aside from their minds the decision they had already reached and expressed in the award, and re-think the situation in the light of Mr Sutherland's further submissions. I would certainly not come to the conclusion (and nobody has invited me to do so) that this board would do other than seek to approach the matter with a fresh mind. I am sure they will. But they will obviously have difficulties.

However, I think that it is not really a proper exercise of my discretion in the peculiar circumstances of this case to remit this award at all, and that it must be set aside. The decision point was not mentioned by Mr Sutherland, who does not understand these things, through no fault of his own for he is not a lawyer, and Mr Godfrey had no opportunity of taking the point before I made it anyway. That point is whether there was any arbitration agreement at all in this case. In my view there was not. I am not able to decide this between the parties because I have here a motion to remit and set aside. I have no writ claiming a declaration that there is no agreement to arbitrate and that the award is a nullity. However it is a factor, indeed it is *the* factor, which decides me upon setting the award aside as opposed to remitting it. In my judgment both parties have misconstrued the customer agreement. The customer agreement, as I read it, provides in the clearest possible terms that all transactions undertaken by Altco on behalf of their customer, Mr Sutherland, shall be subject to the constitution, by-laws, rules, regulations, customs and usages of the exchange or market and its clearing house, if any, where executed, but clause 1 has no bearing at all upon the contractual rights and obligations of the customer and Altco. It is true that when Altco seek an indemnity against a customer the rules of the particular market come into consideration, because they have to show that they have incurred liabilities under those rules, and it would not be open to the customer to say 'You should not have contracted under those rules'. Clause 1 is their authority for contracting under those rules with the third party, be it buyer or seller of the commodity. But I cannot see that the language which talks about 'All transactions shall be subject to the rules of the market ... where executed' has any application to the customer agreement if 'where executed' in that context refers to where the customer agreement was executed. If, alternatively, it refers—as Mr Godfrey rather suggested it refers—to the market in which the particular underlying commodity transactions were executed, there would be very surprising consequences. Disputes between the customer and the broker may and probably will be as to balances arising out of dealings in a number of markets (there must be about twenty markets mentioned in a slip which is attached to the brokers' contract notes), so that presumably balances could arise on dealings in twenty different markets. The parties would then have to submit the dispute to twenty different arbitration tribunals or opt for one of them. It is perfectly true that in the present case all the underlying transactions were on the cocoa market, but they did not have to be. Thus if I looked only at clause 1, I should have no doubt whatever that the arbitration agreements under the different commodity association rules had no application to relations as between customer and broker. But the matter is put beyond a doubt, in my judgment, by clause 7, which says that any controversy arising out of the customer agreement, or in respect of its alleged breach, will be settled by the competent courts of London. That is not a reference to a trade tribunal. It therefore follows that there was no agreement to arbitrate in respect of disputes under the customer agreement.

Then, of course, I have had to consider whether there might not have been some ad hoc agreement made perhaps by conduct. It is perfectly true that such an agreement would be a parol agreement to which the Arbitration Act 1950 would not apply. But I have come to the conclusion that there was no such agreement. What the parties were both doing was conducting themselves on the basis of a mutual mistake that there had already been an agreement. Neither party was making an agreement. Even if I were wrong about that, I think that the pre-existing agreement was so fundamental to their actions that if anything they did subsequently can be construed as making another agreement it is vitiated by the fundamental mutual mistake as to the position in relation to the customer agreement.

That being so, it may very well be that if there is any attempt to re-arbitrate this dispute or to continue this arbitration, Mr Sutherland will wish to take the point that the arbitration award is a nullity anyway because there was no agreement pursuant to which it was made. It would be quite wrong and would produce a highly embarrassing situation if, against that background, I had remitted the award to arbitrators with a direction to hear Mr Sutherland further. I could not possibly make such an order if they are not properly constituted arbitrators. It seems to me that the right course, therefore, in the exercise of the inherent jurisdiction of the court, is to cut the Gordian knot, to set this award aside, and to leave the parties to take whatever course they may be advised . . . .

Award set aside
No order as to costs

An arbitrator cannot be ordered to state a special case after he has made his award (see LPA 12.3)

It is no ground for remitting a case to an arbitrator that he has made an error in law. He cannot be ordered by a court to state a case as a power of law under section 10 of the Arbitration Act 1889 (now section 21 of the Arbitration Act 1950) once he has made his award.

In re Montgomery, Jones & Co and Liebenthal & Co's Arbitration (Court of Appeal, 1898)

> Application to a judge in chambers for the arbitrators to be ordered to state a special case or for an order to remit to the arbitrators on the ground that the arbitrators had entirely omitted to consider or apply the ordinary rules of law as to the measure of damages. The judge refused to make any order and the respondent appealed.

SMITH LJ: In this case the parties entered into an agreement for the sale and purchase of a cargo of grain. The agreement was contained in a written document dated 18 June 1897, and by that agreement Liebenthal and Co. agreed to sell a cargo of wheat to Montgomery, Jones and Co. The agreement contained an arbitration clause, which was as follows:

> All disputes from time to time arising out of this contract, including any question of law appearing in the proceedings . . . shall be referred to arbitration according to the rule endorsed on this contract.

That is a perfectly good and valid agreement to submit to arbitration . . . . The seller did not perform his contract, for he did not make a tender in accordance with his contract. The seller not having performed his contract, the matter went to arbitration. This arbitration was held under the provisions of the contract. The buyer was successful in the arbitration and obtained an award for a large amount of damages. The seller then appealed to the appeal committee of the Corn Trade Association and failed in his appeal, the award being confirmed. Throughout the whole proceedings there was no suggestion made by the seller that the arbitrators should state a special case for the opinion of the court. Then the seller, having been defeated in the arbitration, applied to the Queen's Bench Division for an order upon the arbitrators to state a special case upon points of law as to whether their decision was in accordance with the rules of law as to the measure of damages.

That brings us to the consideration of section 19 of the Arbitration Act 1889, which enacts that

> 'any referee, arbitrator, or umpire may at any stage of the proceedings

under a reference, and shall, if so directed by the court or a judge, state in the form of a special case, for the opinion of the court any question of law arising in the course of the reference'.

What is the meaning of that section? Without any authority upon the question, I should say that is applicable only to a case where the question of law is raised during the pendency of the reference, and that a party cannot wait and then, after the whole matter has been decided and finished in the arbitration, ask that a special case shall be stated. My view of section 19 is that it gives the court jurisdiction to order a special case to be stated when an application to state a case is made during the pendency of the arbitration, and that the section does not apply when the application is first made after the arbitration has been concluded and the arbitrators are *functi officio*.

There is, moreover, authority for that view. There is the authority of Lord Halsbury LC and Lord Watson in *Tabernacle Permanent Building Society* v *Knight* (1892). Lord Halsbury LC there says:

'I think the object of the Arbitration Act 1889, though in one sense it may be said to have for its object the same result, was rather to hold a control over the arbitration while it was proceeding by the courts, and not to allow the parties to be concluded by the award, when, as it is said, parties may be precluded by the arbitrator's bad law once the award is made, although they may have had a right to repudiate the arbitrator if they had done so before the completion of the award.'

Lord Watson also said:

'Section 19 only authorises the intervention of the court during the dependence of the reference, and does not warrant an order being made upon an arbitrator to state a case after his award has been duly completed'.

In the latest case—*Re Palmer and Co and Hosken and Co* (1898) Chitty LJ said:

'Section 19 empowers the arbitrator to state a case "at any stage of the proceedings", but not after the award has been completed, and the power of the court or a judge to compel him to state a case under that section standing alone is, on the construction of the section, limited in like manner.'

Those authorities support the view which I have expressed. Two cases have been referred to, in which it was said that a special case was stated after the award had been made: *Re Gough and the Mayor of Liverpool* (1898) in which the point was not taken; and *Re Kirkleatham Local Board* which was a case under section 10. I have no doubt, therefore, that the appellant cannot resort to section 19, and that the arbitrators cannot be ordered to state a special case under that section.

It is then contended that, if the arbitrators cannot be ordered to state a special case, the matter can be sent back to them for reconsideration, under section 10. I think that counsel for the respondents has correctly stated the law under that section. It was so laid down in *Re Keighley, Maxted and Co and Durant and Co* (1893). I for my part have always understood the general rule to be that the parties took their arbitrators for better or for worse, both as to decisions of fact and decisions of law. That is clearly the law. There are, however, certain grounds upon which the matter may be remitted to the arbitrator for reconsideration. Those grounds have been correctly stated by counsel for the respondents, and I will not recapitulate them. This case does not come within any of those grounds. The only contention of the appellant is simply that the arbitrators have gone wrong on a point of law, and they cannot come to the court for a remedy upon that ground. The appeal therefore fails, and must be dismissed.

CHITTY LJ: I am of the same opinion. I have already expressed my opinion as to the meaning of section 19 of the Arbitration Act 1889, in *Re Palmer and Co and Hosken and Co (supra)* which opinion was founded upon the opinions expressed by Lord Halsbury LC and Lord Watson, in *Tabernacle Permanent Building Society v Knight (supra)* With regard to section 10 of the act, I agree that there are four grounds upon which the matter can be remitted to an arbitrator for reconsideration. Those grounds are: (1) where the award is bad on the face of it; (2) where there has been misconduct on the part of the arbitrator; (3) where there has been an admitted mistake, and the arbitrator himself asks that the matter may be remitted; and (4) where additional evidence has been discovered after the making of the award. Upon the principle on which the case of *Keighley, Maxted, and Co and Durant and Co (supra)* was decided. I cannot find any other ground upon which the court will act under section 10. It is not, however, now necessary to limit the operation of section 10 to those four grounds, for we are asked to remit the matter to the arbitrators solely upon the ground that they have gone wrong on a point of law. That, if it came within any part of the Arbitration Act, would come within section 19 and within section 10. I agree that the appeal fails, and must be dismissed.

COLLINS LJ: I am of the same opinion. . . .

Appeal dismissed.

What is error on the face of an award? (see LPA 12.5)

In a statutory arbitration under the Agricultural Holdings Act 1948, the arbitrator, unlike an ordinary arbitrator, can be required to furnish a statement of the reasons for his decision (section 12(1)). No different principles of law are applicable, however, and an award can only be set aside for 'an error on the face' of it.

To determine whether or not there is an error on the face of the award, a judge is not entitled to look at the statements of the cases or receive affidavits of evidence.

In re Allen and Matthews' Arbitration (Queen's Bench Division 1971)

> Motion to set aside the award of an arbitrator appointed by the Minister under the provisions of paragraph 1 of Schedule 6 to the Agricultural Holdings Act 1948. The facts appear from the judgment.

MOCATTA J: This is a motion dated 14 August 1970 to set aside an award made between the parties by Mr P.C. Handley on the ground that the award on the face thereof was bad in law. The motion has given rise to interesting arguments and it raises a somewhat novel issue.

The respondent to the motion is Mr Frank Allen, the owner of Barrow Farms, Lincolnshire, comprising 324.86 acres. The applicant on the motion is Mr J.C. Matthews, the surviving partner of Messrs F.E. Baker & Sons, and the tenant of Barrow Farms. On 17 March 1969 the respondent, the landlord, pursuant to the provisions of section 8(1) of the Agricultural Holdings Act 1948, requested a reference to arbitration. Section 8 provides:

> '(1) Subject to the provisions of this section, the landlord . . . . of an agricultural holding may, ... by notice in writing served on his tenant . . . demand a reference to arbitration under this Act of the question what rent should be payable in respect of the holding as from the next ensuing day on which the tenancy could have been determined by notice to quit given at the date of demanding the reference, and on a reference under this subsection the arbitrator shall determine what rent should be properly payable in respect of the holding at the date of the reference and accordingly shall, as from the day aforesaid, increase or reduce the rent previously payable or direct that it continue unchanged.'

The parties were unable to agree amongst themselves on the appointment of an arbitrator. On 12 March 1970 they requested the Minister to appoint an arbitrator pursuant to the provisions of paragraph 1 of Schedule 6 to the Act of 1948. The Minister of Agriculture, Fisheries and Food, by a document in writing dated 1 April 1970, appointed Mr P.C. Handley FRICS as arbitrator. The arbitrator, having on 20 May 1970 sat and heard evidence and argument put forward on behalf of the parties, made his award on 15 June 1970. In that award he determined that:

> 'The rent to be paid for the said Barrow Farms, now comprising 324.86 acres more or less, is the sum of £2,325 per annum, such rent to commence to run from 6 April 1970.'

The previous rental award had been of £6 9s 3d, an acre, and the particular figure I have just mentioned I am told works out at £7 3s 3d per acre.

At the hearing, pursuant to section 12(1)(a) of the Tribunals and Inquiries Act 1958, the solicitor appearing before the arbitrator for the tenant requested the arbitrator to furnish a statement of his reasons for his decision. Section 12(1) provides that:

> '(a) any such tribunal as is specified in Schedule 1 to this Act . . . shall . . . furnish a statement . . . of the reasons for the decision [given by it] if requested, on or before the giving or notification of the decision, to state the reasons.'

Schedule 1 makes that provision applicable to 'arbitrators appointed (otherwise than by agreement) under Schedule 6 to the Agricultural Holdings Act 1948'. Mr Handley, was, of course, such an arbitrator. Section 12(3) provides that '. . . the reasons [so given] . . . shall be taken to form part of the decision and accordingly to be incorporated in the record'. Pursuant to that request of the tenant, the arbitrator in his award, after having given his decision and made certain directions as to the payment of the costs, stated as follows:

> 'The reasons for this award are that from my own knowledge and experience, in the light of the evidence presented to me and my inspection of the holding, and of the comparable holdings as requested by the tenant's counsel, I am of the opinion that the rent specified is the rent at which, having regard to the terms of the tenancy (other than those relating to rent) the holding might reasonably be expected to be let in the open market by a willing landlord to a willing tenant and disregarding any effect on rent of the fact that the tenant, who is a party to an arbitration, is in occupation of the land.'

In order to appreciate the importance of that phraseology, it is helpful to read the second paragraph of section 8(1) of the Agricultural Holdings Act 1948, as amended by section 2 of the Agriculture Act 1958. That paragraph reads:

> 'For the purposes of this subsection the rent properly payable in respect of a holding shall be the rent at which, having regard to the terms of the tenancy (other than those relating to rent), the holding might reasonably be expected to be let in the open market by a willing landlord to a willing tenant, there being disregarded (in addition to the matters referred to in the next following subsection) any effect on rent of the fact that the tenant who is a party to the arbitration is in occupation of the holding.'

The next following subsection referred to in that paragraph has a number of provisions in it. I will not read them all fully, but I will have to deal with the first in some detail. Sub-section 8(2):

'On a reference under the foregoing sub-section the arbitrator—(a) shall not take into account any increase in the rental value of the holding which is due to—(i) improvements which have been executed thereon, in so far as they were executed wholly or partly at the expense of the tenant (whether or not that expense has been or will be reimbursed by a grant out of moneys provided by Parliament) without any equivalent allowance or benefit made or given by the landlord in consideration of their execution and have not been executed under an obligation imposed on the tenant by the terms of his contract of tenancy . . . .'

Section 8(2) (b) and (c) deal with other matters which shall not be taken into account by the arbitrator.

It will be noted that the reasons given by the arbitrator in his award make no express reference to section 8(2)(a)(i) or its provisions. The applicant tenant has submitted through his counsel that the award contains an error of law upon its face since evidence was adduced before the arbitrator at the hearing that the tenant had, after the previous award some three years previously, with the approval of the Ministry, which made a grant for the purpose, inserted a tile and mole drainage system in 82 acres of the farms, in part at his own expense. Indeed, from the affidavits before me, it appeared that the tenant may have spent as much as £1,400 on this drainage out of his own money. This new drainage system, it was said, must have improved the rental value of the farms, and the reasons given in the award, because of their failure to mention this matter, either indicated that the arbitrator had wholly overlooked the point (which was not only the subject of evidence but of argument before him), or had failed, in arriving at his conclusion on the rental, to disregard the improvements to the property consequent upon the execution of the drainage, contrary to section 8(2)(a)(i).

The award, as I have already indicated, makes no reference whatever to the matter of the execution of the drainage works by the tenant, and the court is only made aware that any such works had been carried out as the result of being referred to a considerable body of affidavit evidence. In fact there were filed and read to the court five affidavits sworn on behalf of the tenant and three sworn on behalf of the landlord; some of them had exhibits attached to them. In addition there were read to me the statements of case before the arbitrator of both the landlord and the tenant, both of which, incidentally, made no reference whatever to the drainage work. All these documents were put in *de bene esse*, Mr Woods reserving his position as to their admissibility on the hearing of this motion.

I have already mentioned that the issue in this case is a somewhat novel one. A comparable but not a precisely similar point arose in *In re Poyser and Mills' Arbitration* (1963) before Megaw J. That concerned an award made by an arbitrator appointed by the Minister under the Agricultural Holdings Act 1948. The facts of the case differed from the facts of the present case in that there the landlord, pursuant to section 24(2) of the act, had served the tenant with a notice requiring him to remedy certain breaches of the tenancy agreement and had subsequently served on the tenant a notice to quit on the grounds that the tenant had failed to comply with the notice to remedy the alleged breaches. The arbitrator was requested, on behalf of the tenant, to state the reasons for the decisions in his award. He in fact awarded on behalf of the landlord. He set out his reasons in a letter of some length, which is set out in full in the judgment. I only read the last paragraph of it where the arbitrator said:

> 'I found faults in the notice to remedy in respect of certain items, and ignored those items, but I found as a fact that there was sufficient work required in the notice which ought to have been done and was not done on the relevant date to justify the notice to quit.'

Megaw J referred to section 12 of the Tribunals and Inquiries Act 1958 and said that the whole purpose of that section:

> 'was to enable persons whose property, or whose interests, were being affected by some administrative decision or some statutory arbitration to know, if the decision was against them, what the reasons for it were. Up to then, people's property and other interests might by gravely affected by a decision of some official. The decision might be perfectly right, but the person against whom it was made was left with the real grievance that he was not told why the decision had been made. The purpose of section 12 was to remedy that, and to remedy it in relation to arbitration under this Act. Parliament provided that reasons shall be given, and in my view that must be read as meaning that proper, adequate reasons must be given. The reasons that are set out must be reasons which will not only be intelligible, but which deal with the substantial points that have been raised. In my view, it is right to consider that statutory provision as being a provision as to the form which the arbitration award shall take. If those reasons do not fairly comply with that which Parliament intended, then that is an error on the face of the award. It is a material error of form . . . . I do not say that any minor or trivial error, or failure to give reasons in relation to every particular point that has been raised at the hearing, would be sufficient ground for invoking the jurisdiction of this court. I think there must be something substantially wrong or inadequate in the reasons that are given in order to enable the jurisdiction of this court to be invoked. In my view, in the present case paragraph 3 gives insufficient and incomplete information as to the grounds of the decision; and, accordingly, I hold that there is an error of law on the face of the award, that the motion suceeds and the award must be set aside.'

It is noticeable that the only documents referred to in that judgment were the award and the reasons for the decision in the award, which by the Act of 1958 were deemed to be incorporated within it, and the notice to remedy which was itself referred to in the reasons. At the beginning of his judgment Megaw J said:

> '. . . cases were submitted on behalf of the landlord and the tenant which

have, I suspect rightly, not been referred to by either party at this hearing because it may well be that they are not properly admissible in evidence on the motion at present before me.'

It seems to me that there is nothing whatever in that judgment to suggest that, in considering a motion to set aside the award of an arbitrator appointed by the Minister under the Agricultural Holdings Act 1948, different principles of law apply as to what the court is entitled to look at from those which apply when the court is considering a motion to set aside a non-statutory arbitration on the grounds of an error of law on its face. The novelty of the decision is that the judge treated a defect in the reasons, being a defect of inadequacy or of insufficient or incomplete information and not a wrong statement of law on a point of law, as constituting an error of law on the face of the award by reason of the provisions of the Tribunals and Inquiries Act 1958.

Mr Woods drew my attention to a number of well-known authorities in relation to the very narrow ambit of the inherent jurisdiction of the court to set aside an award on the grounds of an error of law upon its face. The mere existence of the jurisdiction has often been regretted: see *per* Williams J in *Hodgkinson* v *Fernie* (1857). However, it undoubtedly exists, but it is only to be exercised within narrow and strict limits. I was referred to *James Clark (Brush Materials) Ltd* v *Carters (Merchants) Ltd* (1944) where Tucker J said:

'To succeed on this motion the buyers must show that there is a decision of law patent on the face of the award, and that that decision is necessarily wrong. As the result of the authorities, where parties choose to go to arbitration—and more especially, I would emphasise, where they arbitrate before a lay arbitrator, and agree to accept his decision—and they do not ask for a case to be stated on a point of law which arises during arbitration—as they are entitled to do—they cannot complain if they get something which may not appear to them to be justice unless they substantiate the very stringent grounds on which an award can be remitted or set aside for error of law appearing on the face of it . . . It is my duty to look at the award in the way most favourable to its preservation, and, looking at it from that angle, I find it impossible to say, because the arbitrator has not set out these facts, that they have not been proved to his satisfaction.'

Before leaving that authority I should say, in view of the reference to the right to request that the award be stated in the form of a special case, that there are similar provisions in Schedule 6 to the Agricultural Holdings Act 1948: see paragraph 24 of that schedule.

I was further referred by Mr Woods to the recent well-known case of *Giacomo Costa Fu Andrea* v *British Italian Trading Co Ltd (supra)*. There the very narrow nature of this jurisdiction was emphasised and the extreme difficulty of making reference to documents not themselves incorporated in the award. Diplock LJ said:

'But I think we are driven back to first principles in this matter, namely, that an award can only be set aside for error which is on its face.'

Again, the issue being to what extent the parties could refer to the contract itself which was not set out in the award, Diplock LJ said:

> 'The principle of reading contracts or other documents into the award is not, in my judgment, one to be encouraged or extended, and in my view we are not entitled in this court, on an award where there is a purely general reference to "contract"—and a reference only in that part of the award which deals with the consequences of the finding of fact—to look at the contract and search it in order to see whether there is an error of law.'

Finally, at the end of his judgment, Diplock LJ said:

> 'I strongly deprecate . . . any suggestion that awards made by commercial arbitrators have got to be examined with a toothcomb to make sure that they have used the exactly correct technical legal terms of art.'

It is of interest to observe that there was a decision of the Court of Appeal in 1922, *In re Jones and Carter's Arbitration* (1922) establishing that under the Agricultural Holdings Act 1908 (which in this respect did not differ from the Act of 1948) the High Court had an inherent jurisdiction to set aside the award of an arbitrator on the grounds of an error of law on its face. The Court of Appeal took the view that the jurisdiction of the High Court in relation to arbitrations under the act, to which the Arbitration Act 1889 did not apply, existed and applied in the same way as in the case of arbitrations to which the Arbitration Act 1889 did apply. It was, of course, following that decision that Megaw J acted when he set aside the award in *In re Poyser and Mills' Arbitration* (1964).

In the present case Mr Otton can only begin to raise an argument as to an error of law on the face of this award by referring the court to a substantial body of affidavit evidence. The affidavits filed in this case are to some extent, but not wholly, conflicting on the question of the drainage works carried out by the tenant. They might have been wholly conflicting so that it would have been impossible for the court to have arrived at any conclusion whatever as to either the evidence or the arguments adduced before the arbitrator on the question of improvements by the tenant without the deponents being called before the court and cross-examined. The fact that from the eight affidavits which I have read it appears without any doubt that drainage was carried out by the tenant to 82 acres, that he got a grant from the Ministry who approved that work, and that he made a substantial payment towards it out of his own pocket does not, in my judgment, affect the principle which I have to apply. I have already said that there is nothing in the judgment of Megaw J (novel though that decision was in applying the principles of the inherent jurisdiction of the court to set aside on the basis of an error of law on the face of the award to an inadequate reason given pursuant to a request to state reasons under the Tribunals and Inquiries Act 1958) which, so far as I read it, extends the principles which otherwise apply to the exercise by the court of its inherent jurisdiction. I have already mentioned the passage earlier in this judgment where he expressed the view *obiter* that in all probability the court was not entitled to look at the two statements of case by the respective parties before the arbitrator.

In my judgment, I am not entitled to look at the affidavits in this case, other, of course, than the affidavit exhibiting the award. If I do not look at the affidavits, I find nothing whatever on the face of the award to indicate any error of law on the part of the arbitrator. Mr Otton, quite rightly, in my judgment, did not contend that the mere absence of any reference in the reasons given by the arbitrator to section 8(2)(a), (b) and (c), without there being either anything in the award itself of admissible evidence aliunde showing that those points had been raised, could be a ground for saying that the award contained an error of law on its face.

Accordingly, in my judgment, this motion fails. . . .

Motion dismissed

'Thus I have shewn you the whole Law of Arbitrement by Method and Rule, wherein if you find some things twice, either relating to the Method or to the Matter of the Award, it is not without reason.'

Arbitrium Redivivam (1694)

Table of Statutes and Statutory Instruments

List of Abbreviations used in Reports

AC *(preceded by date)* — Law Reports, Appeal Cases, House of Lords, since 1890 (eg, [1891] AC)

Alc & N — Alcock & Napier's Reports, 1831-33

All ER *(preceded by date)* — All England Law Reports, since 1936 to presentday (eg, [1936] 1 All ER)

All ER Rep *(preceded by date)* — All England Law Reports Reprint series (eg, [1824-1834] All ER Rep)

App Cas — Law Reports, Appeal Cases, House of Lords, 15 volumes, 1875-90

Atk — Atkyns' Chancery Reports, 1736-55

Beav — Beavan's Reports, 36 volumes, 1838-66

Bing NC — Bingam's New Cases (CP), 6 volumes, 1834-40

Bos & P — Bosanquet & Puller's Reports, 3 volumes 1796-1804; Bosanquet & Puller's New Reports, 2 volumes, 1804-07

Bro CC — Brown (by Belt), Chancery, 4 volumes 1778-94

CB — Common Bench Reports, 18 volumes, 1845-56

CBNS — Common Bench Reports, New Series, 20 volumes 1856-65

Ch *(preceded by date)* — Law Reports, Chancery Division, since 1890, (eg, [1891] 1 Ch)

Ch App — Law Reports, Chancery Appeals, 10 volumes, 1865-75

Com Cas — Commercial Cases, 1895-1941

CPD — Law Reports, Common Pleas Division, 5 volumes, 1875-80

Digest — English and Empire Digest, 44 volumes, 1200-1929; Supplements, Replacement volumes and Continuation volumes to presentday

Dowl — Dowling's Practice Reports, 9 volumes, 1830-41

EG — Estates Gazette

ER — English Reports, 176 volumes, 1220-1865

Fed Rep — United States Federal Reports

Har & W — Harrison & Wollaston's Reports, King's Bench, 2 volumes, 1835-36

H & C — Hurlestone & Coltman's Reports, 3 volumes, 1862-66

HL Cas — House of Lords Cases, 11 volumes, 1847-66

H & N — Hurlestone & Norman's Reports, 7 volumes, 1856-62

JP — Justice of the Peace, 1837 to presentday

KB *(preceded by date)* — Law Reports, Kings Bench Division, since 1900 (eg, [1901] 2 KB)

LGR — Local Government Reports, 1902 onwards

LJCP — Law Journal, Common Pleas, 1822-75

LJCh — Law Journal, Chancery, 1831-1946

LJEx — Law Journal, Exchequer, 1831-75

LJKB or QB — Law Journal, King's Bench or Queen's Bench, 1831-1946

LJPC — Law Journal, Privy Council, 1865-1946

Lofft — Lofft's Reports, Kings Bench, 1 volume, 1772-74

LRCP — Law Reports, Common Pleas, 10 volumes, 1865-75

LR Ind App — Law Reports, Indian Appeals, House of Lords, 77 volumes, 1872-1950

LT — Law Times Reports, 1859-1947

LT(OS) — Law Times Reports, Old Series, 34 volumes, 1843-60

Lloyd's Rep — Lloyd's List Law Reports, 84 volumes from 1919 to 1951. Preceded by date from 1951 onwards (eg, [1951] Lloyd's Rep)

Moore, CP — J.B. Moore's Reports, Common Pleas, 12 volumes 1817-27

PD — The Law Reports, Probate Division, 15 volumes, 1875-90

QB *(preceded by date)* — Law Reports, Queen's Bench Division, since 1891, (eg, [1891] QB)

QBD — Law Reports, Queen's Bench Division, 25 volumes, 1875-90

R. — The Reports, 15 volumes, 1893-95

Sol Jo — Solicitor's Journal, from 1856 onwards

TLR — The Times Law Reports, 1884-1952

Term Rep — Term Reports by Dunford & East, King's Bench, 8 volumes, 1785-1800

Taunt — Taunton's Reports, Common Pleas, 8 volumes, 1807-19

WLR *(preceded by date)* — Weekly Law Reports, from 1953 onwards, (eg, [1953] 1 WLR)

WN — Weekly Notes, 1866-1952

WR — Weekly Reporter, 54 volumes, 1852-1906

Table of Cases

References in **heavy** type refer to pages where the judgment of a case
is set out in whole or in part

General Index